PUNISHED
WITH
POVERTY

Produced in the Republic of South Carolina by

SHOTWELL PUBLISHING LLC

Post Office Box 2592

Columbia, So. Carolina 29202

www.ShotwellPublishing.com

Cover: Portrayal of North Carolina & Oklahoma sharecroppers, circa 1935. (Courtesy Library of Congress)

Cover Design: Hazel's Dream

Interior Design: Melinda Moseley

ISBN-13: 978-0997939347

ISBN-10: 0997939346

10 9 8 7 6 5 4 3 2 1

Punished with Poverty

THE SUFFERING SOUTH
Prosperity to Poverty & the Continuing Struggle

James Ronald Kennedy
Walter Donald Kennedy

ACKNOWLEDGEMENTS

The authors wish to thank Betty Kennedy artist; Kent House Plantation, Alexandria, LA, for slave cabin photo; Brian McClure, Commander Northeast LA SCV Brigade, for designing maps; Lori Huckabay expert review and recommendations; Dr. Clyde Wilson for expert analysis; & Paul C. Graham of Shotwell Publishing.

TABLE OF CONTENTS

Chapter One: Subjugating Southerners 1

Chapter Two: Black & White Southern Poverty—The Punishment Continues 7

Chapter Three: Prosperity Beyond Belief 15

Chapter Four: The Engine of Southern Impoverishment.................................... 33

Chapter Five: Emancipation, the Good, the Bad, and the Ugly 41

Chapter Six: Teaching Hate 51

Chapter Seven: The War to Exterminate Black & White Southerners 69

Chapter Eight: Poverty Imposed by Radical Abolition 89

Chapter Nine: Post-War Economic Exploitation of the South 95

Chapter Ten: Sharecropping—An Even Harsher Form of Slavery 105

Chapter Eleven: Political Poverty—The Death of Southern Statesmanship 121

Chapter Twelve: Two Nations—One Empire 147

Chapter Thirteen: CSA Today: North – South Income Inequality 155

Chapter Fourteen: Reparation for Southern Slavery—Abolishing Poverty 161

Addendum I: Sharecropping: Northern Imposed Post -War Slavery 173

Addendum II: The Yankee Slaver 196

Postscript: Post Reconstruction Politicians & Land Owners 198

Bibliography... 199

Index 205

About the Authors 219

Chapter 1

SUBJUGATING SOUTHERNERS

[A] leading Northern newspaper called for a terrible retribution against Southerners: 'We mean to conquer them, Subjugate them....' Never would traitors be permitted to 'return to peaceful and contented homes'; instead they 'must find **poverty** *at their firesides, and see privation in the anxious eyes of mothers and* **the rags of children.**[1]*

Several years ago an elderly friend of the Kennedy Twins told a story about how his grandmother often stated that "those people tried to starve all of us to death after the War." Two things struck me about this man's story: First, his grandmother lived in North Central Louisiana, a section of the South that was not even physically touched by the War; second, his grandmother was not talking about starvation as a result of military action

From prosperity to poverty—this impoverishment was not accidental—it was the result of invasion, conquest and subjugation of a formerly free and prosperous people. Circa 1935 over 8 million Southern sharecropper slaves. [Photo courtesy Library of Congress(LOC)]

in and around her home but the actions of "those people," that is, Yankees, well after the War. The war was over, what happened to the idea of "with malice toward none," the "North/South reconciliation," and a "reunited" nation with "liberty and

---

1 Simkins, Francis Butler, *A History of The South* (Alfred A. Knopf, NY: 1959), 219.

justice for all"? Was this lady's story unique to her family or was it more general to all the people living in the defeated and occupied nation, the Confederate States of America? Did the nation that spawned the articles quoted above, calling for Northerners to "conquer" and "subjugate" the South and leave the future generations of Southerners to "find poverty at their firesides, and see privation in the anxious eyes of mothers and the rags of children," institute a Reconstruction policy that fulfilled these hideous propositions? One final question that must be asked: "Is the policy of impoverishment and subjugation of Southerners[2] an ongoing political policy of modern America?" Answering these questions will cause much painful reflection and reconsideration of deeply held opinions by the people of the defeated nation, and by the people of the nation that invaded, conquered and occupies the South.

Sgt. Alvin York of Tennessee, WWI Hero (Courtesy LOC)

No section of these United States has been more eager to take up arms in defense of this nation than the people of the South. In the War for American Independence it was Southerners (George Washington, Thomas Jefferson, Patrick Henry, just to name a few) that led the way to American Independence. In both the War of 1812 and the Mexican War, the South, while having less free population, provided more men to defend the nation than did the North. In the Mississippi Territory during the War of 1812, the Territorial Governor had to draft young men to stay home because too many of the local militia were volunteering to serve in the army, leaving the territory undefended. Even after the defeat of the South by the Federal government during the War for Southern Independence, Southerners were first in line when the call came for men to defend the nation. In WW I it was a Southerner, Alvin York of Tennessee, who became the most decorated American soldier of that war; during WW II it was Audie Murphy of Texas who held the honor of most decorated American Soldier. Even today (2016) it has been

2 The use of the label "Southerners" is inclusive of all Southerners regardless of color.

reported that Southerners comprised 38% of Iraq and 47% of Afghanistan casualties.[3] The point is that most Southerners do not feel as if they are a conquered people but rather they feel like equals of all other Americans. Yet, as we shall demonstrate in the following pages, the South has not been accepted as an economic, political, or cultural equal with "those people." Southerners of each and every succeeding generation have been used and misused by those who desired from the very beginning of the War for Southern Independence to see them finding only, "*poverty* at their firesides, and . . . privation in the anxious eyes of mothers and the rags of children." Notice that no distinction was made between black or white children dressed only in "rags."

For a people accustomed to displaying their loyalty to the United States by flying "Old Glory," advocating a strong military, encouraging their children to consider the military as a lofty job opportunity, and promoting American heroes such as Lincoln, the thought of being misused by the ruling Northern elite of the Federal government will challenge their natural patriotic inclinations. To add salt to a fresh wound, pointing out that these actions are being taken against Southerners because they are members of a defeated nation, the Confederate States of America, leaves these patriotic Americans in a state of astonished shock. This shock is displayed by a vigorous denial of the reality of their subjugation, much like a drug addict denying his bondage to drugs. The intervention of love by family members in such situations is not pretty and can become very ugly. The drug addict does not wish to give up his beloved habit and will strike out at his family as they implement the intervention that may save his life. Likewise, explaining to Southerners who see themselves as 100% patriotic Americans that they are citizens of a defeated and conquered nation may not always be pretty, but if *liberty is to survive*, intervention must take place.

For Northerners who view themselves *via* standard establishment propaganda as grand defenders of the downtrodden and promoters of freedom, reading about how the war against the South was instituted in order to secure profits and power for the North's ruling elite, will not be gleefully embraced. Nevertheless, there is a silver lining in the dark cloud composing the South's conquest and subjugation. Today no American, Southern or Northern, black or white, is a free citizen in a free country. As a result of the defeat of the South, the destruction of REAL States' Rights was secured. Most of the men who wore the Blue of the Union army had no desire to

3 Coulter, Ann, "The Wrath of Kahn," http://www.anncoulter.com/columns/2016-08-03.html (Accessed 8/4/2016).

destroy their state's right to run its own affairs. Regardless of what they desired, the result of the defeat of the South was the death of REAL States' Rights.[4] As a result, modern Americans living in California may pass by an overwhelming vote a resolution recognizing marriage as a union between one man and one woman, but the supreme Federal government can over-turn the democratic will of the people of the once sovereign state of California. Also, the people of Arizona can attempt to enforce standing Federal laws on immigration, but the supreme Federal government *orders* the once sovereign state to cease and desist from its lawful action. These are but two of thousands of such Constitutional and lawful actions of "we the people" that were overruled by the Federal government. These un-Constitutional acts of the Federal government, committed against people of *non*-Southern states, would have never happened if REAL States' Rights were alive and well. What happened to REAL States' Rights? Let a Radical Republican and a Union officer give us the answer: "The great stumbling block, the great obstruction in Lincoln's way and in the way of thousands, was the old doctrine of States' Rights."[5] Today the guarantees of the Declaration of Independence that the people have the right to "alter or abolish" any government they disapprove of is no longer viable; the guarantee that a free people have the right to consent to the form of government they live under is no longer alive and well; and the idea that "we the people" have a right to establish a form of government pleasing to the people, and that all of these rights are "inalienable," died with the defeat of the South at Appomattox. Appomattox sounded the death knell for the type of government America's forefathers, North and South, established in 1776. From 1775, the time by which all Royal (English) authority had been expelled from their colony—this action was performed by the people of each colony, acting on its own behalf and for its own benefit—the people of each state were the ones that judged how they would be governed. Until 1860 the people of each separate colony

---

4 REAL States' Rights are those rights belonging to the states as announced by Thomas Jefferson and James Madison in the Kentucky and Virginia Resolves of '98 (1798); St. George Tucker of Virginia in his work on the Virginia and United States Constitutions, 1803; William Rawle of Pennsylvania in his textbook on the United States Constitution, 1825. These are merely a representative sample of those Americans who explained that "we the people" of each state are sovereign and acting in concert with other sovereign states created our agent the Federal government. REAL States' Rights provides the people at the local level with weapons necessary to force their agent, the Federal government, to abide by the Constitution. These weapons include interposition, nullification, and secession. REAL States' Rights was destroyed by the defeat of the South. What is called States' Rights today is nothing more than states' privileges—the states are allowed to do only those things approved of by the Federal government.

5 Ingersoll, Robert G. as cited in Benson and Kennedy, *Lincoln's Marxists* (Pelican Publishing Co., Gretna, La.: 2011), 280.

(after 1776, a sovereign state) were solely responsible in determining how they should be governed. Today it is not the people at the local (state) level who determine how they shall be governed, but, rather, it is an all-powerful Federal government that sets and enforces that agenda. Thus we see the demise of a Republic of free men in sovereign states and the rise of an all-powerful Federal Empire which holds claim to absolute sovereignty on the lives and property of its citizens—who are no longer citizens but now subjects of an empire. Americans may not acknowledge it (and here is the silver lining), but whether residing in the North or the South they have reached the point Alexander Stephens prophesied about after the conquest of the Confederate States of America: "The only hope, in my view, now for its preservation and maintenance [Constitutional Liberty] on this Continent, is, that another like cry shall hereafter be raised, and go forth, *The cause of the South is the Cause of us all!*"[6]

Surely the people of these United States who now hold their government in derision; who live in fear of the IRS, EPA, BLM, EEOC, NSA; who see their tax monies being spent to support projects and nations that they do not agree with; who see how they can vote for one idea and Washington's elite can veto the will of the people; and who see a mountain of debt being passed on to their children's children—surely these people will understand that "the cause of the South is the Cause of us all." But what if "those people," acting like spoiled children, refuse to embrace the Cause of the South as the Cause of all Americans? As was written many years ago, "If we cannot convince our Northern neighbors to reform this current, overgrown, and unresponsive government of their making, then we shall work for the re-establishment of a Constitutional Republic known as the Confederate States of America."[7] When hearing such radical declarations most Americans and far too many Southerners recoil as if handed a snake. But for liberty's sake it is time to divest ourselves of the false notion that it is a radical idea for Americans to reclaim their unalienable right of self-government via a return to real states' rights, inclusive of the rights of nullification and secession. Southerners have been so well indoctrinated by the Federal Empire's propaganda that the first word out of many mouths on hearing the above declaration is, "treason!" The timid and skeptical should not be unmindful of the fact that this very insult was hurled at George Washington, Thomas Jefferson,

---

6 Stephens, Alexander H., *The War Between the States* (1870, Sprinkle Publications, Harrisonburg, VA: 1994), Vol. II, 666.

7 Kennedy and Kennedy, *The South Was Right!* (Pelican Publishing Co., Gretna, La.: 1994), 10-11.

and Patrick Henry when their state seceded from its union with Great Britain. In May of 1765 when he warned King George III of what had happened to other tyrants, Tories (those loyal to the central government in London) hurled the charge of "treason" at Patrick Henry. Henry's response to the charge of treason should inspire all lovers of liberty: "If this be treason, let us make the most of it." Our founding fathers were not dissuaded by such insults but rather gave to us a republic of republics where liberty always trumps government. Patrick Henry placed the role of liberty and government correctly when he noted, "The first thing I have at heart is American *liberty*, the second is American *union*."[8] As the Declaration of Independence notes, the rights and liberties of the people always trump government. Patrick Henry was right. The one great question in today's political and cultural environment is simply this: "Will this generation of Americans have the 'right stuff' like the generation of 1776?" Simply stated, is liberty more important than government to modern Southerners and Americans? Their "subjugation" and impoverishment have fallen hard on both black and white citizens of the South. Our redemption will come only when all Southerners understand how and why we stand impoverished and virtually defenseless before an all-powerful big government. Prosperity follows liberty!

---

8 *Patrick Henry: Life, Correspondence and Speeches*, W.W. Henry, ed. (Sprinkle Publishing: Harrisonburg, VA: 1993), Vol. III, 449.

Chapter 2

BLACK AND WHITE SOUTHERN POVERTY— THE PUNISHMENT CONTINUES

*Every secessionist…has received as the **penalty** of defeat only poverty. It is the mildest **punishment** ever inflicted after an unsuccessful civil war….* [9]

Today, the people of the South are the poorest people in the United States.[10] While the opposite was true prior to Lincoln's war of aggression, poverty has been the reality for the Southern people ever since the invasion, conquest and occupation of the South. We the people of Dixie have gone from North America's richest folks per capita to the poorest, yet no one dare ask pointed questions such as: Why did poverty become the norm for Dixie's people? What

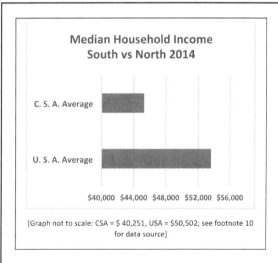

[Graph not to scale: CSA = $ 40,251, USA = $50,502; see footnote 10 for data source]

---

9 Higginson, Thomas W., "Some War Scenes Revisited" in, Smith, John David, ed., *A Just and Lasting Peace* (Signet Classics, New York: 2013), 527. Higginson was a Unitarian minister from Rhode Island.

10 "SELECTED ECONOMIC CHARACTERISTICS 2010-2014 American Community Survey 1-Year Estimates." U.S. Census Bureau. Retrieved 2016-02-12. As listed at: https://en.wikipedia.org/wiki/List_of_U.S._states_by_income accessed 6/20/2016. [CSA includes OK, MO, WV, KY, and MD.] Note: graph does not begin at zero due to space limitations; U.S. median household income 20% greater than median household income for the South.

caused this radical transformation? What can be done to correct this unacknowledged income inequality[11] between the South and the rest of the United States of America?

Black and white Southerners share in this intentional impoverishment—this was punishment for the sin of asking to live in a country ordered upon *the consent of the governed* and simply to be left alone. The South's impoverishment will not be corrected by improving one part (black or white) of the South's population while leaving the other in poverty. Southerners will either rise or continue to fall together. The propagandists for the Federal Empire have done a masterful job in convincing black Southerners that if the white South gains then the black South will lose. This false Yankee narrative began during the War and Reconstruction and continues today. Yet the only way to explain black and white Southern impoverishment is to first understand the reality of the Federal Empire's invasion, conquest, occupation and continuing exploitation of all Southerners—black and white.

When Southerners try to explain the horrors of the so called "Civil War," they are often cut short by an expression of "that was then, this is now." The meaning of course is that something that happened a century and a half in the past has no bearing on the everyday life of people today. But nothing could be further from the truth—*especially for black Southerners!* The poverty inflicted upon the South by Yankee conquerors fell harshly upon all Southerners, but especially upon the poorest section of the Southern population—the newly freed slaves. The Northern desire to put Southern children in "rags"[12] was not directed just at white Southerners but it was directed at all Southerners, both white and black. Today black Southerners still suffer a greater degree of impoverishment resulting from generations of false promises made by national politicians. The impoverishment imposed on black Southerners by the Federal Empire is not just monetary, but it includes spiritual impoverishment caused by an *unnatural* environment of crime, drugs, fatherless families, and sexually transmitted disease such as AIDs. Whether it was the Reconstruction Republican promise of "forty acres and a mule" or the contemporary Democratic promise to solve black poverty—national politicians have created an environment that assures

---

11 The liberal/socialist term "income inequality" is used to demonstrate the calloused indifference the progressive left has toward the Federal Empire's imposed impoverishment of the South. In reality there is no place where income equality exists. In a true free market economy, by definition a market where crony capitalism is not allowed to develop, all have the opportunity to achieve. See Kennedy & Kennedy, *Nullifying Tyranny* (Pelican Publishing Co., Gretna, LA, 2010), 85-91.

12 Simkins, 219.

that black Southerners will remain faithfully on Uncle Sam's plantation.[13]   On Uncle Sam's plantation black Southerners exchange their votes for a continuing stream of promises—yet over a century and a half after "emancipation" poverty, with all its dreadful outcomes, remains a major part of the legacy of black Southerners.   Glory, Glory, Hallelujah!   Yankee "justice for all" marches on.

Defenders of national politicians and their liberal policies are constantly blaming black impoverishment on the "legacy of slavery" and the "legacy of segregation." They do this in order to turn black Southern attention away from the ongoing policy failures of national politicians. Their intention is, and has been since 1865, to create an atmosphere of hate, fear, and mistrust between black and white Southerners. The aim of Republicans at the end of the War for Southern Independence was to turn natural friends into ferocious adversaries.[14]   National politicians (Democrat and Republican) use the votes of black and white Southerners to assure continuation of the political careers of Washington elites and their crony capitalists running dogs who control and enjoy the Federal Empire's perks, privileges and power. Since the mid-1960s National Democrats rely on the votes of black Southerners, while National Republicans rely on the votes of white Southerners to win control of the Federal government.   All Southerners, black and white, are given false promises by their respective national political party but the end is always the same—Southerners remain the poorest people in the Federal Empire.

Black conservative scholar Thomas Sowell noted that the evidence is clear that black Americans *were* doing better "100 years after slavery"[15]   (1865-1965) *than* in the "50 years since…1965."[16]   During the height of Jim Crow segregation in the 1950s, the homicide rate among blacks was going down, but after massive government intervention beginning in 1965—War on Poverty, etc.—the downward

---

13 The term "Uncle Sam's Plantation" is from a book by that title written by Star Parker, a black conservative.

14 It is worth celebrating the significant fact that, while the Federal Empire's propagandists have been largely successful in dividing black and white Southerners along political lines, we still are friends in our social relations. We worship the same God, we enjoy similar foods, we work together, we go to school together and in many places we attend the same churches. Racial division in the South is unnatural and must be generated and constantly maintained by vicious anti-South propaganda taught in public schools and universities and promoted by Hollywood.

15 Sowell, Thomas, "Race, Politics and Lies," May 5, 2015, https://www.creators.com/read/thomas-sowell/05/15/race-politics-and-lies (Accessed May 5, 2015).

16 *Ibid.*

trend reversed and to this day it continues at extreme levels. These levels would not be tolerated if they were occurring in white Northern communities. Prior to 1965 most black children were raised in two-parent families, but today such families are the minority in black communities. As Dr. Sowell noted, the environment created by politicians who claimed they would help black communities has actually caused the destruction of those communities. "Behavior matters and facts matter, more than the prevailing social visions or political empires built on those visions."[17]

Walter Williams, another black conservative scholar, explained that the so-called good intentions of liberals have been destructive of black education as well. Americans typically think of education as a key pathway out of poverty. Yet education is helpful only if society produces employment opportunities and the educational system produces potential employees capable of mastering the technology required by the prospective employer. The modern day education system has failed blacks and has been a key element in keeping them on Uncle Sam's plantation. Dr. Williams points to the deplorable fact that when it comes to math only 33% of American eighth-graders scored acceptable levels but blacks scored even lower at 13%! Reading scores for American eighth-graders were only 34% at acceptable levels but again blacks scored even lower at a mere 16%.[18] Is the problem a racial problem—blacks cannot successfully compete against whites—or is it a system (political) failure? Is it actually a symptom of a failure of political leadership? This political system has worked to the great disadvantage of black Southerners. Dr. Williams points out that prior to massive government intervention beginning in 1965 blacks were not only successfully competing but in some cases actually doing better than their white contemporaries. "Paul Laurence Dunbar High School is a black public school in Washington, D.C. As early as 1899, its students scored higher on citywide tests than any of the city's white schools."[19]

Defenders of national politicians will dismiss these two black scholars as being "Uncle Toms," doing the work of white conservatives who, as Vice President Joe Biden assured his black audience in North Carolina, "want to put you all back in chains." But a report from the liberal Schott Foundation for Public Education, titled "Black Lives Matter: The Schott 50 State Report on Public Education and Black

---

17 *Ibid.*

18 Williams, Walter, "Education Disaster," November 18, 2015, https://www.creators.com/read/walter-williams/11/15/education-disaster (Accessed 11/18/2015).

19 *Ibid.*

Males," documented that the graduation "gap between black males and their white peers has widened."[20]   The report documented the sad fact that while 80% of white males for the school year 2012-13 graduated, only 59% of black males graduated. The report noted that "the low graduation rates in southern states were a cause of concern because the majority of black students were enrolled in southern schools."[21] Progressives, liberals and socialists will rush to complain that the problem is that we are not spending enough money on education. But it has been demonstrated that schools in Utah spend far less per student than schools in Washington, D.C., yet Utah students score far above students in Washington.[22]   The problem is the failure of the educational and political system imposed upon black and white Southerners by the ruling elites of both national political parties. The ruling elite in both national political parties are always more concerned with gaining and maintaining power than they are with the success or failure of their enacted liberal policies. The failure of America's system of public education is but one example.

The Federal Empire's ruling elites have always worked to drive a wedge of mistrust and hatred between black and white Southerners and then use that division to assure the Federal Empire's continuing domination and exploitation of the conquered South. Southern poet-philosopher Donald Grady Davidson in the late 1920s recognized the unnatural environment in which the modern Southerner (black or white) found himself. He described the modern Southerner as being "trapped in a distasteful urban environment, subjecting the phenomena of the *disordered present* to the comparison with the heroic past."[23]   While Southern sycophants and lackeys of the Federal Empire boastfully proclaimed the emergence of a "New South," men such as Davidson realized that the New South was "purchased at the cost of our civility, self-respect, and humanity."[24]   Again it must be emphasized that the intentional impoverishment of the South by the Federal Empire was more than material

---

20 "Black Lives Matter: The Schott 50 State Report on Public Education and Black Males," as cited in Superville, Denisa R., *Graduation Rates Rise; Gap Between Black and White Males Grows, Report Says*, February 11, 2016, http://blogs.edweek.org/edweek/District_Dossier/2015/02/as_nation_graduation_rate_grew.html (Accessed 3/12/2016).

21 *Ibid.*

22 Kennedy, James Ronald, *Reclaiming Liberty* (Pelican Publishing Co., Gretna, LA: 2005), 156.

23 *I'll Take My Stand* (1930, LSU Press, Baton Rouge, LA: 1983), 373.

24 Malvasi, Mark, "Philosopher-Poet of the Rednecks: Donald Davidson and the Defense of the Agrarian South," http://www.theimaginativeconservative.org/2013/06/philosopher-poet-donald-davidson-agrarian-south.html (Accessed 3/02/2016).

impoverishment, it was also an effort to impose spiritual impoverishment upon the South—a spiritual impoverishment that demonstrates its hold on black communities via murder, assaults, drugs, unwed mothers, disease, and talented, creative, entrepreneurial young people with little hope of a full, productive and fulfilling life.

Today black and white Southerners are governed by an Empire that rules over 305 million people. Once every four years the Empire's ruling elite and their propagandists in the mainline media assure these millions of people that they enjoy self-rule by participating in "democratic" elections. But votes are bought and traded in the Empire's mass democracy, and the end results are always the same—the ruling elite of both national political parties and their crony capitalist allies remain in power enjoying the Empire's perks, privileges, and power, while we the people pay an increasingly unbearable tax, inflation, and national debt cost. Wall Street and K-Street (Washington, D.C. headquarters for lobbyists) dominate and are destroying main street.

The U.S.A. is too large to govern as a republic but the Empire can govern by the use or threat of government force. In the first Congress (1789) there was one representative for every 60,000 people and even that was considered too large. Thus, the sovereign states retained the vast majority of rights, leaving a limited Federal government with few, enumerated and specific duties. But Lincoln's Federal Empire changed that equation. Today Americans live not in sovereign states that determine public policy questions. Today Americans live in a mass democracy in which one vote means virtually nothing—it serves only as a pacifier for those who think the status quo will be fundamentally changed by elections. How can "voting" secure personal liberties when today the Federal Empire has one representative for every 700,000 people![25] Today there are 435 members in the House of Representatives. If the same ratio of representatives to population that was used in the first Congress was used today there would be over 5,000 members in the House of Representatives. The system has evolved to secure the status quo—to maintain the ruling elite and their friends in control while we the people pay tribute to our masters in Washington, D.C. The reason that black poverty rate is so high is not due to Southern racism but due to the greed and political ambitions of the ruling elite in Washington. The reason traditional Southern Christian values are publicly ridiculed is not failure to elect "good" conservatives but due to the fact that the current system of governance is

---

25 See Livingston, Donald, "American Republicanism and the Forgotten Question of Size," *Rethinking the American Union for the Twenty-First Century* (Pelican Publishing Co., Gretna, LA: 2012), 145.

designed to maintain the status quo.[26]   Resolving Southern poverty and returning to a civil society based upon traditional Judeo-Christian values will never occur as long as the Federal Empire remains the status quo for America's system of government.

All Southerners were and still are punished with poverty.   The ruling elite's propagandists and lackeys perform their work of protecting the Federal Empire by keeping in place the wedge of racial distrust between black and white Southerners. This allows the Federal Empire to use the technique of "divide and rule" to control the South and use black and white Southern votes to keep the Federal Empire's ruling elites in power. "Divide and rule" was used by the British Empire to successfully control the conquered people of its far-flung empire.[27] They did it in India by dividing India's Hindu and Muslim populations; they did the same to the Clans of Scotland; and to the Protestant and Catholic Celts of Northern Ireland.   Old England's descendants in New England and the North have done the same thing to black and white people of the South. The Federal Empire's ruling elites have been successful in their declared goal: *"We mean to conquer them, Subjugate them.... Never would traitors be permitted to return to peaceful and contented homes; instead they must find **poverty** at their firesides, and see privation in the anxious eyes of mothers and the **rags of children**."*[28]

Northern punishment inflicted on Southern children seventy years after their glorious victory in the so called "Civil War." Photo on left Alabama circa 1935; photo on right North Carolina circa 1935. (Courtesy LOC)

26 Kennedy, *Nullification: Why and How* (Available as free pdf download at: http://www.kennedytwins. com/Nullification_Book_2012.pdf)

27 Johnson, Chalmers, *The Sorrows of Empire* (Henry Holt and Co., New York: 2004), 131: "setting one in-digenous ethnic or religious group against another have often made the policing of a subordinate people easier and less expensive."

28 Simkins, 219.

Chapter 3

PROSPERITY BEYOND BELIEF

During the colonial era Southerners had average income well "above those of
New England or the Middle Colonies."[29] In fact Southern colonial wealth
and riches does not surprise those who have researched this subject but it may
surprise some that "even average free labor earnings were higher in the South."[30]

Americans in general and Southerners in particular instinctively view the South as a traditionally poverty-ridden society. Regardless in which generation one is born, baby boomers to the latest generation capable of reason, Americans commonly hold the view that the South is a place of poverty, ignorance, and racism. Yet, as shall be demonstrated throughout this work,

Middleton Place Charleston, SC, an example of Southern Colonial wealth (Courtesy LOC)

at one time the South was the center of American wealth, a more open and diverse society than its Northern nemesis, and a very well-educated society.

---

29 Lindert, Peter H., (University of California—Davis) and Williamson, Jeffrey G., (Harvard University and the University of Wisconsin), "American Incomes 1774-1860," 14, http://eml.berkeley.edu/~webfac/cromer/e211_f12/LindertWilliamson.pdf (Accessed 3/21/2016).

30 *Ibid.*

The Colonial South—The Growth of a People and Their Wealth

A quick look at the South, first during the colonial and then the antebellum era, will lay bare and destroy the false premise of poverty, ignorance and racism in the colonial and antebellum South. As Lindert and Williamson point out in their survey of Colonial American income, during the colonial era it was the South that was the most prosperous section of America. Not only were the large plantation owners doing very well, but as Lindert and Williamson noted, "even average free labor earnings were higher in the South."[31] The unspoken point being made here is that rank poverty, where people had little food, poor health, poor housing, and a very difficult life, was virtually unheard of at this time. In observing the life-style of the plain folk[32] of the Old South, where mutual help was part of their society, Frank L. Owsley notes: "There was this great advantage: that, while none were very wealthy, few were poor enough to suffer want."[33] Contrary to popular belief, Owsley explains that it was these "plain folks" who comprised the bulk of the population throughout the South from colonial through the antebellum era and: "They, and not the poor whites, comprised the bulk of the Southern population from the Revolution to the Civil War."[34] Another Southern historian, Francis B. Simkins, suggests that even in colonial times, "the owners of plantations and slaves were outnumbered by small farmers who tilled the soil with their own hands."[35]

The genesis of that which ultimately became known as "the South" or "Dixie," is traced back to the first permanent English settlers who arrived in Virginia in 1607—thirteen years *before* the Mayflower landed in New England. The founding fathers of the South were well established in what would become known as the South some thirteen years before New England was settled. Following the establishment of Virginia in 1607, other Southern colonies were established: Maryland in 1634, North Carolina 1653, South Carolina 1670, and Georgia 1733. While each colony was very Southern, each was located in varying degrees in different Southern climates and soils. While each colony looked to agricultural interests as a means of maintaining its economic

---

31 *Ibid.*

32 The term "plain folk" was popularized by historian Frank L. Owsley. It refers to the middle-class white people of the Old South. These people were neither rich nor poor, did not suffer want and were not objects of abuse from rich plantation owners. Their primary occupation was as herdsmen and in limited agricultural holdings.

33 Owsley, Frank L., *Plain Folk of the Old South* (1949, LSU Press, Baton, Rouge, LA: 1982), 132.

34 *Ibid.*

35 Simkins, 59.

viability, each cultivated a different mixture of crops. With John Rolfe's introduction of a sweet Caribbean tobacco to Virginia in 1612 and Sir Walter Raleigh's making the consumption of tobacco a widely held diversion for English society, Virginia and later North Carolina and Maryland established themselves as the tobacco kings of the British Empire. In the more southern regions where tobacco did not grow well, such as South Carolina, rice became the cash crop. With the expansion of South Carolina away from the costal tidewater area, indigo cultivation took the place of rice as the main cash crop in those regions of the colony. Indigo became the mainstay cash crop not only for South Carolina's "up country" but also for Georgia, the last Southern colony to be established.

From the establishment of the first English colonies in North America in 1607 (Virginia) to the founding of the last Southern colony in 1733 (Georgia), a pattern of wealth creation was established that out-stripped anything in the other English colonies. For example, by 1627 (three years before the founding of Massachusetts Bay Colony) Virginia was exporting 500,000 pounds of tobacco. Likewise, by 1630 (while the bare bones blue blood Puritans of Massachusetts were still experimenting with socialism and starving in the process), Maryland had joined in the growing and export of tobacco.[36] By the early 1700s, South Carolina had a thriving economy based upon the cultivation of rice. It was noted that many investors were making up to a 40% return on rice cultivation. By 1744 the discovery of how to make a much sought-after blue dye from the indigo plant led to many indigo plantations and accumulation of great wealth from that commerce.

The cultivation of these labor intensive crops had two important consequences for the South: (1) the movement of large numbers of indentured servants into the colonies; and (2) the establishment of African slavery on large plantations. Indentured servants were white freemen who, for the price of passage to the new world and maintenance during a term as an indentured servant, would work for a landowner from four to fourteen years. After this time, the worker would usually move into the plain folk status and become a small landowner. With the increase in plain folk population in the never-ending wilderness of the Southern colonies, additional people of the British Empire sought a better life in the American South. Having reached the South not as indentured servants but as freemen, they quickly filled the ranks of the plain folks of the colonial South. This and other measures, such as the Hundred and Headright systems of land grants, promoted the movement of free white men and families into the Southern colonies.

---

36 *Ibid.*, 60.

While much wealth was created on the Southern plantations, another means of wealth production unrelated to direct agriculture was land speculation. This system was common throughout the colonies but seems to have been more active and lasting in the South from the colonial period to the advent of the War for Southern Independence (no doubt due to the vast expanse of Southern forest and prairie). As late as the 1830s, one hundred years after the settlement of the last Southern colony, in Mississippi the Kennedy family and their kith and ken were involved in land speculation.[37]

Another means of gaining wealth was the production of food and of livestock. For example, in 1649 Virginia was said to have 20,000 head of cattle. Sixteen years later Virginia was home to 100,000 head of cattle. This figure does not include those animals slaughtered for home consumption. Open range cattle and hog production was a common method of gaining a means of existence for the plain folks of the non-plantation South. What is demonstrated here in these early days of the colonial South is a slow but steady growth of wealth that was not solely concentrated in the hands of a few very rich men. True, there were men of much wealth, but those men were never perceived by the plain folk as harsh competitors and enemies. These plain folks were slowly beginning to make up the bulk of white Southern society. Simkins describes the relationship between the plain folks and plantation owners:

> It would be a misunderstanding of the whole course of Southern history, to assume that the dissatisfaction of the hinterlanders [plain folks] was caused by a desire to revolt against the social values of the coastal region. The [plain folks] were not opposed to slavery, plantation leisure, hedonistic living, and other aristocratic practices. They wished to be rid of the oppressions of the tidewater oligarchs so that they too might move forward in keeping with Southern standards already established on the eastern seaboard.[38]

According to historians such as Frank L. Owsley, Francis B. Simkins, and Grady McWhiney, the South was not a place of dire poverty during the early stages of its history. Just a few years after their founding, the Southern Colonies were exporters of tobacco, rice, indigo, and producing food in the form of grains and cattle for both home and foreign consumption. Non-Southerners also have verified the South's position as

---

37 Kennedy, Doris L. C., *The Kennedy Family of Copiah County, Mississippi and Their Kinfolks* (Self-Publishing, Jackson MS: 2002), 19.

38 Simkins, 55.

a wealthy area of not just the thirteen original colonies but also on a par with Great Britain.[39] Southern Colonial wealth was so great as to make the South "much richer than the North."[40] Looking at net personal incomes, Lindert and Williamson place 1774 personal income for the New England Colonies, Middle Colonies, and Southern Colonies in millions of dollars at around: N.E., $35; M.C., $36; S.C., $91.[41] Here we see, according to these non-Southern statisticians, that the South is almost three times as wealthy as New England and over twice as wealthy as the middle colonies. By 1800 after the disruption of the War for American Independence, the South still held the leading position in property and total income. By 1800, the South was only twice as wealthy as New England,[42] but, nevertheless, still the wealthiest portion of the United States. In looking at what Lindert and Williamson describe as "Real Product per Capita" for the time frame of 1774 to 1860, the fact of a glaring loss of wealth in the South is made obvious. According to Lindert and Williamson's report from 1788, the date of the adoption of the Constitution, to the eve of Southern secession (1860), the South experienced a steady loss of wealth. After 1840 the Southern wealth fell behind that of New England and the Middle Atlantic North, and has never recovered to this day.[43]

By no means does this drop in wealth indicate rank poverty in the South during the antebellum period. What it does dramatically demonstrate is that there was a "great sucking sound" of wealth being moved from the South and landing in the North. This transfer of wealth from the South to the North was one of the major fears of the Southern Founding Fathers as they debated the wisdom of ratifying the Constitution. For example, George Mason of Virginia warned of the danger of going into a government with the North because: "Northern States have interests different from Southern States....The Southern States had therefore grounds for suspicions."[44] Hugh Williamson of NC warned: "Southern interests must be extremely endangered by the present arrangement."[45] Again it

---

39 Lindert and Williamson, 1.

40 *Ibid.*

41 *Ibid.*, 28.

42 *Ibid.*

43 *Ibid.*, 29.

44 George Mason as cited in Bledsoe, *Is Davis a Traitor?* (1866, Fletcher & Fletcher Publishing, SC: 1995), 261.

45 Hugh Williamson, *Ibid.*

must be pointed out that although the South did lose its place as the wealthiest section of the nation, it by no means sank into anything faintly similar to the poverty that black and white Southerners were saddled with after the invasion and conquest of the Confederate States of America by the United States of America.

The Antebellum South—"Treasures Unjustly Taken from the South"[46]

In accordance to the officially recorded and promoted view of the Antebellum South, most Americans view secession as a struggle by the South to prevent the freeing of their slaves by the loving hands of noble Northern abolitionists. This "officially recorded" narrative also paints the South as being ruled by a small group of wealthy plantation owners at the expense of suffering slaves and poor whites. Noted Southern historian Francis Butler Simkins points out that, "Had their Southern rival [the North] not possessed slavery, some other Southern sin could have been shrewdly conjured up for moralizing purposes."[47] Other Southern historians have noted the less than stellar impulse of the North's attack on slavery down South. Dr. Paul Conkin, Distinguished Professor of History at Vanderbilt University, declared that the issue of slavery supplied the North with a "convenient, emotionally charged issue, a mere occasion, for northern imperial conquest of the South." Conkin sums up the result of Yankee victory over the South as causing the South to be economically "impoverished, politically impotent, a dependent colony of the North."[48]

President Jefferson Davis, CSA
(Courtesy LOC)

It was not altruism that was the driving force in the North's attack upon the South but its desire to "milk" the South of wealth. In 1861 Jefferson Davis noted

---

46 Jefferson Davis as cited in Simkins, 190.

47 *Ibid.*

48 Conkin, Paul K., *The Southern Agrarians* (The University of Tennessee Press, Knoxville, TN: 1988), 85.

that the desire of the North was to "convert the government into an engine of Northern aggrandizement. It is that your section may grow in power and prosperity upon *treasures unjustly taken from the South*"[49] [emphasis added]. Simkins points out:

> *Northern capitalism was eagerly imperialistic…. its success was creating a nation*
> *of dollar-worshipers…who regarded themselves as the lords of creation. They tore*
> *down in order that they might rebuild. To tear down the civilization that lay to*
> *their south was but a chapter in their history.*[50]

A grand distinction can be made between the "dollar-worshipers" of the North and Southerners who embraced leisure as a life-style and created a civilization where Southern hospitality became world-famous. As Owsley noted:

> *They [Southerners] practiced the most cordial and unstinted hospitality; and in*
> *case of sorrow or sickness, or need of any kind, there was no limit to the ready*
> *service rendered by neighbors and friends.*[51]

This sense of hospitality and caring for neighbors lives on in the South today. In a 2007 Pew Research poll on per capita charitable giving it was discovered that Southerners are more charitable than Northerners. The State with the highest per capita charitable giving was poor Mississippi, whereas the State with the lowest per capita giving was rich Massachusetts.[52] It would appear that the society of "dollar-worshipers" is alive and well in the State of Massachusetts. As Tocqueville noted in 1830, Yankees were taught from infancy "to place wealth above all the pleasures."[53] This money-grubbing Yankee life style can only be contrasted, not compared, to the Southern life-style of family and leisure. In *Cracker Culture*, historian Grady McWhiney notes that Northerners and Southerners held values that were more than just "different, they were antagonistic."[54] McWhiney rejects the idea of the so-called "Civil War" being a conflict of "brother against

---

49 Jefferson Davis as cited by Simkins 190.

50 Simkins, 191.

51 Owsley, 132.

52 The Pew Research Center, "Trends in Political Values and Core Attitudes: 1987-2007," www.people-press.org (Accessed 03/28/2017).

53 Tocqueville, Alexis de, *Democracy in America* (1838, New York: 1945), I, 411.

54 McWhiney, *Grady, Cracker Culture: Celtic Ways in the Old South* (University of Alabama Press, Tuscaloosa, AL: 1988), 245.

brother," and pronounces it to be a conflict of "culture against culture."[55]

Out of the relationship between these two "antagonistic" cultures has grown several myths that remain to this day and shape the commonly held view of the South. Three of these myths will be discussed here: (1) the South has always been a poverty- ridden region of America; (2) slaves were badly treated and often worked to the point of death; and, (3) Southerners were largely illiterate and backwards.

Southern poverty is so commonplace today that it is hard for most people to accept the idea of a wealthy and prosperous Southland. As has already been pointed out, the colonial South was indeed wealthy beyond the imagination of most modern Americans. Excluding the colonial era, was there a time in the antebellum South when wealth abounded? Yes, according to James McPherson there were more millionaires living in the lower Mississippi Valley than anywhere in the United States by 1860. Most of these millionaires were large plantation owners. Other Southern millionaires were merchants, bankers, and land speculators. At this point most modern historians will place the bulk of the remaining non-slave owning white society in the "poor white" classification. Yet, as already pointed out, these plain folks of the Old South were neither rich nor poor. These people owned large quantities of livestock which were being raised on the open range of the Old South. For example, in 1860 the South's open range livestock was worth over one-half billion dollars, or nearly twice the value of that year's cotton crop and equal to the total of all crops for that year.[56] Americans who love Western folklore are familiar with the famous Chisholm Trail. Over this trail cattle were driven from Texas north to markets during the 1870s and 1880s. On the average about 280,000 head of cattle per year passed over the Chisholm to market. During the antebellum period in South, the plain folk drove to market around 4,500,000 head of hogs per year (this number does not include those used for home consumption). According to Federal records, around 1,000,000 head of cattle were also driven to market by farmers of Mississippi, Louisiana, and Alabama during this time period.[57] This vast amount of hogs and cattle was not being produced by "poor whites," but rather by a prosperous and stable middle-class, aka, "plain folk." They were not in competition with the rich plantation owners, nor did

---

55 *Ibid.*, xiv.

56 McWhiney, 52.

57 *Ibid.*, 55.

they feel threatened by their richer fellow Southerners. Yes, they had a different life-style than their wealthy fellow Southerners but they were not at odds with them. [58]

Confederate General E. Porter Alexander points out how on his father's Georgia plantation it was not uncommon to buy hogs from men who were driving large droves to market: "If he had not raised enough hogs of his own, my father would buy from ten to thirty, from 'droves' which were brought down from Kentucky & Tennessee by hundreds—driven slowly & kept fat on the way."[59] This is an example of the mutually beneficial relationship between the planter class and the plain folks of the antebellum South. The prevalence of open range stock-raising by the plain folk of the old South was observed by the father of American landscape architecture, Frederick Law Olmsted. In his travels through the South during the antebellum era, Olmsted noted how the "hills generally afforded an excellent range, and the mast [nuts and fruits from forest trees] is usually good....Horses, mules, cattle, and swine, are raised extensively, and sheep and goats in smaller number...afford almost the only articles of agricultural export."[60] As both Owsley and McWhiney point out, the open range grazing of cattle and hogs provided both a low labor-intensive income and a comfortable life-style for the plain folks. As Olmsted (a Northerner not to be confused with Owsley the Southerner) and Alexander point out, these plain folks of the old South provided for themselves by marketing their hogs and cattle to local plantations and foreign markets.

It should be noted that the open range system of cattle production was somewhat unique to the Southern forest and terrain. Dr. McWhiney explains that "the open range method of herding and the leisure ethic were integral parts of...antebellum southern culture."[61] As late as 1850 only around 10% of the South's immense land had been cleared and put into cultivation. In the older states of the South, such as Virginia and Kentucky, up to 20% of the land was cleared and cultivated, but in the newer states such as Texas and Florida only about 1% was cleared and under cultivation. Clearly the bulk of land was used for purposes other than growing cotton, rice, tobacco or other labor intensive crops. Comparatively, twice as much farm land in the North

---

58 Simkins, 55.

59 Alexander, Edward Porter, *Fighting for the Confederacy* (The University of North Carolina Press, Chapel Hill, NC: 1989), 5.

60 Olmsted, Frederick Law, *A Journey in the Back Country* (New York: 1860), 222-23.

61 McWhiney, 62.

was cleared, or, as Northerners would describe it, "improved," as in the South.[62]

McWhiney's description of a South where an "open range method of herding and the leisure ethic were integral parts" of Southern society is 180 degrees removed from the description of Yankees as a "nation of dollar-worshipers" given by Simkins. As many have pointed out, the life-style of Southerners produced a unique society in its day and in ours. Richard Weaver suggests that the South was *the last non-materialist civilization in the western World*."[63] The pursuit of a leisure life-style as opposed to a money-grubbing one produced a society with a sense of time and place, a "refuge of sentiments and values, of spiritual congeniality, of belief in the word, of reverence for symbolism."[64] In such a society money and wealth were important but not of ultimate value. In the South honor, both giving and receiving respect, was a value that would trump wealth. No monetary price can be placed upon such a value system, nor would any true Southerner try to place a price on it. In the conclusion of his work, The *Southern Tradition at Bay*, Weaver proclaims that from the "bleakness" of bureaucratic socialism, sooner or later people will seek something "stirring" as they decide to live "strenuously or romantically."[65] In other words, like our Southern forefathers, people will learn to enjoy life and live it with honor as did Southerners in the leisure-orientated society of the antebellum South. Nowhere in that society do we see any evidence of sickly starving poor white or black people so typically seen in the South after the invasion and conquest of the Confederate States of America.

Alex de Tocqueville
(Courtesy LOC)

Slavery, Race and the South

"In the South...the negroes are less carefully kept apart...the whites consent to intermix with them."[66] In the late 1830s Alex de Tocqueville wrote *Democracy In America*.

---

62 *Ibid.*

63 Weaver, Richard M., *The Southern Tradition at Bay* (Arlington House, New Rochelle, NY: 1968), 391.

64 *Ibid.*

65 *Ibid.*, 396.

66 Tocqueville, *Democracy In America*, I, 340.

Tocqueville, a French political thinker, historian and writer, traveled throughout the United States in the 1830s and left us one of the most detailed and interesting overviews of American society of that age. His observation on race and race relationships in both the North and the South is so shocking to modern Americans that it is often ignored or ridiculed. Tocqueville notes that slavery is abolished not for the benefit of the black slave but to benefit white society: "It is not for the good of the negroes, but for that of the whites, that measures are taken to abolish slavery in the United States."[67] He also points out that racial prejudice is stronger in the North than in the South: "The prejudice of the race appears to be stronger in the States which have abolished slavery [Northern States], than in those where it still exists [Southern States]; and nowhere is it so intolerant as in those States [the Midwest] where servitude has never been known."[68] Remember, these observations are being made by a foreign traveler, not a partisan Southerner; yet, his observations run counter to the accepted "truth" which is taught from academic lectern to political podium. Tocqueville, being a non-Southern observer, is quoted as a representative sample of numerous foreign and even Northern witnesses to this view of race in early America. Frederick Law Olmsted, a journalist and social critic from Connecticut, toured the South and published his findings after his journey. Olmsted's observations on the close relationship between the races in the Old South is shocking to those bound to the modern politically correct (p.c.) idea of a racist South. Olmsted was stunned by the "close cohabitation and association of black and white" Southerners. He continues his description of the close interaction between the races in the South: "Negro women are carrying black and white babies together in their arms; black and white children are playing together, black and white faces are constantly thrust together out of doors, to see the train go by."[69] This is going on down South while up North, in the land of so-called "freedom," few if any white men would be seen in public acknowledging a black man, let alone shaking his hand.

Southern historian Francis B. Simkins, also, noted the close relationship that existed among black and white Southerners during the antebellum era: "Social intimacy between the children of the two races was unimpaired by race consciousness."[70] Simkins continues his discussion of the close relationship

---

67 *Ibid.*, 340-41.

68 *Ibid.*, 339.

69 Olmsted as cited in Simkins, 126.

70 Simkins, 145.

between black and white children, noting that as they grew and matured a unique relationship was formed: "With adulthood race consciousness became definite, but the genuine Southerner felt no physical repulsion for colored people."[71] The warm bond of friendship established by the sharing of each other's life and space was noted by William Faulkner, winner of Nobel Prize for Literature (1949). Faulkner asserts that the slave-holder and slave of the antebellum South were only superficially different from each other. They both shared a common life style:

> The identical music from identical instruments, crude fiddles and guitars, now in the
> big house with candles and silk dresses and champagne, now in dirt-floored cabins with
> smoking pine knots and calico and water sweetened with molasses.[72]

As already stated, this view of slavery in the Old South runs counter to the accepted politically correct view of a racist hate-filled South. Equally true, Tocqueville's view of a racist North filled with people who detested the thought of equality with black Americans also runs counter to the modern politically correct view.

Standard Politically Correct history informs a gullible public that slavery down South was harsh to the point of early death, hunger, sickness, rape, and torture. This disgustingly harsh life is said to be the common lot of the wretched slaves in the Old South. Yet as many investigators have pointed out, there is more to the story of slavery down South than the well-hyped propaganda miniseries such as "Roots"[73] or the fictional Uncle Tom's Cabin.

African slavery began in the Western Hemisphere 135 years before its introduction into what would become the South. Sugar and not cotton was the driving force that brought the African slaves to the Western Hemisphere; Spain and not England began the movement of Africans to its sugar plantations in the Caribbean and South America. Of the millions of Africans brought to the Western Hemisphere, only 6% made it to what was to become the United States. A full 94% of Africans were sold into slavery somewhere other than the United States. In what was to become the United States, it was the Colony of Massachusetts and not a Southern colony that first legalized slavery by an act of its assembly in 1643. Most Americans are shocked

---

71 *Ibid.*

72 William Faulkner as cited in *Ibid.*

73 When the creator of "Roots" was challenged regarding the truthfulness of his narrative he dismissed the criticism by declaring "I was just trying to give my people a myth to live by." Cited by Thomas Sowell in *Wealth, Poverty, and Politics* (Basic Books, New York: 2015), 86.

to the point of disbelief when they are informed that slavery existed in Massachusetts for 72 years longer (1643—1780) than it existed in Mississippi (1800—1865).

There were two major differences between slavery in the Old South and slavery in the sugar colonies of Spain: (1) The sugar plantations were usually very large enterprises with *absentee* landlords—whereas in the South plantations were run by planters living alongside their slaves; (2) A large number of small slave-holders (five or fewer slaves) lived and worked alongside their slaves in the South—this was virtually unheard of in the sugar plantations of the Caribbean. When comparing the life of slaves introduced to the Caribbean large plantations and the smaller Southern plantations, U.B. Phillips noted that slaves fared much better in the Old South because they were introduced into a small rather than a large plantation system. This small plantation system offered "better food, and surely better care by reason of the domestic tone of the regime in contrast with the absentee commercialism of the islands."[74] By introducing the new slaves into a small plantation system where he lived alongside his slaves and treated them as his extended family, the master was rewarded with healthy workers and the slave was spared high mortality and morbidity rates so common in the Caribbean. As Phillips points out, treating his slaves well proved a boon to the master because "adequate food and shelter, together perhaps with something of a sense of being cherished, brought to most of them [slaves] a will to live, to mate and to multiply." [75]

This of good treatment and closeness with slaves began to produce a paternal or near family-like relationship which shocked Yankees before and during the War for Southern Independence and today appalls P.C. advocates of racial hatred in the South. Nevertheless, this close relationship was noted even after the War by Yankee General Carl Schurz. In late 1865 Schurz was sent to investigate the condition of the South and

Gen. Carl Schurz, radical socialist and Republican. He was astonished that former slaves did not hate white Southerners.   (Courtesy LOC)

---

74 Phillips, Ulrich B., *Life and Labor in the Old South* (Grosset & Dunlap, NY: 1929), 193.

75 *Ibid.*, 194.

report back to Washington. One of his findings as it relates to the former slaves is of interest. Schurz notes that: "Centuries of slavery have not been sufficient to make them the enemies of the white man."[76] That former Southern slaves were not enemies of the white Southerner was something that Northerners, raised upon a steady diet of the evils of Southern slavery, could not digest. What these Yankees did not understand and what most modern Americans cannot grasp is that the slaves did not like slavery but they did not hate white people, not even their former masters. (This is a generalized statement for surely there were evil and cruel masters who were indeed hated by their slaves, but these were the exception to the rule, not the general rule.)

Poor treatment of slaves to the point of "working them to death" is a standard charge flung against the South. Yet, when looking at the life expectancy of slave and average white American, one notes that in 1850 the slave had a life expectancy of 90% of the rest of America. In comparison to other workers in the civilized world, the slave's life expectancy was equal to that of Italy and greater than that of workers in Austria, Chile, and Manchester, England.[77] Economist Robert Fogel notes that the slave in the South had "much longer life expectations" than workers in Northern factories and in the industries of Europe.[78] Fogel points out that while infant death rates were a little higher for new- born slave children as compared to white children, maternal death rates for slave women were lower than those of white women.

One reason the life expectancy was high for the Southern slave was his consumption of a large volume of nutritious foods. Fogel demonstrates that slaves were given abundant food that exceeded the recommended daily levels necessary for normal health.[79] To the amazement of many, the average daily food consumption of a slave in 1860 exceeded that of all Americans in 1879.[80] The housing of slaves was also important in maintaining good health and a stable marriage bond, which was encouraged by most masters. The average slave cabin in the antebellum South provided more sleeping space per person than the space available to workers in New York City in the late 1890s—notice that this is almost 25 years after the end of

---

76 Schultz, Carl, "Report of Carl Schurz," *A Just and Lasting Peace* (Signet Classics, New York: 2013), 140.

77 Fogel, Robert W., and Engerman, Stanley L., *Time on the Cross* (Little, Brown, and Co., Boston: 1974), 125

78 *Ibid.*, 126.

79 *Ibid.*, 114-15.

80 *Ibid.*, 112.

slavery.[81] While not being motivated by altruism, i.e., doing good for others without expectation of reward, these efforts by the master class improved the life of the slave to a condition unknown in the rest of the Western Hemisphere. In the American South slave population increased without a substantial addition of fresh imports from Africa, something unheard of in the rest of the Western Hemisphere. After 1808 most of the large increase in the number of slaves in the South were from American births. Thus, slave society became more of an African-American culture than a purely African one.[82]

The above-mentioned facts must not be construed as a defense of slavery or to indicate that slaves were happy with their condition. Nevertheless, it points out that the master class, for whatever reason, was compelled to act in a benevolent manner toward their slaves. A plantation is not long lived if it is not profitable. Antebellum masters used the preverbal "carrot and stick" to encourage a smooth-running and therefore profitable plantation. The carrot consisted of good food, health care, care for the sick and infirm, and as much pleasure time as feasible according to the calendar. The "stick" or lash was always in sight, carried by the overseer or otherwise on prominent display, to remind a wayward individual that he was under the authority of the overseer. This "stick" or lash was far less commonly used than modern T.V. miniseries or Hollywood movies would have one believe. Indeed, many Northerners who traveled into the South were astonished by the laxity of discipline applied to slaves. As one Northerner noted: "The slaves do not go about looking unhappy, and are with difficulty, I fancy, persuaded to feel so."[83] This man also suggested that "whips and chains, oaths and brutality" were no more common in the South than in the North. He also states that his travels had brought him far into the South "without seeing the first sign of Negro misery or white tyranny."[84] Another good source of information on life in the Old South is found in the two volumes of Joseph H. Ingraham's *The South-West By a Yankee*, published in 1835. Ingraham also describes slavery as a much more paternal relationship than that which is so commonly described today.[85]

Again it must be pointed out that giving an alternate view on the subject

---

81 *Ibid.*, 116.

82 Smith, Mark M., *Debating Slavery: Economy and Society in the Antebellum American South* (Cambridge University Press, Cambridge, UK: 1998), 7-8.

83 Charles E. Norton as cited in *Ibid.*, 213.

84 *Ibid.*

85 Ingraham, Joseph Holt, *The South-West By A Yankee* (Harper & Brothers, NY: 1835), II, 241-43.

of antebellum slavery is not an attempt to defend slavery. Our desire is to demonstrate the living conditions of Southerners both slave and free during the antebellum era. Having established the true nature of antebellum life, we will then compare it to the life- style of Southern slaves under the post-Appomattox sharecropping system. It is our contention that these post-Appomattox slaves were greater in number, consisting of white as well as black Southerners. Slavery in any of its forms, domestic, civil, or political, is never a defensible institution and must be opposed by those who place liberty above government or wealth.

Another slanderous myth about the South is that it was a place full of uneducated and illiterate people. It is often asserted that one benefit the Yankees brought to the South as a result of the War was education. Were Southerners backward, uneducated and illiterate prior to Yankee invasion and conquest? Research on the men who volunteered for Confederate service in the 28th Louisiana Infantry reveals that 80% of the men were literate. These men were drawn from the most primitive area of North Central Louisiana which was still considered a frontier region in 1860. Yet, these men still had a literacy rate of 80%, or an *illiteracy* rate of 20%. Owsley reports that in the 1860s illiteracy rates in New England were 1.8%, Northwest 5%, and the South 8.27%.[86] At first glance it would appear that the South was more "illiterate" than the rest of the nation, although it was not very far behind the Northwest. But how does the South compare with the rest of the civilized world? In 1860 Great Britain had an illiteracy rate of (male population) 24.6%, an illiteracy rate greater than the South.[87] This places the "illiterate and uneducated" South ahead of every nation in the world other than the Northern section of the United States! In *Emancipating Slaves and Enslaving Free Men*, Jeffery Hummel notes that other than Sweden and Denmark, the South had a literacy rate higher than all European nations.[88] Even the men of a frontier region of the South, North Central Louisiana, possessed a literacy rate greater than all other nations of the world including Great Britain—which cannot logically be described as "backward and uneducated."

Another way to judge the state of education of a society is to measure the number of college students within a given population. In 1860 there was one

---

86 Owsley, 146.

87 Brown, Richard, "Literacy: Looking at History," http://richardjohnbr.blogspot.com/2011/01/literacy-revised-version.html (Accessed 4/14/2016).

88 Jeffery R. Hummel, *Emancipating Slaves, and Enslaving Free Men*, (Open Court, Chicago: 1996), 315.

college student for every 247 people in the South. At the same time there was one college student for every 703 people in the North.[89] This demonstrates that there were more college students per capita in the South than in the North—but the South is said to be "backward and uneducated." It should be noted than many of the students in the North were actually from the South as it was a common practice for upper-class Southerners to send their sons to Northern universities and colleges. The facts speak for themselves; the South was not a region of illiterate, backward and uneducated people as so often portrayed by Hollywood and the media.

From colonial days through the antebellum era, the South was prosperous, healthy, and educated. The one great fear from early in its history was that as a minority within the Union, the South would become the "milch cow"[90] of the North. This fear was announced by none other than Patrick Henry during the debate over adoption of the Constitution. During the antebellum era many Southerners declared that the warnings of early Southern patriots were becoming a reality and the South was being reduced to a second class political and economic region of a greater Yankee Empire.

---

89 Owsley, 148.

90 "Milch" is a Middle English term or archaic term for milking. The term "milch cow" is used to denote a cow that is kept for milking purposes or used as a term to denote easy gain at the "cow's" expense.

Chapter 4

THE ENGINE OF SOUTHERN IMPOVERISHMENT

*We shall then be taxed by those who bear no part of the taxes themselves, and
who consequently will be regardless of our interest in imposing them upon us.*[91]

In June of 1788 a convention of the
people of Virginia was called to consider if
they would adopt a new form of government as
outlined in the proposed Federal Constitution.
One man stood head and shoulders above
all others both in style, force of oration and
in his wisdom and ability in sounding the
depths of the danger of the proposed new
government—that man was Patrick Henry.
As noted by the citation above, Henry
believed that Virginia and the South, being
a minority in the new government, would
be used as a tax source for the benefit of the
North. When assured by Federalists (those in
favor of the new government) that Virginia

Patrick Henry's warning of the tyranny
of a Northern majority in Congress
became a disastrous Southern reality by
1861 & continues today. (Courtesy LOC)

and the South would have representatives in congress to protect their interests and
those representatives would be held responsible for any taxes passed, he replied:

*When oppressions may take place, our representatives may tell us, We contended
for your interest, but we could not carry our point, because the representatives
from Massachusetts, New Hampshire, Connecticut, etc., were against us.*

---

[91] *Patrick Henry: Life, Correspondence and Speeches*, Vol. III, 519.

Thus, sir, you may see there is no real responsibility.[92]

Here, Henry is pointing out that when in the minority, a group's rights and interests are not protected and secured just because they have elected a few representatives. The danger faced by the South from uniting in a government with the Northern majority motivated Henry's opposition to adopting the Constitution. It was not the Constitution that Henry feared as much as it was the people with whom the South would be uniting because the new government would hand every issue to the "Northern majority."[93]   Patrick Henry warned Southerners that the Northern majority, having a need to pass legislation favorable to its commerce and industry, even if it was harmful to the South, would eagerly do so. Henry predicted that by acceding to the new union as a minority section, the South was placing "unbounded power over our property"[94] in the hands of those to whose benefit it would be to plunder and loot that property. Of great significance is Henry's warning about an "oppressive mode of taxation"[95] that the Northern majority could place upon Southerners because the South would not have enough votes in congress to prevent such oppressive taxation.   Henry then gives an inspired warning: "Sir, this is a picture *so horrid, so wretched, so dreadful,* that I need no longer dwell upon it"[96] [emphasis added].   Taxation with unlimited power in the hands of the Northern majority and not slavery is what Henry is warning Americans in general and

Southerners in particular to fear. When Christians today decry the use of Federal power to enforce secular humanist views upon the nation, they should be reminded that it was Patrick Henry who warned Southerners what could and would happen in a democracy if one finds himself in the minority status.   Henry was not alone in his warning about the South becoming the "milch cow" of the Union.

William Grayson, a delegate to the Virginia Constitutional Convention, also warned Southerners of the danger of Northern majority rule. He noted that there was a great difference between the States of the North and the States of the South. Like Henry, Grayson's argument rested not upon the issue of slavery but upon economics

---

92 *Ibid.,* 513.

93 *Ibid.,* 520.

94 *Ibid.*

95 *Ibid.*

96 *Ibid.*

and taxation. It should be remembered that slavery ("slavery" also includes the African slave-trade) existed in the vast majority of Northern States at that time and therefore was not a purely "Southern" issue. Grayson explains, "The interests of the carrying States [Northern States] are strikingly different from those of the productive States [Southern States]....The carrying States will assuredly unite and our situation will then be wretched indeed. We ought to be wise enough to guard against the abuse of such a government."[97] Both Henry and Grayson are warning of the inherent danger of the South being "unequally yoked together" with a Northern majority. As noted in chapter 3, the South was wealthy if not the wealthiest section of the new nation and these men believed they had just cause to fear the looting of the South by the Northern majority.

It was not just the Virginians who feared the tyranny of the Northern majority. A representative sample of other Southern statesmen who feared the tyranny of a Northern majority will demonstrate this widely held Southern fear. From North Carolina Hugh Williamson was so concerned about the Northern majority's ability to rob the South by "unequal taxes,"[98] that he even suggested secession as an alternative to such abuse.[99] Williamson not only warns that the North at that time (1789) was in the majority but it possessed the "means of perpetuating it."[100] Timothy Bloodworth, another North Carolinian, warned of the danger of the new government: "This Constitution, if adopted in its present mode, must end in the subversion of our liberties."[101] Joseph Taylor of North Carolina warned, "We see plainly that men who come from New England are different from us....They cannot with safety legislate for us."[102] Following up on Taylor's statement, William Lancaster questioned the wisdom of placing taxing power in the hands of "Northern majorities...to overburden Southern agriculture."[103] From South Carolina General Charles Cotesworth Pinckney warned that [the South]

---

97 William Grayson as cited in Bledsoe, Albert T., *Is Davis a Traitor?* (1866, The Advocate Publishing House :1879), 262.

98 Hugh Williamson as cited in Bradford, M. E., *Founding Fathers* (University of Kansas Press, Lawrence, Kansas: 1994), 178.

99 *Ibid.*

100 Hugh Williamson as cited in Bledsoe, 262.

101 Timothy Bloodworth as cited in *The Debates in the Several State Conventions on the Adoption of the Federal Constitution as Recommended by the General Convention at Philadelphia in 1787*, ed., Jonathan Elliot (J. B. Lippincott, NY: 1876), IV, 286, 316.

102 Joseph Taylor as cited in Bradford, M. E., *Original Intentions: On the Making and Ratification of the United States Constitution*, (University of Georgia Press, Athens, GA: 1993), 80.

103 *Ibid.*

"will be nothing more than overseers for the Northern States"[104] if it entered into a government with the North as a minority partner. Rawlins Lowndes of South Carolina feared that the North's majority in the new government would destroy any pretense of the Southern States living in a republic.[105] Lowndes fear of the tyranny of the Northern majority in the new government under the Constitution is displayed in his assessment of the future of the South in this statement: "when this new Constitution should be adopted, the sun of the Southern States would set, never to rise again."[106]

The fear expressed by these Southern Founding Fathers was real. In 1789 the Congress of the new government consisted of 26 senators and 65 representatives. In 1789 out of the 26 senators, 14 were from the North and 12 from the South. In the House of Representatives, the 65 congressmen consisted of 35 Northerners and 30 Southerners. This clearly demonstrates that, yes indeed, the South was already in the minority—that is, it could be out voted by the Northern majority.

Rawlins Lowndes, SC. In 1788 he foresaw the sun of the South setting never to rise again. (Courtesy of South Carolina Legislative Manual)

But these same Southern Founding Fathers warned that not only was the North in the majority in Congress but they also had the "means of perpetuating it."[107] Thirty-four years after the meeting of the first Congress of the United States the following breakdown of Senators and Representatives by region proves that Williamson was correct in predicting the South would remain a minority in the Union. In 1823 there were 24 states with 48 Senators and 213 Representatives. The breakdown was 24 North and 24 South in the Senate and, in the House of Representatives 123 from the North and 90 from the South. Notice that only in the Senate has the South maintained equality with the North, but in the House the North has a major "majority" advantage. The

---

104 Bledsoe, 262.

105 Bradford, *Original Intentions*, 64.

106 Rawlins Lowndes as cited in *Ibid.*, 66.

107 Williamson as cited in Bledsoe.

one thing desired by the North at this time was to control the Senate as well as the House of Representatives. But how could they do that if for every time a Northern State was added to the Union a Southern State was added? In the fevered mind of a Northern radical the answer oozed forth, slavery! Deny the movement of slaves into the territories, teach Northerners to hate not only slavery but also Southerners, and fewer Southerners would settle in the new territories. With fewer Southern settlers than Northern settlers moving into the territories, Northerners could outvote Southerners in the new states. The new states would be "free" states, that is, free of Southerners, free of African-Americans, and free of new Southern Senators!

Although the Southern opponents of the new Constitution failed in their attempt to keep the South out of a union with the Northern majority, they were very successful in one major area of American Constitutional history. The Bill of Rights exists today because of the fear of a consolidated and centralized Federal government that could not be controlled by "we the people" of the states. The first ten amendments of the Constitution, known as the Bill of Rights, was an attempt to boldly define where the Federal government could not assert its power. Notice that the very first words of the First Amendment states, "Congress shall make no law…." These words are followed in the Second Amendment by noting that since a free State must have an armed militia, therefore the people's right to "keep and bear Arms shall not be infringed." The Third Amendment puts the Federal government on notice that: "No Soldier shall, in time of peace, be quartered in any house, without the consent of the Owner, nor in time of war, but in a manner to be prescribed by law." Remember, the only standing army, i.e., soldiers, allowed by the Constitution were Federal; therefore the Third Amendment is another limitation on Federal power. A final and bold limitation on Federal power is asserted in the Ninth and Tenth Amendments. These Amendments are a clear warning to the new Federal government that it holds only *delegated* powers and all undelegated powers remain with the people of the states of the union to be used by them at their volition. In 1789, just two years after the adoption of the Constitution, an attempt was made to have the Bill of Rights applied to the States as well as the Federal government but that effort was rejected by Congress.[108] The fact that the Bill of Rights applied only to the Federal government was confirmed

---

108 McDonald, Forrest, *A Constitutional History of the United States* (Robert E. Krieger Publishing Co., Malabar, FL: 1982), 37.

in 1833 by none other than the Federal Supreme Court in *Barron v. Baltimore*. [109]

The Anti-Federalists' warnings of an all-powerful Federal government under the proposed constitution were surmounted only by a conditional ratification. Not only did the Anti-Federalists obtain the assurance of the addition of the Bill of Rights but they also ratified the Constitution by asserting that each state was acting as a sovereign and could at its volition recall any "delegated" right or power. These measures won over enough Anti-Federalists to assure the adoption of the Constitution, but as history proves, men such as Patrick Henry ("a picture so horrid, so wretched, so dreadful") and Rawlins Lowndes ("the sun of the Southern States would set") proved to be painfully correct.

Capt. Raphael Semmes, CSN
(Courtesy LOC)

The great fear of these men, that the new government would be used by the Northern majority to enrich itself at the expense, that is, the impoverishment, of the South, was soon to be realized. By using their control of the Federal Congress, Northern politicians began to propose laws and measures that were very advantageous to them while doing damage to the interests of the South. Even the cod and mackerel fishing industries of the New England States were given a "bounty" drawn from the Federal treasury and disproportionately paid for by duties drawn from Southern ports.[110]

The impoverishment of the South began in earnest as the North gained control of Congress. During the years following the adoption of the Constitution a host of schemes, from banking and monetary systems which benefitted the banking and commercial interest of the North to tariffs that protected Northern industry but increased prices for Southern consumers, were passed through the Federal Congress. Raphael Semmes points out the toxic results to the South of these measures: "Under the wholesale system of spoliation, which was now practiced, the South was becoming poorer and poorer."[111] Semmes is

---

109 *Barron v. Baltimore*, 7 Peters 243 (1833).

110 Semmes, Raphael, *Memoirs of Service Afloat*, (1868, The Blue and Gray Press, Secaucus, NJ: 1987), 59.

111 *Ibid.*, 60.

pointing out that economically the South was unfairly losing ground to the North. This economic downturn fell upon not just the rich white plantation owners but also on the average white non-slave holder as well as on the free and enslaved black people of the South—Northern-imposed poverty is an equal opportunity villain.

Long before Semmes wrote his famous memoirs, Thomas Hart Benton, Senator from Missouri, was denouncing the treatment the South was receiving at the hands of the Northern majority. In a speech before the U. S. Senate in 1828 notice how Benton points out that the rich South was being plundered by the Northern majority:

> I feel for the sad changes, which have taken place in the South, during the last fifty years. Before the Revolution, it was the seat of wealth, as well as hospitality. Money, and all it commanded, abounded there. But how is it now? All this is reversed. Wealth has fled from the South, and settled in regions north of the Potomac; and this in the face of the fact, that the South, in four staples alone, has exported produce, since the Revolution, to the value of eight hundred millions, of dollars;[112] and the North has exported comparatively nothing....Under Federal legislation, the exports of the South have been the basis of the Federal revenue....Virginia, the two Carolinas, and Georgia, may be said to defray three-fourths, of the annual expense of supporting the Federal Government; and of this great sum, annually furnished by them, nothing, or next to nothing is returned to them, in the shape of government expenditures. That expenditure flows in an opposite direction—it flows northwardly, in one uniform, uninterrupted, and perennial stream. This is the reason why wealth disappears from the South and rises up in the North...taking from the South, and returning nothing to it.[113]

Senator Thomas H. Benton, MO. He protested the impoverishment of the South by the Northern majority. (Courtesy LOC)

Senator Benton began his discussion by noting the harmful changes that had taken place in the South during the past fifty years.

---

112 $800,000,000.00 1828 would be well over 17 Billion dollars in current dollars. See, Inflation calculator http://www.westegg.com/inflation/infl.cgi.

113 Benton as cited in Semmes, 57-8.

Benton was speaking in 1828; fifty years prior to his speech would have been 1778, two years after the signing of the Declaration of Independence. As was noted in chapter 3, the South was the wealthiest section of this country during the colonial era. What happened to the wealth? Just as the patriots debating the adoption of the Constitution warned, the Northern majority in Congress began to extract wealth from the South via Federal legislation. The South was not impoverished at this time but it was becoming obvious to Southerners that if something was not done, poverty or near poverty would become commonplace in the South. As Benton noted, "the South must be exhausted of its money, and its property, by a course of legislation....every new tariff increases the force of this action."[114]

Upon recounting Senator Benton's message to Congress in *Memoirs of Service Afloat*, Semmes opined: "No wonder that Mr. Lincoln, when asked "why not let the South go?" replied, "Let the South go! *where then shall we get our revenue?*"[115] Revenue, money, tariffs, and filthy lucre are what pushed Lincoln and the North to wage aggressive war upon the South. Protecting itself from the rapacious hands of those seeking to gain at her expense is what ultimately pushed the South to, in the words of the Declaration of Independence, "alter or abolish" a government they found unsuitable to govern the free and still prosperous people of the South.

114 *Ibid.*

115 *Ibid.*

Chapter 5

EMANCIPATION, THE GOOD, THE BAD, AND THE UGLY

Slavery is an evil at best.[116]

It would be difficult today to find any American who would defend the institution of slavery. But the fact that most Americans cannot fathom is that a similar attitude toward the institution of slavery existed throughout the antebellum South until around the 1830s. Most Americans have been feed a steady diet of radical abolitionist propaganda and embrace the false narrative that from the beginning of the South, Southerners have had a love affair with the institution of slavery. According to this myth, any effort to end slavery would quickly and violently be attacked by slavery-loving Southern bigots. Fantasy is not fact, but when dealing with the issue of American slavery, too often fantasy trumps facts.

Gov. Gerard Brandon of Mississippi. In 1828 he recognized and publicly declared the need to end slavery. (Courtesy LOC)

The first native-born governor of Mississippi, Gerard C. Brandon, spoke out against both slavery and the interstate commerce in slaves. Dealing with the issue of slavery and the abolition of slavery was not a simple issue anywhere in the civilized world of the 1800s. In 1826 Mississippi's legislature even admitted, "However great may be the national evil of slavery, and however much we may regret it, circumstances over which we have no control have rendered it inevitable...."[117] Two years after the Mississippi legislature

---

116 Brandon, Gerard C., Governor Mississippi 1826-32, as cited in Bettersworth, John K., *Mississippi: A History* (The Steck Co., Austin, TX: 1959), 194.

117 Brandon as cited by Bettersworth, 194.

condemned slavery as a "national evil," Governor Brandon addressed the legislature:

> *Slavery is an evil at best, and has invariably operated oppressively on the poorer*
> *class in every community into which it has been introduced....I submit to the*
> *wisdom of the general assembly to say whether the period has not arrived when*
> *Mississippi, in her own defense, should, as far as practicable, prevent the further*
> *introduction of slaves for sale.*[118]

As the desire for the elimination of slavery grew, Virginia in 1832 began exploring means of adopting a gradual emancipation plan to end slavery.[119]

The history of the South's efforts in ending the African slave-trade, freeing at their own expense their slaves and promoting kind and near paternalistic treatment is rejected out of hand by liberal P.C. historians and pundits. Yet these same liberal pundits and historians will embrace Lincoln as a great defender of the black race and promoter of freedom for the slaves. Liberal P.C. pundits seem oblivious to the irony of embracing the same Lincoln who in the famous Lincoln-Douglas debates announced that he was a white supremacist and believed the African was inferior to the white man.[120] In an effort to push forward his desire for the colonization of free blacks, Lincoln meet with five black ministers in August of 1862. This historic first public policy meeting of a black delegation in the White House was not intended to be a discussion between Lincoln and the black ministers. These African-Americans were quickly if not rudely informed that only Mr. Lincoln would be speaking. In no uncertain words they were told that they had not been invited to give advice but to take it. Lincoln quickly set the tone of the meeting:

> *You and we are different races. We have between us a broader difference than*
> *exists between almost any other two races. Whether it is right or wrong I need not*
> *discuss, but this physical difference is a great disadvantage to us both....I think*
> *your race suffers very greatly...by living among us, while ours suffers from your*
> *presence. In a word, we suffer on each side....If this be admitted, it affords a*
> *reason at least why we should be separated.*[121]

---

118 *Ibid.*, 194-95.

119 Simkins; for more information on the South leading the effort to end slavery, see, Kennedy, *Myths of American Slavery* (Pelican Publishing Co., Gretna, LA: 2003) 23-34.

120 For a complete review of Lincoln's racist views see, Kennedy, *Rekilling Lincoln*, (Pelican Publishing Co., Gretna, LA: 2015), 23-71.

121 Abraham Lincoln as cited in Morgan, Robert, Institute for Historical Review, "Abraham Lincoln's Program for Resettlement," http://www.ihr.org/jhr/v13/v13n5p-4_Morgan.html (Accessed 4/17/16).

Lincoln, while speaking to African-Americans, was simply restating his racial views as expressed in the 1858 Lincoln-Douglas debates. In another message to Congress in 1862, Lincoln again spoke in favor of colonization, i.e., removing African-Americans from the U.S. and sending them back to Africa: "I cannot make it better known than it already is, that I strongly favor colonization."[122]

Lincoln's racist opinions mirrored the commonly held Northern view of blacks. (Courtesy LOC)

Modern Americans find it difficult understanding the strong desire of Northerners for the removal of Africans from America. John Adams of Massachusetts, founding father and second President of the United States, throws much light on the subject of removal of Africans from New England. The desire for ending slavery and the removal of Africans from New England society was expressed by Adams when he stated that moral argument:

> might have some weight in the abolition of slavery in Massachusetts, but the real cause was the multiplication of laboring white people, who would no longer suffer the rich to employ these sable rivals so much to their injury. The common people would not suffer the labor, by which alone they could obtain a subsistence, to be done by slaves.[123]

Adams informs us that if slavery had not been abolished, the "common people" who refused to compete with slave labor would "have put the slaves to death, and their masters too perhaps."[124]

The foundation of Northern abolitionism was based not on goodwill for the enslaved African but the desire to rid their society of the African-American even to

---

122 Abraham Lincoln as cited in, Basler, Roy, ed., *The Collected Works of Abraham Lincoln* (Rutgers University Press, Brunswick, NJ: 1953), 685.

123 John Adams as cited in Greene, Lorenzo, Jr., *The Negro in Colonial New England, 1620-1776* (Kennikat Press, Port Washington, NY: 1966), 113, 322.

124 *Ibid.*

the point of putting "the slaves to death." Tocqueville in the 1830s points out: "It is not for the good of the negroes, but for that of the whites, that measures are taken to abolish slavery in the United States."[125] In a shocking revelation of racism in the North, Joanne Pope Melish explains how first New England, quickly followed by other Northern States, embraced the anti-slavery movement as a means of making the North a pure white society.[126] This desire to rid Northern white society of African-Americans is displayed even among strong abolitionists. A noted abolitionist, Thomas Branagan, exposed the feeling of many Northerners as it relates to the presence of African-Americans in the North: "The sons of Africa in America, are the inveterate enemies of America."[127] Even the abolition of the African slave-trade in many Northern States was not predicated upon helping end the horrors of slavery but to assist white workers. The State of New Jersey, for example, ended the importation of slaves in order "that white labor may be protected."[128] Even the title "slave" was changed to "apprenticeship" or something similar in order to avoid the label of slaveholder. As late as 1860 both "apprentices" and slaves were to be found on the census records for the State of New Jersey.[129] Notice the difference between the attitude of the "Free" North and the "Slave" South as it relates to living with African-Americans. The North displayed more racist tendency than the South. As Tocqueville points out, Northerners were shocked and repulsed by the close relationship between the races down South.[130]

While no amount of criticism is spared the South for not ending slavery, it is obvious that even Lincoln was not comfortable with African-Americans living and competing with white Americans. Solving the problems of slavery and race in the 19th century was very problematic and fraught with many obstacles. But as men such as Tocqueville of France and Olmsted of Connecticut observed, the races were much more comfortable living together in the South than the North. The Right Reverend John Henry Hopkins, Anglican Bishop of the Diocese of Vermont, noted: "The South has done more than any people on earth for the

---

125 Tocqueville, 341.

126 Melish, Joanne Pope, *Disowning Slavery: Gradual Emancipation and "Race" in New England, 1780-1860* (Cornell University Press, Ithaca and London: 1998), 230.

127 Thomas Branagan as cited in *Ibid.*, 226.

128 McManus, Edgar J., *Black Bondage in the North* (Syracuse University Press, Syracuse, NY: 1973), 180.

129 *Ibid.*, 181.

130 Tocqueville, 340.

African race."[131]   In 1827 four-fifths of all abolition societies and four-fifths of the members of those societies were in the South.   Many of these Southern societies were founded by Southern slaveholders.[132]   This being the case, the question must be asked and answered: "Where was the Southern emancipation movement in 1861?"

Two events were to take place that stymied and ultimately for all practical purposes killed the Southern abolition movement. First was the horror of the Haitian slave revolt and massacre of the white population. From February until April of 1804 over 4,000 white people were massacred during the Haitian Revolution. All white people regardless of gender or age, slaveholders or non-slaveholders were brutally put to death by roaming bands of rebellious slaves. One feature that was very disconcerting to the majority of non-slave holding Southerners was that in Haiti even white people who were friends of the black population were put to death.[133] Slaveholders and their families, as well as men, women and children of non-slaveholders, all suffered death at the hands of former slaves during this revolutionary period. Is it any wonder that non-slaveholding Southerners were alarmed by the fear of a Haitian-type slave revolt in the South?

A Haitian-style massacre of whites was the radical abolitionist plan for the South. (Photo courtesy Wikimedia Commons, https://commons.wikimedia.org)

The second thing that put an untimely end to the emancipation efforts of Southerners was the extreme and murderous attacks on Southerners by the Radical Abolitionists.[134] From the colonial era until near 1830, "there was little difference between the North and the South in the volume and vigor of antislavery expression."[135] Until the advent and growth of the radical abolition movement,

---

131 John Henry Hopkins as cited in Roper, Gary L., *Antebellum Slavery An Orthodox Christian View* (Gary L. Roper: 2008), xviii. Also see, Hopkins, *A Scriptural, Ecclesiastical, and Historical View of Slavery* (W. I. Pooley and Co., NY), 30, 69.

132 Kennedy, *Myths of American Slavery*, 27-28.

133 Popkin, Jeremy D., *Facing Racial Revolution: Eyewitness Accounts of the Haitian Insurrection* (University of Chicago Press, Chicago: 2010), 363–364.

134 Bettersworth, 192.

135 Simkins, 96.

Southerners and Northerners were happy to work together for the elimination of slavery. A perfect example of Northerners and Southerners working together is displayed in the life of William Rawle of Philadelphia, Pennsylvania. Rawle was a Northern abolitionist who served as president of the Maryland Society for Promoting the Abolition of Slavery from 1818 until his death in 1836. (Maryland was very much a Southern State at this time.) This and other Southern abolition movements were very active until the radical abolitionist's "threat to the South...put an end to most of such activity."[136]

By the mid-1830s radical abolitionists were using the United States mail to flood the South with anti-slavery magazines and tracts that Southerners viewed as an attempt at instigating a Haitian-style slave uprising. President Andrew Jackson condemned this action as a "wicked plan of exciting the negroes to insurrection and to massacre."[137] The radical abolitionist literature denounced slaveholders as:

robbers, manstealers, and thieves who worked their slaves to death in seven years, beat them with many lashes, cropped their ears...threw them to bloodhounds to be chewed, put red pepper, turpentine, and vinegar in their wounds, and failed to give them enough clothes to protect them from the weather.[138]

A Haiti-style slave revolt and massacre was John Brown's vision of emancipation in the South. (Courtesy LOC)

The preceding statement is so full of falsehoods and misinformation as to make it laughable. The statement about slaves being thrown to "bloodhounds to be chewed" is so ridiculous as to beg to be highlighted as an example of Northern gross ignorance and prejudice. The Bloodhound breed of dogs are well known for their ability to follow a scent;

---

136 Bettersworth, 192. Here Bettersworth is speaking specifically of Mississippi, but the same can be said for all Southern States.

137 Andrew Jackson as cited in Simkins, 106.

138 *Ibid.*, 105.

thus they are often used by rescuers to find missing people. Yet, as recognized by dog lovers everywhere, the bloodhound is not an aggressive breed and will more likely lick a person than bite him.[139] The Northerner's "fixation" on the use of the lash and the whipping post was noted by Herman Melville from New York, the author of *Moby-Dick*. He spent his early years as a seaman and was well aware of the use of flogging on board seafaring ships of the day. He quoted John Randolph of Virginia who stated that he (Randolph) saw more whippings during one ocean voyage on board an American man-of-war than he had seen in ten years on his plantation of over 500 slaves. Melville noted that Southern naval officers were much less severe, and much more gentle and gentlemanly in command, than the Northern officers.[140] Bishop Hopkins of Vermont condemned radical abolitionists who depicted Southerners as evil "whipping-post" slaveholders. As he pointed out "The whipping-post was a fixed institution in England and Massachusetts and its discipline administered even to free citizens."[141] Repeated slanderous statements about slaveholders in the South over time morphed into *all* Southerners. At that point even non-slaveholding Southerners became enraged by the activity of the radical abolitionists. With the rise of Northern radical abolitionists non-slave holding Southerners became less concerned about freeing the enslaved and more concerned about protecting their families from slave revolts inspired by radical abolitionists. Radical abolitionism sounded the death knell for the Southern abolition movement. In the South their "incendiary words evoked such fear and anger that a peaceful attainment of his [radical abolitionist] aims was made impossible." [142]

In August of 1831 Nat Turner led a slave uprising in Southampton County, Virginia. All the fears of a slave revolt became a harsh reality that deadly August day. The methodical work of killing white men, women and children began in earnest and by the end of the uprising over fifty white people had been massacred and fifteen homes burned. Under attack, one lady fled her home running and crying, trying to escape. Turner gave chase and caught her. While the lady pleaded for her life, Turner, using his stolen sword, hacked at the lady who refused to die. In desperation Turner seized a fence post and finished the job of killing by beating her to death. Even babies were

---

139 Bloodhound Dogtime.com, http://dogtime.com/dog-breeds/bloodhound (Accessed 4/20/2016).

140 Floan, Howard R., *The South in Northern Eyes 1831-1861*, (McGraw-Hill Book Co., Inc., New York: 1958),

141 Hopkins, 29.

142 Simkins, 104.

not spared. Over ten children were killed; many by decapitation, and their bodies were stacked in a pile.[143] News swept across the South of the horrors inflicted upon white people, even those who had treated their slaves kindly. Stories of white babies being decapitated and white women being beaten to death spread throughout a horrified South. Non-slaveholders as well as slaveholders now felt extremely threatened—but the threat originated not from black Southerners but from bigoted anti-South Yankees!

The South felt under attack every time a petition was made to Congress against slavery (and there were thousands); or when a Northern State refused to abide by its Constitutional obligation regarding the harboring of a fugitive slave. The one great difference was now all the South felt under attack, not just those owning slaves. Just about the time the slavery controversy appeared to be calming, down a new problem would arise. One problem the South was facing in dealing with the North on the subject of slavery was the political alliance between Northern business interests and radical abolitionists. Northern business and commercial interests wanted to decrease the influence of the South in Congress. By seizing on the subject of slavery and fanning the anti-South emotions of Northerners, they promoted the election of members of Congress that would stand against the economic interests of the South and promote Northern business interests.

Throughout the North secret societies were forming to assist radical abolitionist assassins such as John Brown. In the late 1850s Brown attacked and murdered five non-slave holding Southerners in Kansas. For any non-slave holding Southerner who did not believe that Northerners hated all Southerners, here was positive proof that Northerners did indeed hate all Southerners—black or white, non-slaveholders, as well as slaveholders. Brown attacked these Southerners with the shout "The Northern army is upon you," and then, like Nat Turner, hacked the men, young and old, to

John Brown. America's first terrorist "hero." (Courtesy LOC)

143 Oates, Stephen B., "Children of Darkness," *American Heritage*, October 1973, Vol. 24, Issue 6.

death. Such incidents were followed by the infamous raid upon Harper's Ferry, Virginia, financed secretly by wealthy Northerners. (The first person Brown killed was a free man of color.) The fact that Northerners supported Brown and encouraged his bloody work with public celebrations and editorials sealed the issue for Southerners. They now understood that they were hated not because of slavery but because they were Southerners.

In the history of American slavery there is "good" to be reported: Americans freely ended the African slave trade and used their navy to police that nefarious commerce; Americans prohibited slavery in the Northwest territory; Americans, North and South, slaveholders and non-slaveholders, organized societies to begin the effort to end slavery; American States passed laws against reducing a free man (regardless of color) to a slave (man-stealing); and, Americans, especially in the South, freed many of their slaves at their own expense. In addition to these "good" facts about America and slavery, Southern states passed laws to protect slaves from abuse and to protect their right to care after they became old or infirm. In Mississippi for example in 1821 a white man was sentenced to be hanged for the murder of a slave.[144] Even a Northern clergyman in 1863 noted that Southern law holds a master accountable for the death of a slave.[145] All of these "good" acts were done with the full support of the South. Of course these laws did not prevent all abuses of slaves any more than laws against murder prevent all murders. But it does indicate that the general population desired good treatment for the enslaved population. These laws and public scorn of those breaking the moral codes in regard to slavery did go a long way to protect the slave population.

The "bad" was also to be found. Slavery, although often referred to as a "necessary" evil, was an evil just the same. The New Englanders who used slave labor in the early history of their existence and profited from the nefarious African slave trade felt justified in their actions. Southerners who profited from the labor of slaves felt justified, as did the New England merchants, bankers, and industrialists who felt no pangs of remorse in profiting from the merchandising of slave-grown cotton, tobacco, and sugar. So jealous were Northern merchants of their Southern markets that they continually insisted that Congress pass a plethora of protective tariffs. Speaking about slavery, Thomas Jefferson, a slaveholder all his life, mused, "We have the wolf by the ears, and we can neither hold

---

144 Bettersworth, 191.

145 Hopkins, 84.

him, nor safely let him go. Justice is in one scale, and self-preservation in the other."[146]

And now to the "ugly." Once the North found that by using of the power of the Federal government it could enrich itself at the expense of the South, issues were found to support their efforts to control the Federal government. In the modern era the P.C. narrative proclaims that a virtuous North had to contend with an evil South over the issue of ending of slavery. This false narrative is taken for granted as fact and woe be unto he who rejects this view. This false narrative centers almost exclusively on the issue of slavery as the point of contention between the North and the South. Yet, as Simkins so correctly noted, if slavery had not existed "some other sin could have been shrewdly conjured up" to overcome Southern political resistance to Northern ambition—a materialistic ambition motivated by Northern "dollar worship." What was the driving force behind this anti-South effort? As Simkins notes, "Northern industrial and financial leaders wished to destroy the influence of the agrarian South in Washington."[147] The use of race as a weapon against their Southern opponent was born in the minds of those seeking to grow the power and profits of their section of the nation at the expense of the Southern minority. Once established as the majority and finding such a position conducive to the economic well-being of their society, the Northern majority did not look favorably upon losing the benefit of having a minority which had become its milch cow. It has often been reported that in 1861, when Lincoln was asked why he did not just let the South go, his response was, "Let the South go? But where would we get our revenue?" Sixty-three years before Lincoln was reported to have made this statement, Thomas Jefferson was even then (1798) bemoaning that "we are completely under the saddle of Massachusetts and Connecticut, and that they ride us very hard, cruelly insulting our feelings, as well as exhausting our strength and subsistence."[148] The purpose of keeping a "milch cow" is to benefit from its "strength and subsistence" even to the point of "exhausting" the poor cow. Benefits flow to the owner of the "milch cow" and very little if any benefit flows to the cow. In 1861 the Southern "milch cow of the Union" attempted to escape.

---

146 Thomas Jefferson, letter to John Holmes, April 22, 1820 as cited in Thomas Jefferson Foundation, Inc., https://www.monticello.org/site/jefferson/wolf-ear-quotation (Accessed 5/31/2016).

147 Simkins, 190.

148 Thomas Jefferson in letter to John Taylor, June 1, 1798, as cited in, "On Sectional Politics—Possibility of Division," *Letters and Addresses of Thomas Jefferson*, Parker & Viles, eds. (National Jefferson Society, Buffalo, NY: 1903), 123.

Chapter 6

TEACHING HATE

The bitterness and hate created by the late civil strife … would have long since been obliterated in this state, were it not for some unprincipled men who would keep alive the bitterness of the past, and inculcate a hatred between the races, in order that they may aggrandize themselves by office, and its emoluments, to control my people, the effect of which is to degrade them.[149]

The quotation above was written by Senator Hiram Revels in 1875. Who were these people that were attempting to "inculcate a hatred between the races" down South? Those raised upon standard liberal propaganda surely must believe this "inculcating of hate" must be coming from an evil Southern KKK type. If, on the other hand, one has mostly freed himself from liberal propaganda by daily doses of information from conservative "talking-heads" such as Limbaugh, Hannity, Levin, and company, you would likely believe this hate is being inculcated by evil white Southern Democrats. Yet, both the liberal and the conservative answer to this

Senator Hiram Revels, MS. Condemned Republican efforts to foment and use racial hatred as a tool to divide the Southern people and control Congress. (Courtesy LOC)

149 Hiram Revels, "Hiram Revels Letter to President Grant," November 6, 1875 as cited in N C Pedia, http://ncpedia.org/biography/revelsletter (Accessed 4/20/2016).

question are incorrect.[150]

Hiram Revels was the first African-American elected to the United States Senate. Revels was a Republican Senator from Mississippi. He was born in North Carolina as a free person of color and received an education in theology. After the War he moved to Mississippi and worked in the ministry and politics. When he was elected to the Senate many Northerners expected Revels to assist the Radical Republicans in their efforts to punish the South, but they were soon disappointed. Revels understood that in punishing the white South, the black South was also being punished, i.e., harmed. After fighting for the well-being of the people of Mississippi against those who desired only to use black voters to advance the Republican agenda, Revels resigned from the Party. In a letter to President Grant, Senator Revels exposes the misuse of his people (black Southerners) by Republicans:

> A great portion of them [black voters] have learned that they were being used
> as mere tools, and, as in the late election, not being able to correct existing
> evils among themselves, they determined by casting their ballots against those
> unprincipled adventurers, to overthrow them…. My people have been told by
> these schemers [Republican carpetbaggers], when men have been placed on the
> ticket who were notoriously corrupt and dishonest, that they must vote for them;
> that the salvation of the party depended upon it; that the man who scratched
> a ticket was not a Republican. This is only one of the many means these
> unprincipled demagogues have devised to perpetuate the intellectual bondage of
> my people. To defeat this policy, at the late election men, irrespective of race,
> color, or party affiliation, united, and voted together against men known to be
> incompetent and dishonest.[151]

As Senator Revels' letter to Grant resigning from the Republican Party demonstrates, it was not evil white Southerners who were using the newly freed black citizens as "mere tools," nor was it evil Democrats who were engaged in maintaining "the intellectual bondage" of these newly freed black citizens—it was the Republican Party and the ruling elite in Washington. Fast forward 150 years and today it is the

---

150 This is just one of many examples demonstrating that Southerners should not rely on national, i.e. Lincoln-loving, conservatives to protect Southern interest! Their conservative reasoning is founded on a false premise created by the false Yankee narrative about the War for Southern Independence.

151 Hiram Revels as cited in, Garner, James, *Reconstruction in Mississippi* (New York, The Macmillan Co.: 1901), 399-400; http://www.archive.org/stream/reconstructioningarnuoft (Accessed 6/3/2016).

Democrats who are using the black voter "in order that they may aggrandize themselves by office and its emoluments." Is the "modern" Republican doing anything to expose this misuse and abuse of African-Americans by the Democrats? No, they are upset that the Dems have stolen "their" black voters and are doing everything possible to win back their black voters—thus we have Republican Governor Nikki Haley's attack upon all things Confederate. As most tyrants understand, hate is a powerful weapon. Hate, as a weapon, has a long history of being used by the North against the South.

Teaching Northerners to Hate the South

"You have utterly, signally, disastrously—failed to subdue millions of 'rebels,' whom you had taught the people of the North and West not only to hate but to despise."[152] These words were spoken in the U.S. House of Representatives during the United States of America's invasion of a sovereign nation—the Confederate States of America. The fruits of bitter anti-South propaganda were maturing on the tips of bloody Yankee bayonets down South. The unfortunate consequence of the South's union with the North in 1788 had at last come to fruition.

Although it was with some trepidation both in the North and in the South, Americans of 1788 did unite and form a union for their common benefit under the new Constitution. Even though there was a cultural and economic gulf that separated the two sections, the common experience of fighting and defeating the British Empire helped maintain a respectful and polite union between two very divergent people for a short time. But, as Patrick Henry and other Southern patriots warned (see chapter 4), when the "dollar worshipers" of the North discovered they could enrich themselves by passing laws that transferred wealth from the South to the North—economic exploitation

Rep. C. L. Vallandigham, Ohio. Condemned Republicans for having taught the North "not only to hate but to despise [the South]." (Courtesy LOC)

---

152 C. L. Vallandigham, in speech before the United States House of Representatives, January 1863, as cited in *The Record of Hon. C. L. Vallandigham on Abolition, the Union, and the Civil War* (J. Walter and Co., Columbus, OH: 1863), 182.

became the root of political division. But passing laws that would transfer wealth from one section of the country to another cannot be done if the sections are in a close friendly relationship. In such a fraternal relationship the two sections would work together for their common benefit. In the absence of this fraternal relationship, strife with recriminations and counter recriminations began. In an effort to gain the upper hand, radicals in the North began the process of stigmatizing first slavery and then the entire South as evil, barbaric, and less than human. In his January 1863 speech in Congress, Ohio Representative Clement L. Vallandigham notes that radical abolitionists and Republican politicians were successful in their effort to teach Northerners "not only to hate but to despise"[153] the South. From the floor of the United States House of Representatives Vallandigham pointed out that Southern secession:

> was inevitable; because, in the then existing temper of the public mind, and after
> the education through the press, and by the pulpit, the lecture and the political
> canvass for twenty years, of a generation, taught to hate slavery and the South…
> the success of that party [Republican], possessed, as it was, of every engine of
> political, business, social, and religious influence, was certain.[154]

Nothing said about the South or the institution of antebellum slavery which was out of sync with the "hate the South" agenda of Northern radicals was allowed in public discussion. In 1858, a Scotsman, James Stirling, wrote a book based upon his experiences in a recent tour of the South titled *Letters from the Slave States*. Stirling's book was reviewed by the highly acclaimed Boston journal, *North American Review*. Stirling's observation of slavery down South completely refutes the standard Northern narrative of systematic cruelty and habitual abuse of slaves. Stirling's deviation from the standard Northern narrative of slavery down South was noted by the *North American Review* editor: "it entirely lacks the delightful element of recrimination and abuse, without which a work on slavery would fall dead in our market."[155] The editor of this Boston, Massachusetts, journal is admitting that when it came to the issue of slavery and the South, Northerners held the opinion, "Don't bother me with facts, my mind is already made up." Why was it already "made up"? As Vallandigham announced on the floor of Congress in 1863, they had been taught "not only to hate but to despise" Southerners.

---

153 *Ibid.*

154 *Ibid.*, 176.

155 *North American Review*, January 1858, LXXXVI, 290-91.

According to Vallandigham, the secession crisis was made "inevitable" because of the anti-South propaganda spewing forth from different forums in the North. Southerners took notice of how they were being characterized and portrayed by Northern radicals. Up until the late 1830s the number of anti-South radicals in the North were few, but their influence far exceeded their numbers.[156] The South was also very aware of the fact that the vast majority of Northerners, who were not radicals, did little or nothing to defend their fellow countrymen in the South. As Bettersworth, a Mississippi historian, noted, secession was not something new for Mississippians. After all, they remembered that New England called a secession convention during the War of 1812. Mississippi (and the same can be said for all Southern States) acted on the question of secession only after being subjected to a long train of abuse:

> Then came the tariff and the Abolitionists; and embattled Mississippians joined others of the South against the measures and men that threatened the Southland. Secession came by inches—a hint in 1832; a threat in 1851; a fact in 1861.[157]

The feeling this historian is chronicling, that is, that the South was under attack and in danger of being subjugated by the North, was noted in 1863 by Nicholas A. Davis, chaplain of Hood's Texas Brigade. Chaplain Davis wrote that the objective of the North was "to subjugate and despoil—make the South their inferior, and the bearer of their burdens."[158] The immense out-pouring of volunteers to defend the South in 1861 and thereafter is proof positive that feelings of mistrust of Yankee rule were deeply held by most Southerners. It should be noted that regardless of status, slaveholder or non-slaveholder, the men and women of the South stood by their chosen nation—the Confederate States of America. What was generating such feelings in the South?

As already pointed out, radical abolitionist propaganda was teaching Northerners to hate not just slavery or even slaveholders down South but to hate the South itself. On the floor of Congress, Ohio Representative Vallandigham pointed out that for twenty years (one full generation) Northerners had been "taught to hate slavery *and* the South." Ohio Congressman and Radical Republican Joshua Giddings proudly proclaimed his hatred of the South by voicing his desire

---

156 Hummel, 27.

157 Bettersworth, John K., *Mississippi: A History* (The Steck Company, Austin, TX: 1959), 214.

158 Davis, Nicholas A., *The Campaign from Texas to Maryland, with the Battle of Fredericksburg* (Louisiana State University Press, Baton Rouge: 1999), 146.

for the time "when the torch of the incendiary shall light up the towns and cities of the South."[159] Upon hearing about Giddings' desire to see innocent men, women and children of the South massacred, Southerners took this as proof positive that a union of *mutual* benefit and respect was already "gone with the wind." One major leader in the orgy of anti-South blasphemy was William Lloyd Garrison. Howard R. Floan, author of *The South in Northern Eyes 1831-1861*, points out that Garrison's "hatred of slavery became hatred of the slaveholder, and the slaveholder became indistinguishable from the Southerner."[160] Floan asserts that Garrison viewed the North/South conflict as a conflict between God's elect, New England, and the damned, the South. [161]

South hating Ralph Waldo Emerson declared the South to be inhabited not by men but by animals with no prospect for a future. (Courtesy LOC)

In articles and speeches Garrison damned Southerners as "thieves and adulterers...ruffians who insult, pollute and lacerate helpless women and conspirators against the lives and liberties of New England citizens."[162] New England notables such as Ralph Waldo Emerson did not hide their hatred of the South. Emerson described South Carolina as a "troublesome, crime-infested area....We must go there in disguise...making our wills as we go."[163] It was not just South Carolina that Emerson ridiculed and slandered but the entire South. Emerson believed that in the South:

man is an animal, given to pleasure, frivolous, irritable, spending his days in

---

159 Joshua Giddings as cited in Scott, Otto, *The Secret Six*, (Uncommon Books, Murphys, CA: 1993), 309.

160 Floan, 5.

161 *Ibid.*, 9.

162 *Ibid.*, 6.

163 Ralph Waldo Emerson, *Ibid.*, 55. It should be noted that Emerson's great-grandfather, Cornelius Waldo, was a wealthy merchant and Massachusetts slave-trader.

hunting and practicing with deadly weapons to defend himself against his slaves
and against his companions brought up in the same idle and dangerous way.
Such people live for the moment, they have properly no future.[164]

The statement, "they have *properly no future*" tells us the depth of Emerson's hatred of Southerners. Hitler and Stalin believed the same thing about those they hated and turned up the heat in ovens or expanded the Gulag to prove it! Only two years before the secession of the Southern States, Emerson declared that Southerners were "felons who have disentitled themselves to the protection of the law." Hitler and Stalin also believed that those whom they hated were beyond the "protection of the law." Emerson predicted that even if Southerners catch and kill John Brown it would not matter because:

the air [of New England] breeds them [John Browns], every school, every
church...every home of courtesy, genius and conscience is educating haters of him
[Southerners] and his misdeeds.[165]

After the terrorist John Brown's murderous escapades were brought to an end by a length of Virginia rope, Emerson eulogized Brown as "the rarest of heroes, a pure idealist."[166] A very similar eulogy was given throughout the Muslim world for Bin Laden. Both men, John Brown and Osama Bin Laden, were acting on what they believed were the high principles of a "pure idealist." Both men believed in a higher law while rejecting the general rule that civil society follows, which is "live and let live." In the name of doing good (as they defined "good"), *both* men were willing to do great evil—as we say down South, they were just "two peas in a pod!"

In 1826, James Kent of New York explained how the American Union would be held together when he proclaimed: "for on the concurrence and good will of the parts [states] the stability of the whole [union] depends."[167] What would hold the Union together? Not bloody bayonets or trampling upon the rights and liberties of the people but "concurrence and good will." By 1861 "concurrence" (in law this word denotes "a *joint* claim and right") was absent because "good will" among the sections was dead. Without concurrence and good will the Union, as established by the founding fathers, is dead and replaced by the domination of one group by another group. When one

---

164 *Ibid.*, 58.

165 *Ibid.*, 59.

166 *Ibid.*, 56.

167 Kent, James, *Commentaries On American Law* (1826; Da Capo Press, NY: 1971), I, 195-6.

group of people hold another group of people in a relationship against the will of the oppressed group, that is a form of enslavement—otherwise known as slavery.[168] Tyrannical groups often use a simple but effective method to transfer enemies of the dominant group into a category of beings unworthy of consideration as "normal" humans. First, a group is identified as different from the "normal" group; second, the selected group is stigmatized as evil and promoters of all types of problems for the "normal" group; and third, the now evil, problem-causing group is described as less than human.[169] (Human, of course, is measured by the actions, beliefs and life of the dominant group.) Name any 20th century tyrant and this method of gaining and/or maintaining power is displayed in their acts of governing. Compare the actions of 20th century tyrants to the words of Ralph Waldo Emerson of New England when he assailed Southerners as "thieves and adulterers…. [Southern] man is an animal….they have properly no future…disentitled themselves to the protection of the law."[170] From

Gen. Sherman, who declared his intention to exterminate Southerners; "men, women, and children." (Courtesy LOC)

the mouth of "the sage of Concord," Emerson, we see how Southerners were identified, vilified, and ultimately, dehumanized. Southerners were seen as less than human and undeserving of the "protection of law." Therefore, any number of barbaric and hideous acts could then be "legally" carried out upon these "animal" men, women, and children (black and white) of the South.

How did twenty to thirty years of teaching the North "not only to hate but to despise" the South play out once the South was invaded? In a letter to the United States Secretary of War, General William T. Sherman gives us

---

168 St. George Tucker as cited by Kennedy, *Myths of American Slavery*, 235-40.

169 This redefining of "normal" and stigmatizing of the new "non-normal" group is currently being done by secular humanists as they characterize those who hold traditional Christian values as being outside the "normal" for American society, i.e., Christians are politically incorrect and therefore not "normal" Americans.

170 Emerson as cited by Floan, 59.

an insight into how Yankees felt about Southern "animals" in human form: "There is a class of people [Southerners] men, women, and children, who must be killed or banished before you can hope for peace and order."[171] [emphasis added]. Were the authorities in Washington shocked and disgusted by Sherman's suggestion of murdering (exterminating) Southerners including children? NOT AT ALL! Abraham Lincoln's Secretary of War replied to Sherman in the following manner, "Your letter of the 21st of June has just reached me and meets my approval."[172] These unlawful and shocking acts, euphemistically referred to as a "vigorous war policy" by Lincoln, were not just pursued by high ranking officers of the United States Army but permeated the army down to the lowest rank. In Jackson, Louisiana, Celine Fremaux, a fourteen-year-old girl, recounts how these acts of brutality were played out upon Southern civilians. In her diary Fremaux records the story of a neighbor lady who had already lost her husband and six of her seven sons in defense of the South. The neighbor, a Mrs. Fluker, had one sixteen-year-old son living at home who wanted to enlist in the Confederate army. Mrs. Fluker, as so many women of the South of that time did, began making her son a uniform. Needing a few more buttons, she sent her son to town to acquire the needed items. While in town her son noticed that Yankee raiders were approaching town. As he began to leave town, dressed as a civilian and not a member of the military, the Yankee troops gave chase. In the process of escaping the Yankees the young boy's horse fell into a ravine, killing the horse and severely injuring the boy. The Yankees pulled the boy from the ravine and, according to her diary: "There they searched his pockets and his cap. Disappointed at finding nothing of dispatches or signs that he was a soldier, they struck him several blows over the head with the butt of their guns and threw him back in the gully."[173] The young man's mother buried her son in his unfinished (two buttons were missing) Confederate uniform. Mrs. Fluker had given all the male members of her household to the Cause of Southern Independence. This is how a sixteen-year-old boy was treated by those who for over a generation had been taught "not only to hate but to despise" Southerners.

A short time after the murder of Mrs. Fluker's son, a gentleman by the name of Dr. Barkdull was stopped by a Yankee patrol. Dr. Barkdull, the manager of a nearby insane

---

171 William T. Sherman as cited in *Official Records War of the Rebellion*, XXXIX, pt. II, 132.

172 *Ibid.*, 157.

173 Celine Fremaux as cited by Sullivan, Walter, ed., *The War the Women Lived: Female Voices from the Confederate South* (J. S. Sanders & Co., Nashville, TN: 1995), 195.

asylum, had taken the oath of allegiance to the United States in order to obtain food for the residents of the asylum. (Southerners often referred to this detestable act as "swallowing the dog.") Young Fremaux describes what happened as the Yankees accosted Dr. Barkdull:

> He was telling as much [having taken the oath of allegiance] to three or four
> Yankee soldiers and was in the act of pulling his papers from his pocket when a
> corporal came up and cursing, said, 'What is up? Kill him and be done.' So
> saying he leaned far into the buggy and shot twice....Mr. Barkdull fell out, his
> papers [oath of allegiance to the United States] still in his hand. [Several ladies]
> asked the Yankees to help lift him into a house. The men refused saying 'Many
> are buried in a trench, leave him in the gutter, and pile trash over him.[174]

Not satisfied with the amount of insults and death inflicted upon the defenseless local population, a population consisting of old men, women, children and slaves, the Yankees showed up at Dr. Barkdull's burial. Young Fremaux describes an atrocity at the cemetery:

> It happened as they were burying him the Yankees again came. They came into
> the graveyard, and hearing of who was being buried, the murderer was called
> up by his superior officer and then, and there, congratulated on his zeal and
> patriotism.[175]

Such patriotic zeal would make any Nazi Waffen SS officer proud! These incidents were not isolated incidents but rather the common rule of action of the United States (the Federal Empire) as it invaded the Confederate States of America.

Before Sherman's army burned Columbia, South Carolina, Mary S. Whilden, a resident of that city, had a very sick child and sought medical help from a Union doctor. Mrs. Whilden relates her encounter with the Union doctor as she sought medical help for her sick child: "I had an infant who, from exposure, contracted a severe cold and was threatened with a serious illness. I took the child to an army doctor whose headquarters were in the Preston mansion...and asked for medicine. I stood on the front balcony, which was draped with the United States flags. The doctor cursed me as a rebel woman, and said, 'Let the d***** rebel die.'"[176] Hoping to find a more civil physician, she approached a second doctor who seemed to be more willing

---

174 *Ibid.*, 196-97.

175 *Ibid.*

176 Whilden, Mary S. as cited in, Stokes, Karen, *South Carolina Civilians in Sherman's Path* (The History Press, Charleston, SC: 2012), 49.

to assist the desperate mother. The second doctor gave Mrs. Whilden a bottle with instruction to give the child a teaspoonful of the medicine. When she checked the medicine before administering it to her sick child, she noticed that it was laudanum, a very potent narcotic which would have killed the infant.[177]   Now recall the words of Sherman: "There is a class of people [Southerners] men, women, *and children*, who must be killed or banished before you can hope for peace and order."[178]   Notice that the invading Yankees did not ask these Southerners, the young sixteen-year-old boy, the administrator of the asylum or the mother of a sick infant if they owned slaves.

The actions of the United States military during the War for Southern Independence was so horrible and atrocious that even Nazis used it as an example of what Europe could expect at the hands of Americans. In the Nazi propaganda magazine, *Signal*, the Nazis noted that at Appomattox General Lee "surrendered to criminals, not soldiers."[179]   Volumes have been written of these Nazi-like acts of the United States military in its invasion and conquest of the South.[180]   Notice that the invading Yankees did not ask these Southerners if they owned slaves. The only thing that mattered was that morally and intellectually superior Yankees were now in the process of cleansing New England's Southern provinces of the indigenous (black and white) population. This indigenous sub-human population had for too long stood in the way of New England progress. Men such as Giddings, Emerson, and Sherman surely approved of this cleansing work of the conquering Yankee. The war of extermination waged against the Southern people was all done under the authority of "Old Glory," the "Stars and Stripes," the invader's flag! This hatred directed toward black and white Southerners—all under the authority and in the presence of the "Stars and Stripes" or "Old Glory" as the U.S. flag is often called—is the reason that Admiral Raphael Semmes of the CSS *Alabama* referred to the U.S.

---

177 *Ibid.*, 50.

178 Sherman as cited in *Official Records War of the Rebellion*, XXXIX, pt. II, 132.

179 Kiaulehn, Walter, "The Anaconda System," Signal, as cited in, *Hitler's Wartime Picture Magazine*, S.L. Mayer, ed. (Bison Publishing Co., London: 1976).

180 See Sullivan, Walter, ed.,*The War the Women Lived: Female Voices from the Confederate South* (J. S. Sanders & Co., Nashville, TN: 1995); Cisco, Walter Brian, *War Crimes Against Southern Civilians* (Pelican Publishing Co., Gretna, LA: 2008); Keys, Thomas Bland, ed.,*The Uncivil War: Union Army and Navy Excesses in the Official Records* (The Beauvoir Press, Biloxi, MS: 1991); Stokes, *Karen, South Carolina Civilians in Sherman's Path* (The History Press, Charleston, SC: 2012); and Edmonds, David C., ed., *Conduct of Federal Troops in Louisiana* (The Acadiana Press, Lafayette, LA: 1988).

flag as "hate's polluted rag."[181] He made a specific distinction between the "old flag" of the constitutional republic and the "new flag"[182] of the Federal Empire. He knew that even though they looked the same, they did not represent the same government.

A similar emotion about the United States Flag was expressed by the grandson of Francis Scott Key, author of "The Star Spangled Banner." Forty-seven years after Francis Scot Key penned what was to become the national anthem of the United States, his grandson, Francis Key Howard, was forcibly removed from his home by United States soldiers and imprisoned in a military prison at Fort McHenry in Baltimore Harbor. Howard, a civilian not in the active service of the militia, was illegally arrested by the army on orders from Lincoln's administration. Howard, as editor of the *Daily Exchange* of Baltimore, had committed the high crime of writing an editorial opposing Lincoln's un-Constitutional suspension of the *writ of habeas corpus*. The exercise of his First Amendment right of freedom of the press was deemed by the Federal government to be an act of treason, deserving imprisonment. On the first morning of his imprisonment Howard awoke and, looking out of his prison window, he cast his eyes upon the American Flag his grandfather, forty-seven years earlier, had seen as the symbol of freedom. As a political prisoner of the Federal Empire, he no longer viewed the Empire's flag with the same reverence as did his grandfather: Howard noted, "The flag which he [Francis Scott Key] had then so proudly hailed, I saw waving, at the same place, over the victims of as vulgar and brutal a despotism as modern times have witnessed."[183]

Sadly, patriotic Southerners are too reluctant to admit the unpleasant truth which the grandson of Francis Scott Key so clearly understood, that the U. S. flag that was is not the U. S. flag that is! The flag that "was" represented a government that feared the people; whereas, the flag that "is" represents an empire where the people fear the government. Nevertheless, acceptance of this cruel reality is the first step in replacing the *illegitimate* Federal Empire, where the people fear the government, with America's *legitimate* republic of republics where, via real states' rights, the government will fear "we the people" at the local level.

---

181 Semmes, 494.

182 *Ibid.*, 515, 335.

183 Howard, Francis Key, *Fourteen Months in the American Bastilles* (Kelly, Hedian & Piet, Baltimore, MD: 1863), 67.

Teaching Racial Hate

Is racial hatred a natural part of Southern society? If we could ask a black Southerner who was a member of Mississippi's legislature in the 1890s what would he say about race relations in the South as opposed to race relations in the North?

I was born in Mississippi, but raised in a Northern State; associations there led me to regard the Southern white men as dire foes to the Negroes, but receiving such cordial and unprejudiced association upon this floor…these suspicions have been eliminated from the bosoms of these…six and for them I am authorized to speak. You are our best friends…you have shown to be our friends, not our enemies.[184]

Most Americans and unfortunately too many Southerners believe that racial animosity and bitterness is a naturally occurring event down South. But as pointed out in chapter 5, there was less racial hatred and prejudice in the South than in the North. James S. Buckingham, a British abolitionist, makes a shocking observation about race relations in the antebellum United States. Buckingham informs us:

The prejudice of color is not nearly so strong in the South as in the North. [In the South] it is not at all uncommon to see the black slaves of both sexes, shake hands with white people when they meet, and interchange friendly personal inquires; but at the North I do not remember to have witnessed this once; and neither in Boston, New York, or Philadelphia would a white person generally like to be seen shaking hands and talking familiarly with blacks in the streets.[185]

In 1890 Representative Moore, an African-American in the Mississippi Legislature, declared that he had been taught that white Southerners were his enemies, but he now proclaims, "You are our best friends."[186] Moore is speaking about the same South where fifty years earlier a British abolitionist informed the world that there was less racial hatred than the North! According to the modern P.C. liberal narrative of a hate-filled South, these two men's comments cannot be true. Obviously they just did not understand the South as well as modern liberals do. General Carl Schurz, a radical socialist[187] Yankee General, discovered in 1865 that

---

184 Representative Moore as cited in, *Daily Clarion-Ledger,* Jackson, MS, February 23, 1890.

185 Buckingham, J. S., *The Slave States of America,* (Negro University Press, NY: 1968), II, 112.

186 Moore, Ibid.

187 For an overview of Schurz's radical socialist background see Benson and Kennedy, *Lincoln's Marxists* (Pelican Publican Co., Gretna, LA: 2011) ,167-70.

even after centuries of enslavement by whites, the former slaves did not hate white people or their former masters.[188] Once again it must be pointed out that the slaves may not have liked slavery but they did not hate white Southerners. During the war, Northerners began to understand that, even in the mist of war and invasion, black Southerners would not rise up in a Haiti-style revolt. Additionally, they realized that unless disrupted by invading Yankees, the slaves stayed on their plantations and homesteads.

Gen Beauregard, CSA (Courtesy LOC)

Slaves freely choosing to stay on their plantation and in peaceful contact with their "white folks" does not fit the Yankee narrative of slaves longing to be free and hating their masters. Once again and acknowledging being redundant, it must be stated that the slaves may not have liked slavery but they did not hate white Southerners. In the *Federal Writers' Project, 1936-39*, over 2,300 interviews of former slaves were compiled by the Federal government. These interviews are commonly known as the "Slave Narratives." A review of the Narratives will demonstrate that the overwhelming majority of the former slaves describe their life and their master in a positive manner. Yes, there were some former slaves who were mistreated by horrific masters, and these former slaves were more than happy to express their dislike of their masters. But when taken as a whole, a positive feeling was expressed by former slaves for their life as a slave. For example, one told Federal interviewers: "I was born a slave but I ain' neber been one. I'se a worker for good peoples. You would not call dat bein' a slave would you, white folks."[189] Unlike the absentee landlords of huge plantations in the Caribbean or South America, these slaves lived in near proximity to their master, who viewed his slaves more like an extended family than simply chattel. Had this warm (yet very strange by modern

188 Schultz, Carl, "Report of Carl Schurz on the States of South Carolina, Georgia, Alabama, Mississippi and Louisiana (December 19 1865)," Smith, John David, ed., *A Just and Lasting Peace*, (Signet Classic Books, NY: 2013), 140.

189 Roper, Gary L., *Antebellum Slavery: An Orthodox Christian View* (Gary L. Roper: 2008), 189.

standards) relationship not existed among black and white people in the South, a Haitian-style race war would have surely taken place once all the men of military age had been removed from the plantations. Simply put, there was too much love and not enough hate down South for a Haitian-style racial conflict. But, after the war, radicals in the North were very willing to infect the South with their "virus" of racism.[190]

With the adoption of the Thirteenth Amendment and the elimination of slavery, every African-American in the South was counted as one person and not three-fifths of a person for purposes of congressional representation.[191] If the white and black voters of the South united, the Southern and Northern Democrats could possibly control both houses of Congress.[192] The Republican Party went into panic mode—what was to be done? The answer was simple: export racial hatred from the North to the South, with a little twist. Instead of white people being taught to hate black people, as was so common in New England, Republicans would teach Southern black voters to fear and hate Southern white voters. It should be pointed out that most Northern States at that time still prohibited African-Americans from voting. By mobilizing a large bloc of angry black voters and by prohibiting large numbers of white Southern voters from exercising the right to vote, the Republican Party insured its rule in Washington.

The Republican Party's fear of a racially united South was made even more frightening when former Confederate leaders spoke out in favor of black/white unity. Just a few months after the close of the War, from New Orleans, General Beauregard stated:

The Negro is Southern born; with a little education and some property qualifications he can be made to take sufficient interest in the affairs and prosperity of the South to insure an intelligent vote.[193]

No one can question that the Confederate General who is slandered the most as an evil racist is Nathan Bedford Forrest. In a speech to a group of black voters, Forrest reflected the goodwill that had existed before Republican Reconstruction. He states:

---

190 For a more extended look at New England's role in spreading the "virus" of racial hate see Melish, Joan Pope, *Disowning Slavery: Gradual Emancipation and "Race" in New England 1780-1860* (Cornell University Press, Ithaca, London: 1998), 221-37.

191 Counting black Southerners as "3/5 of a person" in the proposed constitution of 1787 was insisted upon by the North in order to keep Southern representation in Congress to a minimum.

192 Melish, 221-37.

193 Harry, William T., *P. G. T. Beauregard: Napoleon in Gray* (Louisiana State University Press, Baton Rouge: 1995), 266-67.

Gen. N. B. Forrest, CSA
(Courtesy LOC)

We were born on the same soil, breathe the same air, live in the same land, and why should we not be brothers and sisters....I want you to do as I do—go to the polls and select the best men to vote for....Although we differ in color, we should not differ in sentiment....Do your duty as citizens, and if any are oppressed, I will be your friend.[194]

Notice the claim of Forrest that he "will be your *friend*" and reconsider the words of an African-American Representative from Mississippi speaking to his white associates, "you are our best friends."

The use of race-hatred became a very successful Republican tool to divide the South into warring parties. These warring parties, both black and white, failed to realize that in the process of enriching Republican industrialists, bankers and politicians, they were at the same time impoverishing themselves. This was the message that Senator Revels delivered to the Republican Party when he resigned from that cabal of thieves and bigots. French journalist and literary critic Jean-Baptiste Alphonse Karr is noted for his epigram, "The more things change, the more they stay the same." Karr would surely agree that in the 20th and 21st centuries American politics reflects his little truism. The only change is in the name of the political party that is the most dedicated to keeping the races in a high pitch of animosity. This has been a win-win for the Federal Empire. As long as Southerners continue fighting each other, they will never recognize who is really benefitting from continued racial hatred. Being thus distracted, the defeated, conquered, and occupied people of the Confederate States of America are much less likely to follow the lead of other occupied nations and demand the right to govern themselves as happened in Hungary in 1956.

Tiring of Soviet communist domination, in the summer of 1956 the defeated, conquered, and occupied people of Hungary expelled the Russian Communist tyrants from their country and proclaimed they were once again a free and independent

---

194 Forrest as cited by Seabrook, Lochlainn, *A Rebel Born; A Defense of Nathan Bedford Forrest* (Sea Raven Press, Franklin, TN, 2010) 483-4.

nation. The Russian response was swift and deadly. Russian tanks and troop poured into Hungary and soon crushed the freedom fighters. Shortly thereafter every Hungarian historical monument, flag, and even song that reminded the people of the time when they ruled their own homeland was destroyed or forbidden. Imre Nagy, the leader of the Hungarian freedom movement, was captured, executed and buried in an undisclosed location so as to prevent his grave from being a reminder of freedom that once existed in Hungary. Why did the Russians work so hard to cleanse Hungary of any historical remembrance of past freedom? The answer is very revealing of today's anti-South P.C. environment. The Communist tyrants of Russia feared anything that was out of keeping with the accepted narrative of the Communist Party because it might stir people to remember what real freedom was all about and once again seek to be free. The parallels between the ongoing campaign of cultural cleansing of the South and the Islamic radicals of ISIS, Nazi book burning, and communist tyrants suppressing freedom of speech to protect their evil empire should make every Southerner question: "Are we really free?"

The effort to destroy the South so well underway before the secession of the Southern States continued unabated during the War and Reconstruction. Communist author James S. Allen acknowledged this fact when he wrote:

> Reconstruction was the continuation of the Civil War into a new phase, in which the revolution passed from the stage of armed conflict into primarily a political struggle which sought to consolidate the Northern triumph."[195]

The constant attack upon the South was recognized by Southerners from all walks of life. Even famous Western "outlaws" such as John Wesley Hardin of Texas noted the impact of Northern conquest and occupation: "I became a fugitive, not from justice be it known, but from the injustice and misrule of the people who had subjugated the South."[196]

The topic of "subjugation" is not something often discussed in the South up until now. Nevertheless, even men such John W. Hardin understood what the relationship between the defeated South and the Federal Empire meant. Today when Alabama is "ordered" by the Federal Empire to remove the Ten Commandments from court houses, when the United States Supreme Court protects the right of the

---

195 Allen, James S., *Reconstruction: The Battle for Democracy* (International Publisher, NY: 1937), 175-76.

196 McCubbin, Robert G., ed., *The Life of John Wesley Hardin* (University of Oklahoma Press, Norman, OK: 1961), xvii, 6-7. Hardin was an "outlaw" from Yankee Reconstruction "justice."

descendants of Buffalo Soldiers to display a car tag that honors their ancestors but denies the same right to descendants of Confederate soldiers, and when Southern States demand that males use male bathrooms and stay out of the girls' bathroom, and are ridiculed and blasted as bigots, it is past time for Southerners to revisit Mr. Hardin's thesis. For surely, a truly free people who are living in a government formed and sustained "by the consent"[197] of the governed and who enjoy the American right to "alter or abolish"[198] any government that does not suit the people—surely such a courageous people will not abide living as a subjugated nation forever!

---

197 See Declaration of Independence, second through fourth sentences.

198 *Ibid.*

Chapter 7

THE WAR TO EXTERMINATE
BLACK AND WHITE SOUTHERNERS

[Treat the South] as conquered provinces and **settle them with new men** *and* **exterminate** *or drive out the present rebels as exiles.*[199] *Congressman Thaddaeus Stevens (R-Penn.)*

We believe in a war of **extermination**....*Brig. Gen. James H. Lane, U.S.A.*[200]

In this chapter we will see how the intentional elimination of black and white Southerners was the official policy of the United States of America under Lincoln and Radical Republicans[201] in Congress. Their goal was to "exterminate" enough of the native Southern population to allow the southern part of the United States to be "repopulated" with Northerners who would then support the expanding Federal Empire.[202] Their intention was to completely remake the South into a second class image of the North.[203]

---

199 Fleming, Walter Lynwood, *The Sequel of Appomattox* (Glasgow, Brook & Co., Toronto, Canada: 1970), 59.

200 Cisco, 27.

201 The term "Radical Republican" is used by national historians in an attempt to distinguish between Republicans during the War/Reconstruction and current day national Republicans. The truth is that there is no difference because the current Republican Party has never renounced its radical past and currently is a leader in the ongoing efforts to *exterminate* Southern heritage. Republican Governor Nikki Haley's removal of the Confederate Battle Flag and the GOP- controlled Congress's vote May 2016 to prohibit descendants of CSA veterans from displaying the Confederate flag in U.S. National cemeteries are but two examples. Republican anti-South Radicalism used in the 1860s to enhance and exploit political opportunity continues today—same song, different verse.

202 Tourgee, Albion W., *A Fool's Errand* (1879, The Belknap Press, Cambridge, MA: 1961), 24, 27. (Just one of many examples of Northern intent to "repopulate" the conquered South—an effort that continues today!)

203 *Ibid.*, 27, 381; also see 386, 402, demonstrating the Yankee view of a "sick" South that would not cure itself and had to be forcefully cured of its Southern disease by the North; and 381 showing their desire to "remake" the South. Albion Tourgee was a carpetbagger from Ohio who spent time in New England and New York prior to the war.

Never again would Southern political power be allowed to stand in the way of protective tariffs or other "progressive" federal legislation. The North used an aggressive war to exterminate its traditional Southern political adversary. This "vigorous" war policy was endorsed and encouraged by Lincoln and Congress then under Republican control.

One of the primary reasons for post-war Southern poverty was the death of over a million black and white Southerners in the war and post-war period. This loss of valuable Southern "human capital" would hinder Southern economic development for generations to come.[204] Thanks to Lincoln's aggressive war waged against a sovereign nation—the Confederate States of America—the Southern states would never again attain economic or political parity with the other states in Lincoln's newly-created Federal Empire. We the people of the South have been reduced from prosperity to virtual peonage to the economically successful North—a second class Southern economy for a second class people! The Federal Empire's unofficial motto would hence forth be: *Vae victis*—Woe to the vanquished!

When Americans think of "wars of extermination" they never consider that the United States of America might be guilty of such atrocities. Yet, as we shall see, this was one the United States' primary goals as it invaded, conquered and occupied its smaller neighbor, the Confederate States of America. It has been estimated that the number of Southerners "murdered" by the U.S. Army would be equal to 3.5 million souls if "standardized for the South's 2010 population."[205] The death toll of invasion and occupation for black Southerners alone has been estimated to be between 400,000 to one million.[206] Accurate records do not exist due to the utter destruction caused by the Federal invaders, but their intentions are well documented. In the winter of 1863-4 the Governor of Louisiana, Henry Watkins Allen, issued a report stating that more blacks had died in Louisiana due to the effects of invasion in the previous year

---

204 The importance of human capital was noted by economist Sowell: "Human capital is important, not just in helping a country recover from devastating losses of physical capital, such as after war. It is also a major factor in economic progress in normal times." Sowell, Thomas, *Wealth, Poverty, and Politics* (Basic Books, NY: 2015), 83.

205 DiLorenzo, Thomas, "The Founding Fathers of Constitutional Subversion," *Rethinking The American Union* (Pelican Publishing Co., Gretna, LA: 2013), 80.

206 Graham, John, *A Constitutional History of Secession* (Pelican Publishing Co, Gretna, LA: 2002), 385. A Connecticut "intellectual" estimated that 3.5 million former slaves were put at risk after the war due to the way in which the United States handled emancipation. Downs, Jim, *Sick from Freedom; African-American Illness and Suffering during the Civil War and Reconstruction* (Oxford University Press, New York: 2012), 21.

than the total of white deaths in both armies![207] A Mississippi Unionist stated during Reconstruction that 50% of blacks in Mississippi died during the war.[208] Taken at face value the prior estimate would seem unreasonable. But when viewed in light of the events in the "Devil's Punchbowl" at Natchez, Mississippi, it becomes believable. The "Devil's Punchbowl" was the name given to a contraband, actually concentration, camp established by the Union army after it occupied Natchez. Over 20,000 "freed" slaves died in the Union army's concentration camp in the year following the Union army's occupation of Natchez. The camp was walled off by the Union army to prevent escape.[209] Most, if not all, historians schooled in the Northern narrative of the war— that narrative being a biased depiction of an "evil" South fighting to keep blacks in slavery while the virtuous North willingly shed its blood to free their black brothers— such historians pass off atrocity claims as being no more than mere Confederate "wartime propaganda" designed to inflame Southerners.[210] But as one scholar discovered:

> As my research progressed, however, I found similar accounts of the same outrages in the extant papers of planters, clergy....But the most persuasive evidence is in the letters and diaries of the Northern soldiers....the circumstances described by Union onlookers are frequently even more sordid and deplorable than those depicted by... Confederate authors.[211]

Northerners had for generations readily consumed an outpouring of biased anti-South propaganda. The hatred of the South that was engendered by this slanderous anti-South propaganda worked its magical effect upon the armed invaders of the South. A Massachusetts colonel wrote the Republican Governor back home, declaring: "The thing we seek is permanent dominion....We must take their ports, their mines, their

---

207 Pollard, Edward A., *Southern History of the War* (1866, The Fairfax Press, New York: 1977), vol. 2, 198.

208 Wilson, Clyde, "Defeat and Occupation: The Cold War Known as Reconstruction," *To Live And Die In Dixie*, 445.

209 http://www.africanamerica.org/topic/during-the-civil-war-authorities-in-natchez-mississippi-forced-tens-of-thousands-of-freed-slaves-into-camps-built-in-what-s-known-as-the-devil-s-punchbowl-of-natchez (Accessed 7/1/2016).

210 Connecticut "intellectual" Downs admitted that "historians fear that any indictment of freedom, would in some way substantiate a claim put forth by slaveholders 200 years ago." See Downs, 181, footnote 13. Fear of the truth is the reason the Federal Empire richly rewards its propagandists (i.e., national historians) for their efforts in maintaining the slanderous, anti-South Yankee narrative about why the United States of America invaded a peaceful, democratic nation in 1861 and turned a sovereign nation into its colonial possession.

211 *The Conduct of Federal Troops In Louisiana* (David Edmonds, ed., The Acadiana Press, Lafayette, LA: 1988, originally published 1865), vii.

water power, the very soil they plow."[212] Nor was this desire to exterminate Southerners only expressed by Union soldiers and United States elected officials. Henry Ward Beecher, a Yankee Radical Abolitionist, while speaking at Exeter Hall in London in 1863, responded thusly when asked why not just let the South go: "Why not let the South go? O that the South would go! But then they must leave us their lands." If this attitude was only a rare exception, then perhaps it could be overlooked. But the facts demonstrate that not only was it *not* rare, it was in fact the official attitude and policy of the United States government—no longer a Republic but now the supreme, all-powerful, Federal Empire. During the War and the Empire's post-war effort to destroy the South's influence in the government of the empire no one, black or white, was safe from the hand of the cruel invader. David Conyngham, a Northern newspaper reporter, described the horrors visited upon the people of the South and bluntly confirmed that, "Color is no protection from these [Yankee] roughriders."[213] The murderous actions of the Yankee invader against the black population when found alone led to the practice of always having a white person with a black traveler. Benjamin S. Stafford describes the precarious condition of black Southerners in South Carolina after Sherman's Army passed through the area: "There were bands of roving bush whacker, Yankee bummers who would not harm [a black person] if he had some white person with him. On the other hand, if he were by himself, they would in most cases simply kill him and take his wagon and [valuables]." [214]

The poverty imposed upon the people of the South by the United States of America resulted from more than merely the loss of material and financial property. The major loss was the tremendous loss of what economists refer to as "human capital." Approximately 25% of the South's white male population became causalities[215] as a result of their heroic efforts to defend their homes and families from a numerically superior, vicious and merciless invader. This "human capital" loss represented a large portion of the South's best and brightest—men who would not be available to help restore a destroyed Southern economy. But direct war causalities are not the only ones to be considered. Added to that number must be the even larger number of black and white Southern civilians—

---

212 Wilson, "Defeat and Occupation," 437.

213 David Conyngham as cited in Stokes, 107.

214 Benjamin S. Stafford as cited in Stokes, 109.

215 Historian J. David Hacker noted that 22.6% of Southern males between the age of 20-24 in 1860 died due to the war. http://www.history.com/news/civil-war-deadlier-than-previously-thought (Accessed 4/13/2016)

men, women, children and infants who died as a result of disease and starvation—a direct result of the Federal Empire's *extermination* policy (euphemistically referred to by Lincoln, Republicans in the U.S. Congress and others as a "vigorous war policy").

Exterminate Southerners

National historians who act as propagandists advancing or defending the Federal Empire's narrative about the "Civil War" are quick to dismiss examples of the Federal Empire's military using extreme measures against Southern civilians. They do this primarily by simply ignoring the Empire's atrocities; if they do mention civilian deaths they dismiss it as a natural part of war—with the implicit assumption that that the "Civil War" was a just war made necessary by an evil South that attacked the North at Ft. Sumter, South Carolina.[216] Occasionally the Empire's propagandists (also known as national historians) will acknowledge a "few" atrocities but insist that they were only isolated events not worthy of scholarly notice. But as we will document, using the Federal government's own records, Lincoln and other high Federal officials encouraged the adoption of a "vigorous" war policy which included not only killing Southern civilians by direct military action but also by the United States government's induced starvation of Confederate civilians—black and white, old and young, male and female, infants and the infirm.

During World War II the "civilized" world deplored acts of the German SS when they punished local civilians in reprisal for local military acts against German targets. Yet, the United States of America (better described as the Federal Empire) engaged in acts against Southern civilians that were no less hideous. Indeed, Germans during World War II were following Union General Sheridan's recommendations to German Chancellor Otto von Bismarck. Prior to World War I, while visiting Bismarck, General Sheridan declared that it was his policy to "leave civilians with nothing but their eyes to weep with."

A war of extermination can be conducted only if the target for extermination (in this case Southerners) has been de-humanized to the point that the exterminator (in this case the Federal Empire, i.e., the United States of America) feels no natural human compassion for his victims. As demonstrated in chapter 6, this was the primary outcome of generations of vicious anti-South propaganda—slanderous attacks that had been readily consumed by the Northern public. The lily white upper class of New England

---

216 For a detailed timeline outlining Lincoln's secret plan to instigate a war with the Confederate States of America see Kennedy, James Ronald, *Uncle Seth Fought the Yankees*, (Pelican Publishing Company, Gretna, LA: 2015), 348-51.

considered white Southerners as nothing less than a mongrel race due to generations of close and relaxed social relations with black Southerners. As previously noted most Northern abolitionists were opposed to slavery not because they loved black folks but because they wanted to rid the country of blacks either by shipping them to another country or by "cooping them up" in the South. Much of their Reconstruction policy was based upon the false and inhuman racial theory of "extinction" in which Northerners thought black Southerners would go extinct once they were freed from chattel slavery.[217]

The people of the North had a firm belief that black Southerners would become extinct if they—the Federal Empire—could "hem him in and coop him up,"[218] thereby leaving North America for "the white man."[219] Their thinking was that, because the black South was going extinct, all that was necessary for a new America made in the image of New England was to rid the U.S.A. of white Southerners. In the "vigorous" war of invasion and conquest thousands of Southerners, both black and white, were permanently removed via death by starvation, illness or direct military action. But just as important to the Federal Empire's ruling elite, the South's political power was utterly exterminated! Southern political power in Congress had for generations posed a constitutional hindrance to the North's vision of a vast, worldwide, commercial, financial, and industrial empire. With the South's political and economic power *exterminated*, the Federal Empire was free to expand, unchecked[220] by the limits imposed by a written constitution or Christian morality.

Extermination via a Vigorous War Policy

The Federal Empire's propagandists in education, the mainline media, and Hollywood present an image of President Abraham Lincoln as a mild-mannered and compassionate person who reluctantly waged a war to preserve the United States of America. According to the Empire's sycophants, Lincoln's war was waged "with malice toward none" and a desire to restore the South to a Union free of

---

217 The Federal Empire's "extinction" theory is discussed by Downs, 15, 97. Downs is a New England, P.C. "intellectual" and by no means a friend of the South.

218 Quote from Shepherd Pike, a correspondent for the *New York Tribune* who hated slavery but cared not in the least for blacks, as cited in Livingston, Donald, "Confederate Emancipation Without War," *To Live and Die in Dixie*, 463-464.

219 *Ibid.*

220 "Since 1865 an agrarian Union has been changed into an industrial empire bent on conquest of the earth's goods and ports to sell them in. This means warfare, a struggle over markets, leading, in the end, to actual military conflict between nations." Lytle, Andrew Nelson, "The Hind Tit," in *I'll Take My Stand*, 202.

slavery. The truth is that Lincoln conspired to instigate a war[221] with a sovereign, peaceful, and democratic nation—the Confederate States of America—and pursued his war with a hideous vengeance from the beginning to the last days of his life.

Union General George B. McClellan received a letter from Major General Henry W. Halleck in Missouri on December 19, 1861, in which Halleck complained about the barbaric acts of Union General James H. Lane in Kansas. Halleck declared: "I receive almost daily complaints of outrages committed by these men in the name of the United States, and the evidence is so conclusive as to leave no doubt of their correctness."[222] When Lincoln read Halleck's letter he penned this as his reply: "An excellent letter, though I am sorry General Halleck is so unfavorably impressed with General Lane. A.L."[223] What would have been the liberal media's reaction had President Nixon given a similar response to the atrocities committed at My Lai during the Vietnam War? Yet here we see the president of the United States of America endorsing the barbaric treatment of his former countrymen. And what was Lincoln's former countrymen's great crime? Southerners dared to ask to be left alone to live in a country of their own choosing, based upon the American principle enshrined in the Declaration of Independence— that *governments receive their just powers from the consent of the governed.* Nor were General Lane's acts of barbarism isolated events. In St. Louis on September 16, 1862, German-born Union Colonel Albert Sigel complained that two Confederate "prisoners were brought in....I felt much chagrined that the pickets had brought in the two...and I reprimanded Lieutenant Kerr...for not obeying my orders...to bring in no prisoners." [224]

When Yankee propagandists are presented with such evidence they try to pass it off as only happening in the wild west of Missouri, but it was actually happening everywhere the Yankee invader found helpless civilians or defenseless Confederate POWs. From Bethel, Tennessee, an officer of the United States Army wrote:

Complaints come to me of their [U.S.A. army troops] having robbed the farmers of all their stock and in some cases of their watches and money....They have in some

---

221 For Lincoln's secret plan to instigate a war with the Confederate States of America see Kennedy, *Uncle Seth,* 348-51.

222 Keys, Thomas Bland, *The Uncivil War: Union Army and Navy Excesses in the Official Records* (The Beauvoir Press, Biloxi, MS: 1991), 12. All of Keys's citations are from the Federal Government's own Official Records of the War of Rebellion.

223 *Ibid.*

224 *Ibid.,* 24.

instances attempted to force the women to cohabit with them when found at home alone.[225]

Aside from actual or attempted rape of defenseless Southern women, it must be noted that "all" farm animals and money was taken away from the civilians. The destruction of livestock, farm buildings, farm equipment and financial resources was done in order to prevent the raising food and thereby produce starvation among the Confederacy's civilian population. In addition, post-war it would assure the impoverishment of black and white Southerners who had managed to survive Yankee attempts of extermination. This was repeated over and over again in every Southern state with the active or passive encouragement of the so-called "compassionate" Lincoln and other United States officials in Lincoln's administration, as well as Republicans in the United States Congress. Halleck admitted as much in his correspondence with United States Secretary of War Stanton: "I have no doubt the U.S. Senator Lane and others will attribute any measures of restraint...to political influence, "[226] but no effective efforts were made by the invaders to halt acts of atrocities against Southern civilians. The people of the United States of America were determined to extract vengeance against the people of the Confederate States of America. According to the testimony of Union Colonel Marc Mundy, a Chicago newspaper complained about a Union officer who had tried to discipline a subordinate who was guilty of conducting a "vigorous" war against the South. Colonel Mundy testified that the Chicago paper's complaint was that the Union officer was:

> *protecting the people [Southern civilians] rather than punishing them....[the paper] seemed to advocate what they called a 'vigorous war policy,' by which they seemed to mean general devastation....I know that plundering has been justified by officers as high or higher in command than myself, in pursuing a policy promulgated by [Union] General Pope in Virginia I thought to have been sanctioned by the administration. A vigorous war policy, as generally understood in the army to which I have been attached, means the adoption of all means not only to crush out the rebellion but to punish indiscriminately all persons who live in a rebellious territory.*[227]

This "vigorous" war policy was nothing less than genocide conducted against the people of a sovereign nation, the Confederate States of

---

225 *Ibid.*, 35.

226 *Ibid.*, 38.

227 Ibid., 41.

America, by the government and people of the United States of America.
The New York World in its December 15, 1862, issue noted:

> *The ragged, half-starved rebels passed through Maryland without disorder or*
> *marauding, without injury to the country, showing their excellent discipline. The*
> *well-fed, well-clothed Union soldiers laid waste to everything before them, plundering*
> *houses, hen-roosts, and hog-pens, showing an utter want of discipline.*[228]

The United States Navy was also an active participant in the United States'
genocidal vigorous war policy. Lieutenant Commander Babcock, *U.S.S. Morse*,
in his official report noted that while patrolling the Mattaponi River in Virginia:

> *rebel artillery opened fire on the U.S. mail boat Swan....Armed crews went on*
> *shore and burned twelve houses in the vicinity, three full of corn, three full of bacon,*
> *three out houses, and three dwelling houses.*[229]

Note that the retribution was made against innocent Southern civilians. Note also that the
United States naval officer thought it important to report to his superiors the fact that civilian
food supplies and homes had been destroyed. Starvation of the Southern people was an
important war policy used by the United States of America in its imperialistic war against the
people and the democratically-elected government of the Confederate States of America.

On more than one occasion General Sherman declared his hope that the South
would be "repopulated" with Northerners. Before you can "repopulate" a nation you
must first "depopulate" it! While invading Georgia on October 9, 1864, Sherman
declared, "Until we can repopulate Georgia, it is useless to occupy it, but the utter
destruction of its roads, houses, and people will cripple their military recourse...."[230]
General Halleck, Chief of Staff in Washington, sent this instruction to General
Hunter: "...make all the valleys south of the Baltimore and Ohio railroad a desert....
every particle of provisions and stock should be removed and the people notified
to move out."[231] And where do people who no longer have food or shelter go? The
Federal Empire did not care—to be precise the United States of America did not care!
Lincoln did not care! The Republican-controlled Congress, and the officers of the

---

228 *Ibid.*, 45.

229 *Ibid.*, 46.

230 *Ibid.*, 90.

231 *Ibid.*, 87-9.

United States Army and Navy did not care! Their mission was to create and expand the Federal Empire by invading and conquering a sovereign nation—the Confederate States of America—and ultimately making the Southern states subservient provinces of the Federal Empire. The lasting effect was to make once free and prosperous citizens of the South into impoverished subjects of the Federal Empire. *Woe to the vanquished!*

United States General Sheridan while at Harrisonburg, Virginia, sent orders to Brigadier General Merritt to "carry out the instructions of Lieutenant-General Grant...leave the Valley a barren waste'"[232] A few weeks later General Sheridan wrote to General Grant regarding Southern resistance to invasion: "I know of no way to exterminate them except to burn out the whole country."[233] Note the use of the word "exterminate" in reference to Southerners and the plan to lay waste to everything necessary for human survival. It is evident that Yankee President Lincoln was not only aware of these tactics but endorsed and encouraged them. Lincoln wrote to General Sheridan: "With great pleasure...my own personal admiration and gratitude for the month's operations in the Shenandoah Valley." [234]

In South Carolina Union Brigadier General Oliver recorded:

There are still a large number of mounted men from this corps...stripping the people of everything that can sustain life. I saw families of women, children, and negroes who had absolutely nothing to eat.[235]

In Louisiana General Grant, near Milliken's Bend, reported:

Rebellion has assumed that shape now that it can only terminate by the complete subjugation of the South....It is our duty, therefore, to use every means to weaken the enemy, by destroying their means of subsistence, withdrawing their means of cultivating their fields, and in every other way possible.[236]

And why was this war against the peaceful people of the South conducted? The answer can be found in a letter from Halleck, General in Chief in Washington, to Grant on March 31, 1863: "We must conquer the rebels....The North must conquer...or become...the

---

232 *Ibid.*, 106.

233 *Ibid.*, 107.

234 *Ibid.*, 108.

235 *Ibid.*, 129.

236 *Ibid.*, 56.

manufacturers…hewers of wood and drawers of water to Southern aristocrats."[237] In 1875, ten years after the end of the War, Massachusetts historian Charles Bancroft admitted the ultimate motive for the invasion and conquest of the Confederate States of America thusly:

> *While so gigantic a war was an immense evil; to allow the right of peaceable*
> *secession would have been ruin to the enterprise and thrift of the industrious laborer,*
> *and keen-eyed businessman of the North. It would have been the greatest calamity of*
> *the age. War was less to be feared.*[238]

And never let it be forgotten that on at least three separate occasions Lincoln was asked why not simply let the South go (and thereby avoid the death and destruction of war) and he responded "Let the South go? Let the South go! Where then shall we gain our revenues?" Numerous Northern newspapers agreed with this sentiment. For example; the *Chicago Times* December 10, 1860, declared:

> *Let the South adopt the free-trade system [Northern] commerce must*
> *be reduced to less than half what it is now.*[239]

The *Newark Daily Advertiser* in its April 2, 1861, edition was even more specific, declaring that low tariffs in Southern ports "must operate to the serious disadvantage of the North" and recommending the use of military force to prevent such a situation. *The Boston Transcript* March 18, 1861, noted that a low Confederate tariff in the Southern ports of New Orleans, Charleston, and Savannah would destroy the greatness of the North and that "The government would be false to its obligations if this state of things were not provided against."[240] The so-called "Civil War" was not a war to free men but a war instigated by the North to *exterminate* their Southern political enemy and maintain the steady stream of tribute forcibly extracted from we the people of the South for the benefit of the Federal Empire's ruling elite and their crony capitalist allies. We the people of the Confederate States of America, both black and white, were impoverished in order to assure the continued enrichment of the Federal Empire's ruling elite and their crony capitalist allies. *Vae victis*—Woe to the vanquished!

---

237 *Ibid.*, 56-7.

238 Bancroft as quoted in, Livingston, Donald, "Confederate Emancipation" *To Live and Die in Dixie*, 485.

239 Scruggs, Leonard M., "The Morrill Tariff: Northern Provocation to Southern Secession," *To Live and Die in Dixie*, 156.

240 *Ibid.*

Exterminating Black Southerners

Camp Nelson was a Union army camp in Kentucky containing between three to four thousand Yankee soldiers and approximately 500 slaves.[241] The black people at Camp Nelson had either escaped chattel slavery or had been forced to leave their plantation home due to its destruction by Union forces, or they were simply lured away by false Yankee promises. Joseph Miller[242] was one of the slaves who came with his family to Camp Nelson. Yankee officials had promised him that if he enlisted in the Union army, the United States would provide for his family. But like so many Yankee promises made to black and white Southerners,[243] the promise to provide for Private Miller's family was broken. In the early hours of November 22, 1864, Union soldiers under orders from General Pry entered the camp where the slave families resided and ordered them to vacate the area immediately. Many of the families were rudely awakened from sleep by white Union soldiers tearing the tents down around them. Private Miller begged for time to arrange shelter for his family, but to no avail. He pleaded with camp authorities telling them that his eight-year-old boy was sick and the displacement of the family might cause his son's death. The Yankee response was "get up in the wagon or he [the Union soldier] would shoot the last one of them." Private Miller's family had neither food nor a place to live. Private Miller walked next to the wagon until he reached the limits of the Union camp—as a soldier he could not leave without an official pass. He watched as six to eight wagons loaded with slave families left the camp—destination unknown. One Yankee soldier noted that "the weather at the time was the coldest of the season. The wind was blowing quite sharp and the women and children were thinly clad and mostly without shoes." Within three weeks Private Miller's eight-year-old son died. Shortly after that his wife, Isabella, and another son, Joseph, Jr, died, followed in death by his daughter, Maria, and his remaining son, Calvin, also died. Private Joseph Miller died January 6, 1865, approximately six weeks after his family's eviction—this brave soldier did not die in battle—he most likely died from a

---

241 Because slavery still existed in the United States during the war and even after the Emancipation Proclamation (Lincoln made it applicable to the Confederate NOT the United States territory), all blacks were still technically "slaves," usually referred to by Yankees as "contraband."

242 The details of this account are from; Downs, *Sick from Freedom; African-American Illness and Suffering during the Civil War and Reconstruction*, 19-21.

243 Not the least of which was the promise made in 1787 to abide by the *limitations* imposed upon the federal government by the original constitution—a promise that was immediately broken. See; Kennedy, *Reclaiming Liberty*, 45-53; Kennedy & Kenedy, *Nullifying Tyranny*, 141-148.

heart pierced through by broken Yankee promises.[244] What price for freedom? A price these black Southerners were forced to pay because the Federal Empire did not allow an opportunity for Confederate Emancipation and integration into our mutually shared Southern society.[245] No one knows what could have been had the South been allowed to go in peace, but as will be shown in the following chapters it could not have been as bad as the transition from 4.5 million chattel slaves in a prosperous South into 8.5 million black and white sharecropping slaves eking out a miserable existence in an impoverished South. [See Sharecropping: Northern Imposed Post War Slavery, p. 175.]

If the Federal Empire would treat the families of its own black soldiers in such a heartless manner as described above, what then would they do to black Southerners who were not part of the invader's army? The answer can be found in the Federal Empire's *Official Records of the War of the Rebellion*. A few examples will demonstrate the Federal Empire's calloused and actually evil attitude toward black Southerners:

- August 13, 1861, Northern Missouri; in a letter to United States Secretary of War Simon Cameron: "soldiers…entering and searching houses, and stealing in many cases; committing rapes on the negroes…." [246]

- August 12, 1862, Woodville, Alabama; "negro women debauched." [247]

- September 1862, West Tennessee; Captain Frank Moore's company (Second Illinois Cavalry) "behaved more like brigands than soldiers. They robbed an old negro man…." [248]

- October 1862, Beaufort, South Carolina; forced conscription of black Southerners " has created a suspicion that the [U.S.] Government has not the interest in the negroes that it has professed, and many of them [black Southerners] sighed yesterday for the 'old fetters' as being better than the new liberty."[249]

- October 29, 1862, Beaufort, South Carolina; Brigadier General Rufus

---

244 Downs, 219, footnote 15.; "As government employed freedmen, the military stipulated that dependents… (would be provided rations) …yet the government failed to fulfill their promise."

245 See Livingston, "Confederate Emancipation," *To Live and Die in Dixie*, 455-89.

246 *Ibid.*, 35.

247 *Ibid.*, 36.

248 *Ibid.*, 22.

249 *Ibid.*, 22.

Saxton, writing to U.S. Secretary of War Stanton: "When the colored regiment was first organized by General Hunter no provision was made for its payment, and the men were discharged after several months' service, receiving nothing for it. In the meantime, their families suffered...." [250]

- November 1862, Newport News, Virginia; "A complaint has been made to me that the colored people who are to go to Craney Island have been forced to remain all night on the wharf without shelter and without food; that one has died, and that others are suffering with disease, and that your men have turned them out of their houses, which they have built themselves, and have robbed some of them of their money and personal effects." [251]

- October 10, 1863, Memphis, Tennessee; General Sherman writing to General- in-Chief Halleck in Washington: "I have your telegram saying the President had read my letter and thought it should be published....I profess...to fight for but one single purpose, to sustain a Government capable of vindicating its just and right authority, independent of niggers, cotton, money or any other earthly interest." [252]

- October 19, 1863, Baton Rouge, Louisiana; white Union officers' cruelty toward black soldiers of the Corps d'Afrique was so bad it caused an uprising among the black troops. There were shouts calling for fellow black Union soldiers to "kill all the damned Yankees." [253]

- March 13, 1864, Fort Leavenworth, Kansas; "A negro man, Sam Marshall, ...yesterday went to get his children....He was arrested by Captain David Johnson....About a dozen of the soldiers did escort him...out of Platte City, where they tied him to a tree, and stripping him to the waist lacerated his back with a cow-skin, the marks of which Sam will carry to his grave...." [254]

- April 7, 1864, Memphis, Tennessee; "The [United States] cavalry broke en masse in the camps of the colored women and are committing all sorts

---

250 *Ibid.*, 44.

251 *Ibid.*, 44.

252 *Ibid.*, 64.

253 *Ibid.*, 63.

254 *Ibid.*, 75.

of outrage."[255]

- September 1, 1864, New Bern, Virginia; "The negroes will not go voluntarily, so I am obliged to force them....The matter of collecting the colored men for laborers has been one of some difficulty....They must be forced to go.... this may be considered a harsh measure, but...we must not stop at trifles."[256]

- November 30, 1864, New Orleans, Louisiana; "Captain Moore Union], his officers and men, had seized a quantity of Louisiana rum and were on a drunken spree, committing various depredations, and that one of his men had attempted to rape a mulatto girl and had shot and killed her for resisting."[257]

- December 30, 1864, Beaufort, South Carolina; "A black man on his way to enlist as a volunteer was stopped by a recruiting party. He told them where he was going and was passing on when he was ordered to halt. He did not stop and was shot dead and left where he fell." [258]

- December 30, 1864, Beaufort, South Carolina (reporting on the actions and attitude of Union troops); "I found the prejudice of race here in full force, and the general feeling of the army of occupation was unfriendly to the blacks. It was manifested in various forms of personal insult and abuse, in depredations on their plantations, stealing and destroying their crops and domestic animals, and robbing them of their money....The women were held as legitimate prey of lust...." [259]

- January 31, 1865, Robertsville, Georgia; "The indiscriminate pillage of houses is disgraceful....houses in this vicinity, of free negroes even, have been stripped...shocking to humanity."[260]

- April 29, 1865, Richmond, Virginia; "A number of cases of atrocious rape by these men [United States troops] have already occurred. Their influence on the colored population is also reported as to be bad." [261]

---

255 *Ibid.*, 73.

256 *Ibid.*, 106.

257 *Ibid.*, 102.

258 *Ibid.*, 113.

259 *Ibid.*, 113

260 *Ibid.*, 123.

261 *Ibid.*, 120.

- June 26, 1865, Augusta, Georgia; "The colored citizens wander around at all hours of the night, and many in consequence have been robbed and abused by scoundrels dressed as U.S. soldiers….The conduct of the Fourth Iowa Cavalry in passing through this district was such as reflects disgrace on both officers and men…. Firing so as to cause a colored woman to lose her arm; likewise committing robberies, etc."[262]

- 1865, South Carolina; "men in my command…encouraged if not assisted by a few officers…have become…highwaymen, with all their cruelty and ferocity….their victims are usually old men, women, and children, and negroes, whom they rob and maltreat without mercy, firing dwellings and outhouses…."[263]

This sample of "official" reports from United States Army and Navy officers as recorded in the Federal Empire's own *Official Records of the War of the Rebellion* stands as evidence to the truthfulness and accuracy of Southern reports about Yankee atrocities during their invasion of the Confederacy. William Gilmore Simms, a famous Southern author who lived through Sherman's invasion, recorded that "regiments, in successive relays" gang-raped scores of black women prior to burning Columbia, South Carolina.[264]   In Georgia a black nurse complained to her mistress:

They [United States soldiers] took everything I had. Honey, I never knowed a
Yankee that wasn't mean as dirt. They would skin a flea for his hide and tallow.
Everybody say the Yankees going to free us. Like a fool I believed them and now this
is what they do. I might a-knowed it. What can you spec from a hog but a grunt.[265]

Despite official United States records and Confederate citizens' and officials' accounts of the Federal government's crimes against black and white Southerners, the Yankee narrative of the war remains the United States' official *excuse* for its war of aggression against its smaller, peaceful neighbor—we the people (black and white) of the Confederate States of America. This officially accepted and enforced narrative (excuse) is used by the Federal Empire's ruling elites of both national political parties to maintain the racial divide in the South and thereby provide the Democratic

---

262 *Ibid.*

263 *Ibid.*, 129

264 Cisco, 181.

265 *Ibid.*, 175.

and Republican parties with a reliable source of black and white Southern voters.

Northern racial indifference and bigotry towards black Southerners was evident in 1898 during the Spanish American War when an Ohio unit used a black child for "target practice." The winner was the white Ohio soldier who shot a hole in the child's sleeve. A riot ensued when a unit of Buffalo Soldiers learned about the cruelty. These black soldiers provided heroic service during the charge on San Juan Hill but very little notice was made in the American press. One General noted the heroic efforts of this black unit, former Confederate General "Fighting" Joe Wheeler. In his official report this Southern officer noted the black soldiers' gallantry thusly, "You forded the San Juan River and gallantly swept over San Juan Hill, driving the army from its crest…you will receive the plaudits of seventy millions of people."[266]   The "plaudits" never came.

Remaking the South in the Image of the North

It was an arrogant, self-righteous and materialistic North that used the Federal government to invade, conquer and exploit the South's human[267] and natural resources.[268] In their self-absorbed arrogance they found it easy to de-humanize the Southern people—a people who dared to resist their imperial embrace. For generations Northerners had been taught that the people of the South were intellectually inferior, racially tainted by prolonged close social relations with the black race, and morally corrupt sinners who needed to be redeemed by conversion to the New England ideal. This New England ideal required the abandonment of traditional Biblical Christianity, the embracing of various trendy "isms" and establishing, by whatever means necessary, an economic system of worldwide commercial dominance. From its earliest days New England had a unique view of its importance in the world. Southern scholar M.E. Bradford noted:

The New England sense of mission rests on a myth of covenant and of a special relation to the Deity. The region's sense of itself as a "second Israel," of its redemptive errand into the wilderness by means of which human history might be transformed, of the zealous labors of God's elect, has been well and thoroughly

---

266 http://www.tbo.com/lifestyle/black-soldiers-faced-prejudice-in-tampa-245732 (Accessed 1/25/2016)

267 Downs, 196, footnote 25, noting Federal government's primary interest was in the freed slaves "labor." Also see similar treatment of Native Americans in an effort to use their labor, describing reservations as a "hybrid of contraband camps," 175.

268 See, "Sharecropping: Northern- Imposed Post War Slavery," Appendix I, p. 173.

described.... [269]

The late 19th century New England Congregationalist minister, Reverend Josiah Strong, described the Yankee race thusly:

> *This race of unequalled energy, with all the majesty of numbers and the might of wealth behind it—the representative, let us hope, of the largest liberty, the purest Christianity, the highest civilization—having developed peculiarly aggressive traits calculated to impress its institutions upon mankind, will spread itself over the earth.* [270]

The New England "City on a Hill" would be populated by the elect of the commercial masters and post-Puritan ideologues of the North. From their exalted vantage point they would rule an empire forced to submit to Northern views and Northern opinions, all the while enriching those aligned to those rulers residing in that Federal "City on a Hill."

After the South's surrender, this "American" arrogance expressed itself in the North's surprise that the exhausted and defeated people of the South would not publicly admit their sins and appeal to their superiors of the North for absolution! The North's post-Puritan mentality demanded punishment for Southern "sinners." The Republican-controlled Reconstruction legislature of South Carolina went so far as to repeal prior legislation providing for thousands of artificial arms and legs for disabled Confederate veterans—after all, sinners deserve their punishment. [271] Republican Thaddeus Stevens, while speaking in the United States House of Representatives prior to the war, promised to punish any Southerner who dared to resist, via secession, Northern demands for protective tariffs. He declared he would "lead an invasion to hang everyone involved." [272] He reasserted his demand to punish the South on January 22, 1862, declaring he wanted the United States to hang the leaders of the Confederacy and to crush the South, observing that "Our generals have a sword in one hand and shackles in the other." [273] The sword with which to kill Southerners and shackles with which to enslave and forever bind we the people of the South to the Yankee's "one nation indivisible" Federal Empire.

269 Bradford, M. E., *Against the Barbarians* (University of Missouri Press, Columbia, MO: 1992), 18-9.

270 Reverend Josiah Strong as cited by; McDonald, Forrest, "Why Yankees Won't (and Can't) Leave the South Alone," http://www.theimaginativeconservative.org/2015/07/why-yankees-wont-and-cant-leave-the-south-alone.html (Accessed 2/9/2016).

271 Wilson, "Defeat and Occupation," *To Live and Die in Dixie*, 444.

272 Scruggs, "The Morrill Tariff," *To Live and Die in Dixie*, 143.

273 Bowers, Claude, *The Tragic Era*, (Halcyon House, New York: 1929), 72.

After the South's surrender at Appomattox, President Lincoln demonstrated the attitude toward the Southern people held by most Northerners when he declared that Southerners could return to the Union just like a "pardoned sinner."[274] United States troops held the opinion that Southerners were "wicked people" who had no rights that the "righteous were bound to respect."[275] But perhaps most telling was General Sherman's declaration equating Southerners with Satan:

Satan and the rebellious saints of Heaven were allowed a continuous existence in hell merely to swell their just punishment. To such as would rebel against a Government so mild and just as ours was in peace, a punishment equal would not be unjust.[276]

Here we see one of Yankeedom's greatest imperialist icons equating we the people of the Confederate States of America with Satan and his rebellion against God. He openly declares that the *punishment* received by the rebels was to remain eternally in Hell. The Federal Empire's inflicted punishment on the South would be a "continuous" punishment as future generations of impoverished Southerners are seated upon the "stools of everlasting repentance." [277]

Henceforth, a politically subservient and docile South would no longer be a political barrier to the North's vision of a worldwide industrial, commercial and financial empire. The reliable votes from impoverished and obedient white and black Southerners would assure the perpetual control of the federal government by a select group of national (Republican and Democratic) elites, while the treasures of Southern natural resources and cheap Southern labor would enrich Northern crony capitalists. In the meantime, impoverished Southern young men seeking to escape Northern-imposed Southern poverty would fill the ranks of the Federal Empire's vast military complex—Southern cannon fodder[278] for the Federal Empire's future wars. *Vae victis*—Woe to the vanquished!

---

274 Johnson, Ludwell H., *North Against South: The American Iliad, 1848-1877*, (Foundation for American Education, Columbia, SC: 1978), 185.

275 *Ibid.*, 187.

276 Sherman quoted in Johnson, 187.

277 Owsley, "The Irrepressible Conflict," *I'll Take My Stand*, 63.

278 Using locals from a conquered nation as cannon fodder is a long established method used by empires to inculcate loyalty to the empire and relieve the empire's population from the burden of imperial military service. See, Johnson, Chalmers, *The Sorrows of Empire*, (Henry Holt and Co., New York: 2004), 131.

Chapter 8

POVERTY IMPOSED BY RADICAL ABOLITION

To the poor whites who fought against us in the blindness of their ignorance....I
would try to raise them up to the idea that honest labor is honorable above all
things.[279]

Many Americans are shocked to find out that Northerners at the very beginning
of the United States were eager to exploit their numerical majority for their own
personal and regional benefit. They willingly exploited the political advantage arising
from their numerical majority in Congress even when it caused economic disaster for
the Southern numerical minority. Northern politicians ignored the interests of the
South when they voted in favor of the 1786 Jay-Gardoqui Treaty—a treaty that would
have prevented Southerners from using the Mississippi River as an outlet for their
goods. The commercial interest of the North would have been served by preventing
Southern commerce from going down the Mississippi River toward Spanish-held
New Orleans. Profit- minded Yankee merchants and Yankee politicians wanted to
use the Federal government to force Southern commerce into Northern ports. This
would have been disastrous for the settlers in Kentucky and Tennessee.[280]   Even
at this early time in American history Southerners had valid reasons to suspect
the veracity and good will of Northerners. Many Southern leaders harbored a
sense of betrayal against their "fellow Americans" of the North due to the North's
reluctance to come to the South's aid during the later stages of the Revolutionary
War. They recalled that when the British moved the war to the South no armies
from Massachusetts, Pennsylvania, or Connecticut came to the South's aid.[281]

The exploitation of the South for the benefit of the North has been a key factor

---

279 Lydia Maria Child, Massachusetts abolitionist in Smith, *A Just and Lasting Peace*, 370. (Note the proud display of Yankee arrogance.)

280 Bradford, *Against the Barbarians*, 94.

281 *Ibid.*, 95.

in the North's emergence as America's center of commerce, capital, and wealth. It is also the reason the South today is the poorest region in the Federal Empire. After the South's surrender in 1865 the North was free to continue its long- established Yankee tradition of exploiting Southern human and natural resources. A major factor of that poverty producing exploitation was the intentional destruction of Southern capital—financial resources—necessary to rebuild the Southern economy that had been shattered by Northern invasion, conquest and occupation.

Land, labor and capital are the key requisites for establishing a prosperous economy.[282] Despite enormous destruction due to Yankee invasion, the South after the war had enough land and labor resources necessary to rebuild a vibrant economy. The one essential item missing was capital—money and/or credit. Imagine the distress an individual would be in if a looter broke into his home, stole all his money, and burned down his home. To make matters worse the bank now viewed him as a credit risk and either refused to lend to him or offered to lend to him only at an enormous interest rate. This was the condition the people of the South found themselves in after 1865.

The manner in which the North forced emancipation upon the South is one of the factors in the loss of Southern investment capital. The problem with stating this *fact* is that it is immediately met with an *emotional* response aimed at intimidating the "fact finder" into silence. It amounts to a declaration by the Federal Empire's propagandists and sycophants that the pro-South *fact* speaker is merely a racist trying to justify African-American slavery. They use emotion because facts do not support the Empire's narrative. Protecting the Federal Empire's false narrative is absolutely necessary because this narrative is the justification for the invasion, conquest and continuing occupation of the South. The Federal Empire's narrative describes Southern slave- holders as being immoral sinners who did not deserve any consideration for the loss of their investments in slaves. But Yankee propagandists never mention that (1) it was Yankee slave merchants who gained enormous profits by selling slaves to the South,[283] (2) when the North abolished slavery they did so in a manner that allowed the Yankee to reclaim his financial investment in

---

282 Mises, Ludwig von, *Human Action; A Treatise on Economics* (1947, Ludwig Von Mises Institute, Auburn, AL: 1998), 637. (There is also a presumption that entrepreneurial talent is available and is allowed to appropriately use these factors of production—which is generally the case in a true free market.)

283 The vast majority (94%) of the Yankee's nefarious slave trade went to the Caribbean; only approximately 6% of the Yankees' slave cargo was sold in the United States; see Kennedy, *Myths of American Slavery*, 44-45.

his slaves by the extended use of their labor as indentured servants or selling the slaves to the South prior to the date of their emancipation, and (3) after abolishing slavery in their states Yankee merchants eagerly purchased slave-grown cotton from the South to be used in their cotton mills—mills that had their financial origins in the nefarious Yankee slave trade. That which was considered essential to the profit-minded Yankee—reclaiming his capital investment in his slaves—was denied, at the point of bloody bayonets, to the South. The North grew rich as a result of their mode of emancipation, but the South was impoverished by the Yankee-imposed method of emancipating Southern slaves. It should be remembered that this Yankee imposed impoverishment fell the most severely upon the newly freed slaves.

Post-emancipation impoverishment of newly freed slaves occurred most cruelly in the South (post 1865) but it also occurred earlier in the North for the few remaining free blacks after the Northern states abolished slavery. As late as 1863 Solomon Northup—the hero in the 1850s book *Twelve Years a Slave*—was living with his wife and son in the home of his son-in-law. They resided in a segregated community in Glen Falls, New York. Solomon, who had been kidnapped by Yankees, had returned to his trade as a carpenter but his son and son-in-law remained unemployed.[284]

One scholar estimated that in 1865 over $2,000,000,000 worth of investment capital vanished overnight as a result of Northern imposed radical emancipation in the South.[285] The South's capital loss in 1865 from slave property alone would be approximately $28,000,000,000 in 2015 dollars! In Louisiana, as an example, over $170,000,000 of invested capital was lost.[286] That would be in excess of $4,063,000,000 in 2015 dollars! Contrast Yankee uncompensated emancipation in the South to the way in which the British emancipated their slaves.

In 1833 the British Parliament, which had new members, many of whom were owners of slaves and textile mills, passed an act freeing over time all slaves and providing over £20,000,000 to compensate slaveholders.[287] This amount has

---

284 Northup, Solomon, *Twelve Years a Slave*, edited by Sue Eakin and Joseph Logsdon, (1853, Louisiana State University Press, Baton Rouge, LA: 1968), xxiii.

285 Fleming, *Sequel of Appomattox*, 2.

286 Winters, *Civil War in Louisiana*, 428.

287 http://www.nationalarchives.gov.uk/pathways/blackhistory/rights/emancipation.htm (Accessed 4/23/2016).

been estimated to be worth £16,500,000,000 today. [288] The British compensated these slave- holders for the loss of their capital investment in slaves even though many, if not most, were absentee landlords and Britain did not need the capital to invest because it already had a well establish industrial economy—unlike the defeated, devastated and occupied South. For example, John Gladstone, who resided in England and was the father of 19th century prime minister William Gladstone, received £106,769 (modern equivalent £83m) for the 2,508 slaves he owned across nine plantations.[289] But even more applicable to the South is the way Lincoln and the United States Congress emancipated slaves in Washington, D.C., during the war.

President Lincoln signed Congressional legislation emancipating slaves in Washington on April 16, 1862. The title of the legislation was "District of Columbia Compensated Emancipation Act." The Act set aside $1 million to compensate slave owners in Washington, D.C. It provided for compensation of $300.00 per slave to D.C. slave holders. The investment cost (price) of a slave was $300.00 in 1804 and had increased to $800.00 by 1860.[290] This D.C. emancipation was done nine months before Lincoln issued his Emancipation Proclamation which declared free those slaves who resided in the territory controlled by the Confederacy but did NOT apply to those slaves who resided in territory or states controlled by the United States. The D.C. Emancipation Act also set aside $100,000.00 to provide each newly freed slave a cash grant of $100.00. But this was not an act of generosity on the part of Lincoln and the United States Congress. The only way a freed slave could obtain the $100.00 was to agree to immediately leave North America![291] As has been pointed out many times, but never by the Federal Empire's propagandists (scholars, mainline media & Hollywood), Lincoln's and the North's (i.e., the Republican Party's) goal was to rid North America of the black race. For example, while debating the emancipation policy in 1862, a Republican-controlled House Committee issued a report that declared in part: "the highest interests of the white race, whether Anglo-Saxon, Celtic, or Scandinavian, requires that the whole country should be held and occupied by these races alone." [292]

---

288 http://www.independent.co.uk/news/uk/home-news/britains-colonial-shame-slave-owners-given-huge-payouts-after-abolition-8508358.html (Accessed 4/23/2016)

289 *Ibid.*

290 https://www.measuringworth.com/slavery.php (Accessed 4/26/2016).

291 https://www.archives.gov/exhibits/featured_documents/dc_emancipation_act (Accessed 5/9/2016).

292 Livingston, "Confederate Emancipation," *To Live and Die In Dixie*, 464.

If the United States had compensated Southern slave owners for the approximately 4.5 million slaves in the South at the same rate that they compensated the owners in Washington, ($300.00 per slave), it would have provided approximately $1,350,000,000 that could have been used to restart the Southern economy. One of the primary reasons for the post-war poverty in occupied Dixie was the lack of investment capital. Even socialist Union Army General Carl Schurz, in a report to the U.S. President on December 19, 1865, noted the lack of "pecuniary means" (money to pay workers) to support free labor.[293] This type of compensation could have been provided by Congress with the stipulation that it be used to pay "field hands" or as investment capital for entrepreneurial commercial/industrial activities that would have provide employment for black and white Southerners. Had this been done a major part of post-war Southern impoverishment could have been avoided. But an economically strong and vibrant South that would naturally be allied with the Democratic Party in the North posed a major political obstacle to the imperial ambitions of the ruling Republican Party. Therefore, an impoverished South was the only solution, and the Republican Party gladly took the opportunity to be the first, but not the last, national political party to exploit impoverished black and white Southern voters. Once the Republican Party had obtained the desired results from Reconstruction (primarily the illegal enactment of the 14th and 15th Amendments)[294] they abandoned black Southerners.[295] They were able to do this because (1) the majority of Northerners did not want to remain in close political contact with blacks[296] and (2) by the end of Reconstruction enough new Republican-controlled Western states had been added to the Union; therefore the Republicans no longer needed the black votes in the Southern states. One Southern scholar noted that the Republican Party abandoned black Southerners in the hope of gaining support from white Southerners —the GOP would have to wait over 100 years before that would happen. Lincoln's "new era

---

293 Schurz, 135. (More detail regarding the lack of capital in post-war Dixie can be found in addendum I: "Sharecropping: Northern-Imposed Post-War Slavery.")

294 Kennedy & Kennedy, *The South Was Right!*, 170-76 & 375-79.

295 Johnson, 206. For Republican use of freed slaves to advance the *national* Republican Party see Downs, *Sick From Freedom*, 208, footnotes 146 & 148.

296 *Harpers Weekly* in its October 1862 issue noted "a mortal antipathy for the negro is entertained by a large class of persons in the North." As cited by Walters, "The Power of a Usurper; Northern Opposition to Lincoln's Emancipation Proclamation," *To Live and Die In Dixie*, 306. Charles Eliot Norton of Massachusetts, Professor at Harvard, declared his support for the free soil movement because it would "confine the Negro within the South." Cited by Livingston in "Why The War Was Not About Slavery," *To Live and Die In Dixie*, 17.

of freedom" meant generations of impoverishment for the newly freed slaves, their former masters, and the vast majority of the white South who had not owned slaves.

Beginning in the early 1830s, radical Yankee abolitionists began to advance the idea of a Haiti-style slave insurrection down South. Their hope was not merely the removal of slavery but the extermination of all Southerners, who they believed had been polluted by the sin of slavery. Failing to exterminate the white South via a Northern- inspired barbaric slave revolt, they then attempted to exterminate the South via direct military action coupled with indirect military action of starvation and disease. Once again the black and white people of the South proved to be more resilient than the Yankee had first imagined. The North's final effort was to exterminate the South politically via impoverishment, reinforced by Northern- inspired racial hatred and division of the black and white South. Once the South's political power was exterminated, the ruling elites of both national political parties were free to take turns controlling the reins of power in Washington. In the meantime, the suffering South became an economic backwater in an otherwise prosperous "one nation indivisible." The Federal Empire would henceforth masquerade as the legitimate United States of America that was established by the founding fathers in 1776. In reality the Federal Empire's ruling elite had destroyed the legitimate, constitutionally limited republic of republics and enthroned an evil empire that would henceforth rule its conquered Southern provinces. *Vae Victis*, Woe to the Vanquished!

Chapter 9

POST-WAR ECONOMIC EXPLOITATION OF THE SOUTH

The sharecropping system was a modification of the slave system....The sharecroppers in the cotton states were thus among the most disadvantaged groups in American society.[297]

During the Great Depression the plight of poor farmers (black and white) in the South was brought to the attention of Henry A. Wallace, U.S. Secretary of Agriculture under President Franklin D. Roosevelt. Wallace dismissed concerns for poor Southern farmers by declaring that their "extremely low standard of living" had existed for a long time.[298] In all of the Federal Empire's "talk" about poverty, no one from Franklin D. Roosevelt (New Deal) to Lyndon B. Johnson (War on Poverty)—has

Southerners have had an "extremely low standard of living" for a long time. Franklin D. Roosevelt's Secretary of Agriculture 1933-40. (Courtesy LOC)

dared to ask "Where did these poor Southerners come from?" The powers-that-be in the Federal Empire dare not ask that question because the truth would point directly back to Washington as being responsible for instigating and maintaining Southern poverty.

---

297 Venkataramani, M.S., "Norman Thomas, Arkansas Sharecroppers, and the Roosevelt Agricultural Policies, 1933-1937," *The Mississippi Valley Historical Review*, Vol. 47, No. 2, (Sept. 1960), 226; downloaded from www.jstor.org 3/7/2016.

298 *Ibid.*, 230.

Unfortunately, there are too many Southerners in particular and Americans in general who believe that the "good ole U.S. of A." is a Christian nation and therefore it could never exploit, impoverish or attempt to exterminate people of a smaller nation. This is another example of the effectiveness of the false Yankee narrative that their propagandists and sycophants constantly advance about *their* Federal government. The "good ole U.S. of A." was not too good to exterminate the American Indians of the Western plains to obtain land that the Yankee had openly declared was to be inhabited exclusively by the white race;[299] nor was "the good ole U.S. of A." too good to invade and seize the formerly free Kingdom of Hawaii;[300] nor did its supposedly virtuous standing among the nations prevent the "good ole U.S. of A." from killing over 200,000 Filipino[301] freedom fighters who, after the end of the Spanish-American War, were actively resisting Yankee reconstruction. These native freedom fighters died in an effort to establish self-government in the Philippines.[302] The 100% American super-patriot may want to read that section of the American Joint Declaration of Independence that declares that governments derive their "just powers from the consent of the governed." The meaning is clear. Any government that is forced upon a people is a violation of this basic American "unalienable" right. Any government forced upon a people in violation of the people's free and unfettered consent is an unjust and therefore illegitimate government. There is no statute of limitations for unjust governments. The mere running of time does not confer legitimately upon an unjust government. Had Hitler ruled France for a thousand years, his rule would still be unjust and his long-standing French puppet government would have still been illegitimate. The same is true for the unjust and illegitimate government forced upon we the people of the Confederate States of America post-1865.

The unacknowledged record of the Federal Empire's imperial adventures—in flagrant violation of the American principle of the consent of the governed—began in 1861 with the invasion of its peaceful neighbor, the Confederate States of

---

299 Lincoln, for example, declared in the seventh debate with Douglas: "our new Territories being in such condition that white men may find a home...as an outlet for free white people...." He received loud applause by the gathered crowd of Northerners. Cited in Walters, Ryan S., "The Powers of a Usurper," in *To Live and Die for Dixie*, 309.

300 Kennedy, *Uncle Seth*, 105-9.

301 Johnson, Chalmers, *The Sorrows of Empire*, (Henry Holt & Co., New York: 2004), 43.

302 "The Philippines are ours forever...and just beyond the Philippines are China's illimitable markets.... The Pacific Ocean is ours." Senator Albert Beveridge of Indiana, as cited by Chalmers Johnson, 43. President McKinley referred to the Filipinos as his "little brown brothers." Johnson, 44.

America. During the United States' 1861-5 foray into militaristic empire building, it managed to steal around 66% of Southern wealth.[303] But even before the invasion of 1861 profit-seeking, Yankees had been busy exploiting the South. The post-war exploitation of the South was merely a more radical continuation of prior exploitation.

In the early 1850s Jefferson Davis was Secretary of War in President Franklin Pierce's administration. Davis understood that the west coast was particularly at risk to foreign invasion due to the lengthy delay it would take to send troops west via slow moving sailing ships of the day. As a matter of national defense, he suggested the construction of a transcontinental railroad from Texas through New Mexico to California. To facilitate the shortest passage, the Pierce Administration completed the Gadsden Purchase of Mexican territory which became part of southwest New Mexico. But the profit-minded Yankees realized that a southern transcontinental railroad route would bring western products to the ports of Texas and especially New Orleans, thereby denying profits to New England ports. Yankee crony capitalists had previously demonstrated their propensity to place personal profits above national security during the War of 1812 when they threatened to secede *during a time of war and sign a separate peace treaty with the British enemy*; and earlier in 1786 when they negotiated a treaty with Spain to close off Southern shipping through the port of New Orleans via the Mississippi River.[304] Thus their successful efforts to halt the consideration of a transcontinental railroad with a Southern route is perfectly consistent with the history of profit-minded Yankees. Understanding the Yankee's *modus operandi* both before and after the so called "Civil War" should make it a little easier to accept—if not understand—the fact that the "good ole U. S. of A." did indeed intentionally impoverish we the people of the South. The Yankee's motive, as always, was their never ending quest for the "almighty dollar." The looting and destruction of the South's emerging industrial base was done not just to further their invasion and imperial conquest, but also to prevent the emergence of industrial competitors down South.

In 1860 railroads were beginning to expand across the South. These railroads were owned by Southern investors and were built to promote Southern commerce. As such they represented a major competitor for Northern owned railroads, especially in the efforts to establish the eastern terminus for the proposed transcontinental line. The

303 James McPherson as cited by DiLorenzo, Thomas, "The Founding Fathers of Constitutional Subversion," *Rethinking The American Union*, (Pelican Publishing Co., Gretna, LA: 2013), 80.

304 Bradford, *Against the Barbarians*, 94.

so-called "Civil War" was a financial and strategic windfall for Northern railroads—not to mention the tariff-protected Northern iron industry. Lincoln's war required a major increase in Northern railroad carrying tonnage consisting of war materials for Northern imperial armies invading the Confederacy—which opportunistic Yankee factory owners realized would result in large and immediate profits! The glittering prospects of such enormous profits solidified Northern crony capitalists' support for Lincoln's imperial war. In addition, it provided these crony capitalists with a "legal" means to destroy their potential Southern railroad competitors. During Lincoln's war over 10,000 miles of Southern railroads were destroyed.[305] These destroyed and bankrupt Southern railroads were confiscated by the Federal government and turned over to "loyal" boards or bought at "fire sale" prices by Northern "investors." Post-war Southern railroads served a distinctly different purpose than their pre-war Southern-owned predecessors. As previously noted, the pre-war Southern-owned railroads were built to

Yankee invaders destroying Southern railroad (Courtesy LOC)

support emerging Southern commercial and industrial activity and thereby facilitated the growth of the Southern economy. Post-war Northern-owned "Southern" railroads were built to haul raw materials away from the South[306] and to transport finished Northern goods into the South.[307] Thanks to Yankee invasion, conquest and occupation, the once prosperous South had become the Federal Empire's first colonial possession. [308]

---

305 For a more detailed discussion and documentation of Northern economic exploitation of the conquered South see herein, "Sharecropping: Northern- Imposed Post- War Slavery."

306 *Clark & Kirwan, The South Since Appomattox*, (Oxford University Press, New York: 1967), 12.

307 *Ibid.*, 270.

308 *Ibid*,. 91. "In many areas the South became a colonial appendage to industrial and grain-growing sections of the country."

One of the many Yankee-engendered reasons for post-war Southern poverty was the lack of Southern capital—financial where-with-all—necessary to re-start destroyed farming and emerging industrial/commercial enterprises.[309] For example; If you were a farmer in 1865, before you could plant a crop you must first purchase seed and fertilizer; you must acquire plows and draft animals, and then you must have enough cash or credit to purchase food for draft animals and yourself/family until the "crop comes in." And of course this scenario presumes that the farmer owns land to cultivate. Capital was virtually non-existent in post-war Dixie. Furthermore, there were very few banks that would loan money on such risky ventures, and those that did make loans to start-up farmers charged extremely high interest rates—some as high as 125%. [310]

Even as late as 1895 there were relatively few banks in the South. In the North there was one bank for every 16,000 people but in the South there was only one bank for every 58,130 people![311] Prior to Yankee invasion, conquest, and occupation the South had $61 million in banking capital, but by 1870 Southern banking capital had withered to a measly $17 million. The currency in circulation prior to Yankee invasion was $51 million, but after the Yankee's glorious victory in the so-called "Civil War" currency in circulation down South had shriveled to $15 million. And who stood to be harmed the most from this loss of investment capital? The poorest of the poor always suffer the most and in this case it was the newly freed slaves. All Southerners, black and white, suffered, but the poorest regardless of their skin color suffered the most. And remember, this Northern- imposed poverty was inflicted upon the black and white people of the South as punishment for resisting the Yankee's imperial embrace.

The Wall Street-created panic of 1907 was used by Northern financiers and industrialists to gain control of emerging Southern iron and steel industries in Tennessee and Alabama. On November 2, 1907, "Robber Baron" J. P. Morgan acquired the Tennessee Coal, Iron, and Railroad Company. He later headed the Moore and Schley Steel Company of Birmingham, Alabama. The otherwise "Trust Busting" Theodore Roosevelt agreed to the purchase and instructed his Attorney General not to interfere with the purchase/merger.[312] This purchase of struggling Southern

---

309 *Ibid.*, 92-3.

310 *Ibid.*, 91. Others state even higher, up to 500%. See details and documentation below: "Sharecropping: Northern- Imposed Post- War Slavery."

311 Clark & Kirwan, 88-9.

312 *Ibid.*, 159.

iron and steel industries prevented the development of competition for Northern companies and put Southern industries under eastern control.[313] Southern industries had been "struggling" due to a chronic lack of investment capital—by 1907 the struggle was over and so was the opportunity to develop iron and steel industries on a par with those mills in the North.

The lack of investment capital in the South was noted by former Union Army officer and outspoken socialist Carl Schurz in his report to the President on December 19, 1865. He wrote that the lack of finances made it difficult to pay day laborers (field hands) and in many cases the newly freed slaves were working and being paid in food.[314] As a direct result of the Federal Empire's destruction, exploitation, and

J. P. Morgan, one of many Northern crony capitalists who used the panic of 1907 to purchase Southern industries. (Courtesy LOC)

confiscation of Southern investment capital there were few paying jobs available for black and white Southerners post-war. A person moving dirt with a shovel works harder than the person operating a dirt-moving machine and is paid less—investment capital in the free market allows for the development/acquisition of technology for more productive output per unit of investment, lower cost for consumers and higher paying jobs for workers. Unfortunately, this was not the case in post-war Dixie. Due to Yankee invasion and occupation, capital was removed from the South and now resides on Wall Street and other points in the North.

It was noted that agricultural workers in the South in the late 1890s were working with implements no better than the ones used in India. In 1880 the output per person was 20% less than in 1860.[315] Recall that part of Lincoln's "vigorous war

---

313 *Ibid.*, 160.

314 Schurz, 135.

315 *Ibid.*

policies" was to destroy all cattle, horses, mules, and agricultural implements in addition to homes, barns, and out- buildings. Replacing private property and rebuilding infrastructure destroyed by Lincoln's invading armies would have required a substantial capital investment. But by the end of the war and Reconstruction, very little Southern capital had escaped the grasp of "those people"[316] who worship the "almighty dollar." The amount of destruction inflicted upon we the people of

Richmond, VA 1865. The Marshall Plan helped Germany to overcome greater destruction within five years after WWII. There was no Marshall Plan for the people of the South. (Courtesy LOC)

the Confederate States of America by the Federal Empire was not matched until World War II. Germany and Japan suffered even greater destruction than did the South, but with the Marshall Plan Germany and Japan were rebuilding and back on the road to economic recovery within five years after the end of World War II.[317] But there was no Marshall Plan for we the people of the formerly free and prosperous South. Five years after Appomattox the South was continuing to sink deeper into Northern imposed poverty.

The Federal Empire's ruling elite were well aware of the harsh economic conditions that Southerners were forced to live under. In President Franklin D. Roosevelt's letter dated July 5, 1938, requesting a report on the economic conditions in the South, he acknowledged the South's honorable heritage and its current unfair economic condition:

It is an unbalance that can and must be righted, for the sake of the South and of the Nation. Without going into the long history of how this situation came to be—the long and ironic history of the despoiling of this truly American section

---

316 "Those people" is the term General Robert E. Lee used to describe the invading Yankees.

317 Hummel, 322.

of the country's population—suffice it for the immediate purpose to get a clear

perspective of the task that is presented to us....a population still holding the great

heritages of King's Mountain and Shiloh — the problems presented by the South

's capital resources and the absentee ownership of those resources, and problems

growing out of the new industrial era and, again, of absentee ownership of the

new industries. [318]

The Federal Empire's President was unwilling to acknowledge the fact that the reason for Southern poverty was not lack of human capital or natural resources but lack of self-government in the occupied states of the conquered Confederate States of America. Self-government would have prevented Northern exploitation and the "absentee ownership" of Southern resources and industry. The Federal government even refused to release a report prepared in January 1935 by an attorney from the Federal Agricultural Adjustment Administration that documented increased evictions of sharecropper families due to Federal legislation (Agricultural Adjustment Act).[319]   Roosevelt and the Federal Empire's elites knew that "bad" Southern politicians could be easily bought-off,[320] thereby providing Roosevelt and the Empire's ruling elite political "cover." Socialist Norman Thomas lamented the fact that:

He [President Roosevelt] seems more interested in the labor problems of

Pennsylvania where he needs their votes, than in the South, where he does

not need the votes of the laboring man. [321]

The South's "bad" politicians assured the national Democrats votes from the "Solid South." As payment for abandoning legitimate self-government via real states' rights these "bad" politicians received advancement up the Federal Empire's political ladder. All the while the poor black and white South continued to labor as peasants, serfs, and virtual slaves.   And those Southerners who were not bound to sharecropping slavery were no more than second class subjects of an "indivisible" Federal Empire.

In 1960 Richard A. Easterlin of the University of Pennsylvania published

---

318 "REPORT ON ECONOMIC CONDITIONS OF THE SOUTH Prepared for The President by The National Emergency Council (1938), 1-2," PDF available at: https://ia600202.us.archive.org/21/items/reportoneco-nomic00nati/reportoneconomic00nati.pdf

319 Venkataramani, M.S., 232.

320 *Ibid.*, 236.

321 *Ibid.*, 242.

a study, "Interregional Income Differences."[322] He appeared surprised when his work documented the harsh reality of Southern poverty: "one is struck immediately by the drastic decline between 1840-1880 in relative per capita income."[323] He noted that "in every southern state" the level of wealth had drastically declined from the 1840 level. The most interesting comment was:

Wealth in 1900 America

C.S.A.   U.S.A.

> [T]wo decades after the start of the
> Civil War the South may have been
> little better off than two decades before—attests strikingly to the impact of that
> war and the subsequent disruption on the southern economy.[324]

The sad fact was that there was no trend of economic growth in the South similar to the booming growth in the rest of the United States. In fact, the per capita income in the South was "about the same in 1900 as in 1880."[325] This is remarkably dissimilar to the prosperous condition of the pre-war South as documented herein in Chapter three. In 1840 the per capita income for the South was almost 50% higher than the per capita income for the North.[326] Yet post-war the South was punished with continuing poverty.

Easterlin's research divided the South into three sections—South Atlantic, East South Central, and West South Central. The West South Central section was the section that encompassed the Port of New Orleans, Louisiana. His research demonstrated that in 1840 the West South Central containing New Orleans had a per capita income 144% above the national average but by 1900 it has declined to only 61% of the national average and by 1950 (the

---

322 Interregional Differences in Per Capita Income, Population, and Total income, 1840-1950,

http://www.nber.org/chapters/c2475.pdf (Accessed 7/1/2016)

323 *Ibid.*, 92, using data from footnote 17.

324 *Ibid.*

325 *Ibid.*

326 *Ibid.*

last date of his study) it had risen to only 80% of the national average.[327] "One nation indivisible with liberty and justice for all" except for Southerners!

But "that was then, this is now" the Federal Empire's apologists proclaim as they arrogantly wave off and dismiss contemporary Southern complaints. But even today at the beginning of the 21st century the Southern states remain the poorest states in this "one nation indivisible," certainly not a nation "with liberty and justice for all" if you are a Southerner. As far as the conquering masters of the South are concerned, the only pledge of allegiance Southerners need to recite is: *Vae Victis*—Woe to the Vanquished.

---

327 *Ibid.*, 137.

Contemporary Impact of Northern Imposed Sharecropping Slavery

Understanding the impact of post-war sharecropping slavery is important because the economic reality survives and continues to punish modern-day Southerners. The Federal Empire forced the South to accept a second-class economy which assured future generations, down to today, would live in the poorest section of the United States. Even though sharecropping slavery ended in the 1950s the impact continues today. The maps following the sharecropping photograph section document the continuing impact of Federal invasion and post-war sharecropping slavery. It demonstrates the fact that we the people of the South are indeed a separate, but captive, nation within the current Federal Empire. The following photographs were taken approximately 70 years after the end of the so-called "Civil War." As you review these photographs keep in mind the Yankee promise to punish Southerners with "poverty" and to dress Southern children in "rags." And remember—the economic and politically correct punishment continues.

THE SOUTH   **U.S.A.**

Sam Nichols sharecropper Boone County, Arkansas circa 1935 (Courtesy LOC)

Sharecropper's wife Washington County, Arkansas circa 1935 (Courtesy LOC)

Child labor in sharecropper's cotton field circa 1935 (Courtesy LOC)

Childhood denied as punishment for being a Southerner (Courtesy LOC)

The descendants of the men who wore the Gray—punished with poverty and abandoned by the South's politicians. Circa 1935. (Courtesy LOC)

Lauderdale County Mississippi circa 1935
(Courtesy LOC)

Sharecropper's children Arkansas circa 1935
(Courtesy LOC)

Sharecropper's son
Arkansas circa 1935
(Courtesy LOC)

McIntosh County Oklahoma circa
1935 (Courtesy LOC)

Children of evicted Arkansas
sharecropper circa 1935 (Courtesy LOC)

SHARECROPPER FAMILIES CIRCA 1935

Mother and child Chesnee, South Carolina circa 1935 (Courtesy LOC)

Mother and child Walker County Alabama circa 1935 (Courtesy LOC)

Mother and child Tangipahoa Parish Louisiana circa 1935 (Courtesy LOC)

Mother and child Tangipahoa Parish Louisiana circa 1935 (Courtesy LOC)

Sharecropper Person County, NC (Courtesy LOC)

Sharecropper farther and his first child Person County, NC circa 1935 (Courtesy LOC)

Sharecropping Slave Housing

This is not a chattel slave's cabin but a sharecropper slave's cabin Transylvania Louisiana circa 1935 (Courtesy LOC)

Boone County, Arkansas circa 1935 (Courtesy LOC)

Front porch sharecropper's cabin Alabama circa 1935 (Courtesy LOC)

Arkansas Sharecropper's house circa 1935 (Courtesy LOC)

Sharecropper cabin Coahoma County, MS circa 1935 (Courtesy LOC)

Sharecroppers Macon County, GA circa 1935 (Courtesy LOC)

United States of America

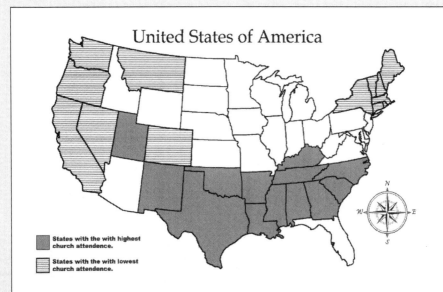

States with the with highest church attendence.

States with the with lowest church attendence.

Fifteen highest and lowest church attendance by state. Map illustration by Brian McClure

Data: http://www.gallup.com/poll/181601/frequent-church-attendance-highest-utah-lowest-vermont.aspx

United States of America

States with unique Southern accent.

Map illustration by Brian McClure. Data: http://thechive.com/2013/06/06/american-accents-beautifully-mapped-22-hq-photos/

Fifteen most conservative states & most liberal states. Note: No Southern state in liberal list. All Southern states more conservative than national average. Map by Brian McClure.

Data: http://www.gallup.com/poll/181505/mississippi-alabama-louisiana-conservative-states.aspx

States with highest and lowest per capita income. No Southern state other than VA & MD above national average. Map by Brian McClure.

Data: https://en.wikipedia.org/wiki/List_of_U.S._states_by_income

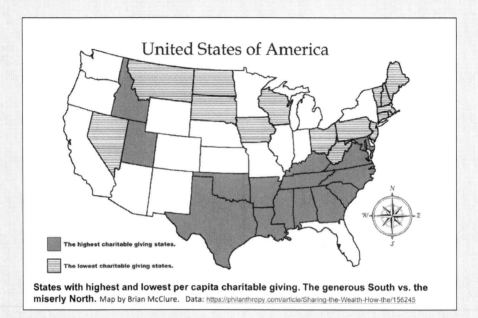

United States of America

The highest charitable giving states.

The lowest charitable giving states.

States with highest and lowest per capita charitable giving. The generous South vs. the miserly North. Map by Brian McClure. Data: https://philanthropy.com/article/Sharing-the-Wealth-How-the/156245

(Left) 1945 Germany: After 35 years both Germany and Japan had recovered from major destruction inflicted on them during World War II. Both became an economic power house in Europe and Asia. Photo: Copyright Unknown, Courtesy of Harry S. Truman Library

(Right) 1865 Richmond, VA: After 35 years the South was still suffering from the punishment of poverty inflicted upon Dixie by the conquering Federal Empire. Even today the South is still the poorest section in the Federal Empire. The punishment continues. (Courtesy LOC)

Governor John Winthrop of Massachusetts: As Governor, Winthrop sanctioned the enslavement of Native Americans and the sale of these Native Americans to the Caribbean Islands in exchange for African slaves. He also coined the phrase "City on a Hill."

New England Puritan Theologian, Jonathan Edwards: Not only did Edwards not condemn slavery in New England but he was an active slave holder during his adult life. In his Last Will and Testimony, Edwards did not free his slaves but bestowed them to his family.

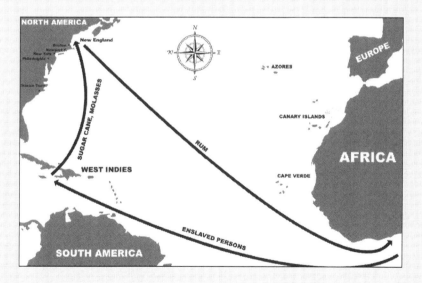

New England's Triangular slave trade was a profitable business that modern Americans do not understand. Profits were made in each of the three exchanges, rum for slaves in Africa, slaves for sugar and molasses in the West Indies, and sugar and molasses for rum and other goods in New England. Note that it was slave-grown sugar and molasses that was the foundation of the numerous New England rum distilleries just like it was slave grown cotton which became the foundation of New England textile mills. Slave grown produce was essential to maintaining New England profits but it is the South that is damned because of slavery.

The Way We Were and The Way We Are

The Federal Empire Punished and Continues to Punish Southerners with Poverty

Wealth in Colonial America

New England   The South

Wealth in 1860 America

New England   The South

Wealth in 1870 America

C.S.A.   U.S.A.

Wealth in 1900 America

C.S.A.   U.S.A.

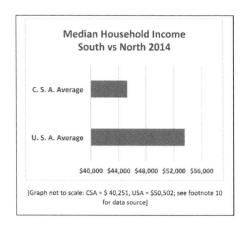

Median Household Income
South vs North 2014

C. S. A. Average

U. S. A. Average

$40,000 $44,000 $48,000 $52,000 $56,000

[Graph not to scale: CSA = $ 40,251, USA = $50,502; see footnote 10
for data source]

From the Colonial era to 1860 the South was the richest section of the United States. The Federal Empire used its victory to impose perpetual poverty upon the Southern people. The punishment continues! [See text for data sources]

Chapter 10

SHARECROPPING— AN EVEN HARSHER FORM OF SLAVERY

Poor Southern farmers for a long time prior to the 1930s had an "<u>extremely low standard of living</u>." —Henry A. Wallace U.S. Secretary of Agriculture in Franklin D. Roosevelt's Administration.[328]

Of all the many slanderous lies about the War for Southern Independence told by the Federal Empire's propagandists and sycophants, the greatest and most universally accepted is that the "Civil War" ended slavery. Antebellum chattel slavery, a system in which approximately 4.5 million blacks were indentured for life—the master owned the individual's labor not the slave's physical body—was abolished. It was replaced by a system of tenant farming, better known as sharecropping, in which approximately 8.5 million Southerners were *enslaved* from the late 1860s until sharecropping died a natural death in the mid to late 1950s. In the 1930s there were around 8.5 million Southerners engaged in sharecropping and close to 66% were white.[329]

Typical Plain Folk Home pre-War. (Betty Kennedy)

---

328 Henry A. Wallace as cited in Venkataramani, M. S., "Norman Thomas, Arkansas Sharecroppers, and the Roosevelt Agricultural Policies, 1933-1937," *The Mississippi Valley Historical Review*, Vol. 47, No. 2 (Sept., 1960), 230. [Emphasis added in above quotation.]

329 Clark & Kirwan, *The South Since Appomattox*, (Oxford University Press, New York: 1967), 104; Also see Agee, James, *Cotton Tenants*, (1936, Melville House Publishing, New York: 2013), 205.

Northern-imposed[330] sharecropping was a system of post-war slavery worse even than the system of pre-war chattel slavery.[331]

As documented in chapters 7, 8, 9 and Addendum I, the destruction of a substantial part of the South's human, physical, and financial capital created a situation in which investment capital needed to restart the economy was virtually absent in post-war Dixie. The war also destroyed a large portion of the simple but comfortable homes as well as hogs and cattle belonging to the plain folk.[332] Their hogs and cattle had freely roamed the South's open range. But Reconstruction legislatures closed off most of the open range,[333] and Northern investors purchased large tracts to harvest the South's virgin forests.[334] Therefore, a majority of the South's white population—primarily plain folk—who were not part of the plantation system were forced into poverty as a result of the invasion, conquest, and occupation of the Confederate States of America. The North's "punishment of poverty"[335] fell the hardest upon innocent people—former slaves and non-slave holding whites—who had not been a part of the plantation system so slandered and derided by radical Northern abolitionists. But such insignificant facts did not matter because Northern propagandists had

Mississippi Sharecroppers (Courtesy LOC)

---

330 For a more detailed description see herein, "Sharecropping: Northern- Imposed Post-War Slavery."

331 Some may object to "slavery" being used to describe sharecropping, but Bishop Anthony Durier specifically referred to sharecropping as "a new form of slavery" in a Pastoral Letter. See, Hair, William Ivy, *Bourbonism and Agrarian Protest* (LSU Press, Baton Rouge, LA: 1969), 52. "The sharecropping system was a modification of the slave system of pre-Civil War days...." Venkataramani, 226. McDonald & Mc-Whiney refer to sharecropping as "peonage," "The South from Self-Sufficiency to Peonage: An Interpretation," *The American Historical Review*, Vol. 85, No. 5, (Dec. 1980), 1111, 1118.

332 Hummel, 278. "Down to 1940 the South still had a great deficiency of livestock of every variety." Clark & Kirwan, 104.

333 McDonald & McWhiney, 1116.

334 Hair, 48. The trees on the open range provided much of the food source for hogs roaming the range.

335 "Every secessionist...has received as the penalty of defeat only poverty. It is the mildest punishment ever inflicted after an unsuccessful civil war." Rev. Thomas W. Higginson, Unitarian minister from Rhode Island, *A Just and Lasting Peace*, 527.

branded all Southerners as evil sinners[336]   not worthy of communion with the racially pure and intellectually superior New Englander who dwells in that exalted "City on a Hill." Therefore, such people (black and white Southerners) are fit for extermination or, at a minimum, total domination by their Northern betters.

During the Great Depression (not to be confused with Obama's Great Recession), James Agee, a liberal/progressive who lived among the sharecroppers while doing research, was compelled to admit the dreadful condition that "his" government had allowed:

> *A civilization which for any reason puts a human life at a disadvantage; or a civilization which can exist only by putting human life at a disadvantage; is worthy neither of the name nor of continuance.*[337]

Agee lamented an uncaring society that would put others at an inhuman disadvantage in order for the people of the uncaring society to prosper. Of course Agee's answer, as typical of progressives/socialists, was to jettison the free market and embrace big government socialism. Being thoroughly schooled in the Northern narrative of the War for Southern Independence, he could not realize that the sharecroppers whom he studied and lived with were the primary victims of the ultimate American big government—the Federal Empire. The Mississippi sharecroppers in the adjacent photo are typical. In the 1930s Franklin D. Roosevelt's "President's Committee" reported

Alabama sharecroppers circa 1934. Note the "rags" of the children and the only one with shoes is the "field hand." Recall FDR's Secretary of Agriculture who brushed aside concerns regarding the South's sharecroppers' "extremely low standard of living." But did the descendants of the men who wore the Gray while defending their homes deserve such "punishment" from the United States of America? (Courtesy LOC)

---

336 U.S. President Lincoln in March 1865 offered to pardon "repentant sinners." Johnson, 185.

337 Agee, 34; as a progressive/liberal he was not able to see the true cause of Southern poverty, but he was moved by the harsh conditions he found. Like most progressives he sought a "socialist" solution for poverty—a solution that has never worked!

that most sharecroppers were living "below any level of decency."[338]   The New York *Times* April 15, 1936, noted that Southern sharecroppers' lives were made even worse by Federal legislation giving them "a lower standard of living, if the hand-to-mouth existence they have led *since the War between the States* may be called a living at all."[339]

Transylvania, LA sharecropper mother teaching her children (Photo courtesy LOC)

In 1937 the Federal government issued a moderately worded report in which it declared that one (Southern) sharecropper family out of four "occupies a position in the Nation's social and economic structure that is precarious and should not be tolerated."[340] Debt peonage[341] was enforced by civil law and by the laws of economics. The sharecropper had little resources of his own and therefore had to rely upon the landlord to supply him and his family during the lean times after harvest and before the beginning of the next planting season. This "credit" was issued at extremely high interest rates, and when added to the money advanced to pay for the sharecropper's half of the seed and fertilizer, etc.—the result was that the sharecropper was perpetually in debt. Debt peonage is not that different from the condition of someone held as an indentured servant for life—a slave. But a slave master must provide food, shelter, clothing, and medicine for his slaves, while the sharecropper was responsible for such "amenities of life."

"I just want to go to High School." Earle, Arkansas circa 1933 (Courtesy LOC)

338 *Farm Tenancy: Report of the President's Committee* as cited in, Venkataramani, 226.

339 *Ibid.*, 236.

340 *Ibid.*, 242.

341 Debt slavery or debt peonage was one of the means to bind the sharecropper and his family to his "master."

The Children—Childhood Denied

The children of sharecroppers grew-up with little hope of breaking the cycle of debt bondage. There were many who wanted to further their minimal education. But because "making a crop" was paramount to the family's survival, the education of children took second place to working in the field. This is not to say that all sharecroppers were illiterate. Many sharecropping children were "home schooled" within the limits of their parent's ability. The young man in the photograph from Earle, Arkansas, (1930s) was asked by the photographer what he wanted the most. His answer was that he wanted to go to high school. But debt peonage, i.e., sharecropping-slavery demanded that he stay in the field working with his family to hopefully make

(Courtesy LOC)

a good crop. The Transylvania, Louisiana, mother in the photo above is doing all within her ability to lift her children out of ignorance and perhaps, in some small way, gain a better life for themselves. Just like any loving parent, she hoped for a life for her children that would be better than the one her sharecropper parents were able to offer her. The photo was taken in the 1930s, but even today East Carroll Parish, where Transylvania is located, is the poorest Parish in the state of Louisiana. It also has one of the largest African-American populations per capita for Louisiana parishes.

Life for the children of sharecroppers was extremely harsh. The photographs of these children were taken in the 1930s in Arkansas, Louisiana and Alabama. It should bring to mind the quote on page 5 in which a Northern newspaper promised that Southerners would "find poverty at their firesides, and see privation in the anxious eyes of mothers and the rags of their children." The promise to conquer and impoverish the South was the one Yankee promise that was kept and continues even today. Recall that sharecropping was not a system freely selected by black and white Southerners—it was the only means left to stave off starvation. Note the "rags" on the children and notice how most of these folks are not wearing shoes. This is what motivated Agee to write his harsh criticism of the government previously quoted. These photographs taken in the

1930s and held by the Library of Congress explain more than words could ever explain. They demonstrate why the liberal/progressive Agee had such harsh words for "any" government or people who would exploit another people for their own materialistic advantage. Those who would willingly reduce a formerly free and prosperous people to living in "rags" are less than civilized folk and could only

Mississippi sharecropping family late 1930s. Prior to the War Mississippi was one of the richest states in the Union. Today it is the poorest state in the Union. Punishment for resisting Northern imperialism. (Courtesy LOC)

be viewed as arrogant, evil, imperialists. Agee inferred that people who allowed their nation to exploit the people of a smaller nation are human beings in name only and are in fact no better than pernicious parasites living at the expense of the oppressed. The progressive/liberal Agee did not properly diagnose[342] the origins of the Southern poverty he beheld in 1933 Alabama, but he, nonetheless, knew intuitively that something tragic, outside of the control of the sharecropper, had occurred. What Agee saw was summarized by historian Kenneth Stampp describing the results of Yankee victory over the South: "The most striking products of their crusade were the shoddy aristocracy of the North and the *ragged children of the South*"[343] [emphasis added]. What great evil did these Southern children do to deserve such harsh punishment? By what right does the Federal Empire force them to remain forever upon the "stools of everlasting repentance"[344] where they serve as the Federal Empire's "whipping-boy?" Southern captives in the Federal Empire are required to constantly repent for the sins

---

342 Agee's sympathetic yet incorrect diagnosis of Southern poverty is yet one more example of the evil result of the false Northern narrative about the so called "Civil War." The narrative establishes a false premise from which "intellectuals" attempt to make logical determination of cause and effect. Agee could not make a correct diagnosis of Southern poverty because his frame of reference was distorted by the false Northern narrative. What was true for Agee in the 1930s is true for politically correct "scholars" and media personalities today.

343 Kenneth Stampp as quoted in Woodward, C. Vann, *The Burden of Southern History*, (Louisiana State University Press, Baton Rouge, LA: 1960), 207.

344 Owsley in *I'll Take My Stand*, 63.

Sick Texas sharecropper child. Mother treating him with "milk" made by mixing flour and water.(Courtesy LOC)

of slavery and racism—sins that originated not in the South but in New England and were made inevitable in the South by Northern- imposed cultural distortion.[345]

Malnutrition and Disease among Sharecropper Slaves

Post-war malnutrition and disease became very common in Dixie. Most Southern diseases, such as malaria, had been known prior to the war. The Northern-imposed impoverishment inflicted upon the Southern people made it difficult to control and treat these known diseases and therefore more people were exposed and died. But one disease was new to the South. It was almost an exclusively Southern disease—Pellagra. Even the Federal government admitted: "The scourge of pellagra, that affects the South almost exclusively."[346] This "South only" disease was rarely seen before the War but began appearing across Dixie subsequent to war and Reconstruction. By the early 1900s it had become epidemic. Crop failures and an economic down turn caused a radical increase in the occurrence of Pellagra in the South—but Pellagra was almost unknown outside of Dixie. Therefore, very little attention was given to this "Southern" problem. One can only imagine what would have been the reaction by the Federal Empire if its elites in New England, New York or other commercial centers of Northern states were suffering from this horrifying disease. Note the lesions on the hands of the man in the photo. It was determined that Pellagra was found among vulnerable people such as those whose diets were

Man suffering from Pellagra (Photo courtesy LOC)

---

345 Kennedy & Kennedy, "Our Re-United Country? The Sad Reality of Reconciliation," *To Live and Die in Dixie*, 501-503.

346 "REPORT ON ECONOMIC CONDITIONS OF THE SOUTH, Prepared for The President by The National Emergency Council (1938)," 32.

N.C. barefooted sharecropping children "their children in rags" (Photo courtesy LOC)

Arkansas sharecropper child suffering from rickets and malnutrition. (Photo courtesy LOC)

severely limited. A researcher, Joseph Goldberger, in 1915 determined that the poor Southerner whose diet consisted primarily of cornbread, molasses, and pork fat was most likely to develop Pellagra. He demonstrated that by giving Pellagra victims a diet of meat, fresh vegetables and milk the symptoms would disappear. Despite his efforts, no one in the national medical or governmental establishment took his finding seriously. It was not until 1937 that another researcher—who this time experimented on dogs instead of Southerners—establish the link between diet and Pellagra. The epidemic lasted for forty years, devastated over 3,000,000 and killed 100,000 people—mostly black and white Southerners. (See below herein describing how Southern food production was greatly hampered by Yankee invasion, conquest and occupation, which was the origin of much Southern disease post "Civil War," especially Pellagra.) It is worth noting that while sharecroppers were suffering from malnutrition, the federal government ordered the slaughtering of six million pigs in an effort to increase pork prices during the depression. [347]

Southern children suffered and had the highest mortality rate in the U.S.A. Because shoes were not commonly worn, children were exposed to hookworm and infections arising from contact with hookworm eggs in the soil. Hookworm eggs in the soil came from unsanitary disposal of human fecal

---

347 Venkataramani, 229. Government "experts" wanted to increase pork prices by decreasing the pork supply—while people were starving! God deliver us from government "experts."

matter.[348] According to one (Northern) source, average life expectancy in the South (circa 1933) was forty-five to fifty years for whites and five to ten years less for blacks.[349] The same source claims that infant mortality was 200 per 1000 live births for blacks and 125-150 per 1000 live births for whites. By comparison, in 2012 the infant mortality for Afghanistan was 150/1000 live births.[350] In 1890 the sickness rate for black sharecroppers was 20% higher than for pre-war slaves.[351] Today (2016) the most current data gives the infant mortality rate for the United

Bathing facilities in a Missouri sharecropper's cabin. The Federal President (FDR) was more concerned about the voters in Pennsylvania than these "forgotten" people. (Courtesy LOC)

States as 6 per 1000 live births.[352] A report published in 2016 in *USA Today* noted that only one Southern state was below the national average for infant mortality.[353] The five states with the highest infant mortality rate were all in the South, whereas the five states with the lowest infant mortality rate were all in the North. In a 2016 report of the best and worst states for underprivileged children, there were only four Southern states in the top 25 (best) while twelve Southern states were in the bottom (worst) twenty-five states. Yes, the punishment continues even today. All of this is evidence that things that happened to the South in the past still impacts the South today. *If you can't leave you are not free, if you are not free you will not be prosperous.*

It is appropriate to ask: "What was Franklin Delano Roosevelt's reaction to Southern poverty?" Norman Thomas, a socialist activist, was one of the few who dared to ask such a question and he also provided the answer:

---

348 http://www.cdc.gov/parasites/hookworm (Accessed 3/28/2016). (See photo of open-back out-house.)

349 Bryan, Dan, https://americanhistoryusa.com/slaverytoserfdom-blackpeople-newsouth (Accessed 5/2/2016).

350 *Ibid.*

351 Fogel & Engerman, 267.

352 http://data.worldbank.org/indicator/SP.DYN.IMRT.IN (Accessed 5/2/2016).

353 *USA Today*, "Mortality Rates by States," George Petras, Mar. 7, 2016

The screen window of a sharecropper's cabin near Marshall, Texas. (Courtesy LOC)

He [FDR] seemed more interested in the labor problems of Pennsylvania where he needed their votes, than in the South, where he does not need the votes.[354]

While Southern poverty and resultant diseases were caused by the Federal Empire, Southern poverty and disease were of no real concern to the ruling elite in Washington. While they may have pretended at times to be concerned, the reality is that they and Southern politicians accepted Southern poverty as normal and did nothing to effectually resolve the problem.[355]

Malaria and other diseases transmitted by flying insects were also a major problem in the hot and humid South. Before the era of air conditioning the only way to cool a house was to open doors and windows to allow "fresh air" in from the outside. But windows and doors without screens on them were an open invitation for flies and mosquitoes. People who owned their homes would invest time and

Slave quarters on the Kent House Plantation in Louisiana (Courtesy of Kent House Plantation Alexandria, LA)

Sharecropper's tenant house 1933, Muskogee, Oklahoma (Courtesy LOC)

---

354 Venkataramani, 242.

355 *Ibid.*, 244: "In theory [yes, but] in reality...only a very small portion of those who might wish to become owners of farms" were helped; also see *Ibid.*, 227, 232, documenting the fact that FDR's Administration knew but did very little to actually help with evictions of homeless tenants due to FDR's policies, which made matters even worse for thousands of sharecroppers.

money into the upkeep, but a tenant could not afford to repair a house that he may not inhabit the following planting season. Thus, the economics of the South's sharecropping system worked against the health and comfort of sharecropper tenants.

Sharecropping Slaves' Housing

During the era of antebellum chattel slavery, the master would provide housing for his slaves. Whether out of Christian compassion or mere business necessity, most slaves were housed in small but reasonably comfortable housing by the standards of the day. As has already been noted, the living space for most Southern slaves exceeded the living space for New York workers in 1893.[356] Another fact that supports the claim that most slaves were well cared for is that Southern slaves had a longer life expectancy than either Northern or European urban industrial workers.[357] Most politically correct (P.C.) indoctrinated Americans find it hard to believe that the housing for post-war sharecropper slaves was worse than the housing provided for pre-war slaves. That is because the P.C. Northern narrative of the war imprints on the minds of Americans the false notion that after the war the North labored to reconstruct the devastated South and provide the newly-freed slaves with freedom and opportunity to participate in the American dream. Nothing could be further from the truth—but truth has never been an obstacle to Northern domination of American and especially Southern history. The truth is that chattel slaves had reasonably good housing—

depending mostly upon how long the plantation had been in operation. Younger plantations were growing and would have less efficient slave housing but housing would improve as the plantation became more financially successful. The slaves understood this, and it is one of the reasons so many slaves identified themselves with "their" plantation. It is

Sharecropper family residence Warner, Oklahoma circa 1933 (Photo courtesy LOC)

---

356 Fogel & Engerman, 116.

357 *Ibid.*, 126.

also the reason economists Robert W. Fogel (Nobel Laureate, 1993) and Stanley Engerman state that slaves (specifically field hands) received over their lifetime the value of upwards of 90% of the income they produced. As bad as chattel slavery was (with respect to violating the principle of self-ownership and

Evicted sharecropper circa 1935. FDR's price support efforts did little to resolve the depressed crop prices but it did cause the displacement of thousands of Southern sharecroppers. (Courtesy LOC)

personal liberty) it was not nearly as bad as sharecropping slavery imposed upon black and white Southerners by the victorious United States of America.

Under the system of sharecropping slavery, the "cropper" received between 30 to 50 percent of the value he produced and then had deducted any money advanced to him by the landlord during the lean times between harvesting and the next planting season, plus interest. The landlord would deduct the value of the tenant house provided to the "cropper" as well. In most cases the "cropper" ended the year in debt—giving rise to the term of Southern "debt peonage." The leftist Swedish economist Gunnar Myrdal, noted the tragic irony in the manner by which black Southerners were treated before and after "Emancipation":

> *Even to many Negroes themselves slavery…was [a] more advantageous*
> *economic arrangement…than…caste status into which they were thrown by*
> *Emancipation.*[358]

The point is not that Emancipation was bad but that the manner in which the North imposed it upon the South was bad. Northern- imposed radical abolition ensured the impoverishment of both black and white Southerners, a relative poverty that remains over a century and a half after the end of the so-called "Civil War." [359]

---

358 *Ibid.*, 262, quoting Gunnar Myrdal.

359 See, "Dixie's Unwelcomed Presence in Rosie O'Donnell's America," in Kennedy & Kennedy, *Nullifying Tyranny*, 187-99.

Homelessness—How the Federal Government Made Matters Worse

At the height of Southern sharecropping there were an estimated 1.8 million sharecropping *families* who had no permanent home. Each year they were subject to being evicted or otherwise compelled to move from one landowner's property to another. This nomadic lifestyle cost approximately $25,000,000 annually.[360]

Evicted Sharecroppers, MO circa 1935. Even though 66% of Sharecroppers were white Southerners, for the most part, black Southerners were the poorest of the poor. (Courtesy LOC)

The cost was born not by the landowner but by the sharecropper. Prior to the War the South did not have a large population living a nomadic lifestyle. Chattel slaves had permanent homes on well managed plantations.[361] If a move was made the cost was born by the plantation owner. The plain folk, prior to the War, had well- established cabins built and owned on the South's open range. But this changed

Evicted Sharecroppers, Arkansas 1935
(Photo courtesy LOC)

post-war. After the War both newly freed slaves and numerous white plain folk were forced to rely on large landowners for shelter. But this necessity gave the landowner a bargaining advantage when it came time to negotiate crop contracts with the

---

360 Clark & Kirwan, 104.

361 Twenty-five per cent of black males pre-war were mangers, professionals and skilled craftsmen, Fogel & Engelman, 40. Apparently race did not make a difference to white Southerners when it came to managing plantations and working with skilled professionals or craftsmen. This provides a hint of what "could have been" in a free and prosperous Confederate States of America. But Yankee invasion, conquest and occupation prevented the flowering of a free and equal Southern society.

sharecropper. The sharecropper always knew that he and his family could be evicted if he did not agree to the landowner's contract. But federal government intervention during the Great Depression made matters even worse for the sharecropper.

In an effort to support crop prices during the Depression the federal government initiated a policy of paying landowners NOT to plant certain crops—hoping to thereby reduce supply and drive up crop prices. As usual with government interventions in the market place, the ruling elite did not foresee the unintended consequences of government meddling. If a landowner is paid not to plant a crop, then the landowner does not need to employ sharecroppers. If the landowner does not employ the sharecropper, then the landowner will evict the homeless sharecropper from his property. Dr. William R. Amberson of the University of Tennessee reported that "between 15 to 20 per cent of sharecroppers had lost their employment as a result of the crop reduction program." [362] Remember that part of the employment contract was the landowner's provision of shelter for the sharecropper and his family. The federal government was made aware of the distress its crop reduction program was causing down South but did very little to resolve the distress. Dr. Calvin B. Hoover of Duke University conducted an investigation at the request of Henry Wallace, Secretary of Agriculture under President Franklin D. Roosevelt. Dr. Hoover reported that the federal government's program had "created a motive for reducing the number of tenants on farms." [363] But despite this and other data received by the federal government, "No concrete action was taken by the Department of Agriculture, however, to safeguard the interest of sharecroppers." [364] It can be argued that the federal government actually hid such information. In January, 1935, Mary Conner Myers, an attorney with the federal government, went to Arkansas to investigate the complaints regarding evictions of sharecroppers due to government crop reduction policy. Her report on the appalling conditions caused by evictions of sharecroppers was not released by the Federal government. [365] In the March 31, 1935, issue of the New York *Times* it was disclosed that: "The Secretary admitted that displacement of tenants had increased and that the operation of the cotton contracts had probably added to their difficulties." [366] Oh well,

---

362 Venkataramani, 231.

363 *Ibid.*, 232.

364 *Ibid.*

365 *Ibid.*

366 *Ibid.*, 238.

what difference did it make? After all, Southern sharecroppers were just poor white and black trash—leftovers from the Federal Empire's extermination policy.

The Federal government's intervention in the marketplace caused the Great Depression[367]—although progressives do all they can to hide this inconvenient fact. During the Depression the "experts" in Washington attempted to solve the problem their intervention had caused by even more government intervention! Their Agricultural Adjustment Act intended to "raise farm prices by curtailing production."[368] But when notified about the sad results, the "experts" refused to discuss publicly its negative impact on Southern sharecroppers.[369]

Northern-Imposed Poverty—It Is Not a Joking Matter

The term "poor white trash" (in slang "pwt") became popular during the era of sharecropping and the "Dust Bowl."[370] It was a harsh term callously applied by Northern journalists, comedians of the day, and politicians. It can be heard even today, long after the era of sharecropping, but the era of anti-South comedians, journalists, and politicians remains. Many a joke has been made about backwoods Southerners and their open-back, unsanitary "outhouses", i.e., privies or toilets. The one pictured may or may not be typical of the era but it should give the reader an understanding of the level of destitution that many of our Southern kith and kin were forced to endure in the nearly 100 years of Northern-imposed post-war sharecropping slavery. Northern imposed

Sharecropper's Outhouse/privy Pace, Mississippi circa 1933 (Courtesy LOC)

punishment for resisting their imperial embrace. *Vae Victis*—Woe to the vanquished.

---

367 Rothbard, Murray, *America's Great Depression*, (1963, The Ludwig von Mises Institute, Auburn, Al: 2000), xxix.

368 Venkataramani, 227.

369 *Ibid*.

370 The Dust Bowl resulted from a drought that struck primarily the panhandles of Oklahoma and Texas and adjacent areas in 1934-7. It added yet another degree of misery to Depression era farmers.

Chapter 11

POLITICAL POVERTY—THE DEATH OF SOUTHERN STATESMANSHIP

The South and former Spanish colonies are similar....In both, the US Supreme
Court specifically sanctions US jurisdiction over territories in which
the people in those territories were denied the fundamental right
to have government based upon their consent.[371]

Southern statesmanship was a key, if not the key, guiding factor in the creation of America's original Constitutionally limited Republic of Republics.[372]   Indeed, the Southern State of Virginia was once known as the mother of presidents. Southerners continued to be at the forefront of the struggle to maintain constitutional liberty for almost a hundred years after the beginning of the American agitation against the British Empire's tyranny.   Every document, every issue, and eventually every key battle surrounding the inception and development of the United States as a republic composed of sovereign states has the imprint of Southern statesmanship, Southern thinking and Southern blood. American thinking on personal freedom and defense against tyrannical central government would be virtually nonexistent if it were not for the words, writings, and actions of Southern Statesmen. Unfortunately, contemporary

---

371 DeRosa, Marshall, "The Rationalization of American Militaristic Imperialism," *To Live and Die In Dixie*, 288. Reference is to Cuba and the Philippians.

372 The Founding Fathers referred to the new government under the proposed Constitution as a "compound republic." See Federalist Papers Number 51. William Rawle used the terms "compound commonwealth" & "union is an association of the people of republics" (note plural), Rawle, William, *A View of the Constitution* (1825 Land & Land, Baton Rouge, LA: 1993), 234; Also described as "an association of republics," Centz, P. C., *The Republic of Republics* (Little, Brown, and Co., Boston, MA: 1881), x .

America suffers from the abandonment of this Southern conservative tradition.[373] In the South today "practical" partisan politics has replaced principled statesmanship. Practical politics has given us an America where we have become slavish subjects to a supreme Federal Empire—a political and financial Empire far more onerous and oppressive than the British Empire[374] from which our Colonial ancestors seceded. [375]

This chapter will review a representative sample of the South's "Good," "Bad," and "Ugly" political leaders, covering the time from the "Good" (1776 to 1865) to current day "Ugly" Southern politicians. Southern statesmen who dominated American and Southern political thought from the inception of the United States up to 1865 represent the "Good" Southern statesmen. The "Good" were true statesmen who were concerned with establishing a limited federal government that would not infringe upon individual liberties, while protecting the new country's borders and (most importantly) leaving "we the people" of the sovereign states alone. The "Bad" were politicians whose policies from 1865 to 1965 established a system of government that drove an unnatural wedge of racial bitterness between white and black Southerners in order to assure first Republican and then Democratic political dominance. The policies of these "Bad" politicians assured the economic and civil impoverishment of black and white Southerners. The "Ugly" politicians are contemporary Southern politicians of both political parties who willingly sacrifice the well-being of the very electorate who vote for them in order to secure a place for themselves in the halls of the ruling elite in Washington. In the process it will be explained that, due to post-Appomattox Northern-imposed cultural distortion, the people of the South are not the proximate cause of the "bad" and "ugly" politicians that have ruled the Southern States since Appomattox. These Southern politicians *willingly*[376] worked within the distorted political system

---

373 Actually it was a classical liberal tradition that stressed a constitutionally limited central government, local self-government, and personal responsibility within the Judeo-Christian tradition.

374 The Colonies revolted when the King placed a tax of around 2 pennies on a pound of tea, but today the Federal Empire extracts close to 50% of our income in direct and indirect taxes! See Kennedy, *Reclaiming Liberty*, 163-183.

375 See Virginia's Resolves of May 1776 declaring "the union" that had heretofore existed between Great Britain and Virginia as being "dissolved," as discussed in Kennedy & Kennedy, *Was Jefferson Davis Right?*, 258.

376 By "willingly" we mean that Bad and Ugly Southern politicians completely abandoned the concept that we the people of the South had and still have a right to establish a government ordered upon our own free and unfettered consent. They rejected liberty and self-government while embracing the perverted, unconstitutional government that rules the United States post-Appomattox. They betrayed and continue to betray our right to be free—our right to be the masters in our own home!

established and foisted upon the South by the Federal Empire. They were and are responsible for the civil and social evils that arose in the South post -Appomattox. These social/economic evils include racial mistrust and hatred, sharecropping peonage, "Jim Crow" white supremacy, and poverty. Post-war Southern politicians' willingness to embrace a culturally distorted Southern society assured the continuation of the social, political, and economic enslavement of black and white Southerners. It assured that the evil enforced by an uncontrollable federal empire continues and threatens the very existence of the little liberty upon which we now barley subsist. But worse of all, it assured continuation of a sharp racial divide and poverty that was imposed upon black and white Southerners by the invading and occupying forces of the Federal Empire.

Distinguishing Between Statesmen and Politicians

Most Americans think that the words "statesman" and "politician" define the same group of people. This misunderstanding is yet one more "progressive" benefit from taxpayer-financed liberal propaganda masquerading as public education. From a traditional conservative Southern point of view, a statesman is someone who has a personal reputation for honesty, integrity and intellectual prowess; a person who is well established in his profession or vocation; and someone who does not seek office but who will sacrifice his time and talents to represent his community. The mark of a true statesman is that when he leaves

John C. Calhoun (Courtesy of Wikimedia Commons)

office neither he, nor any of his friends or family, have been financially enriched by their close connections to the government's treasury. Nashville Agrarian Andrew Nelson Lytle describes a statesman as one who saw his mission to be the person who clarified a given people's alternatives.[377] A statesman declared his political principles, and if the people elected him, then the people could be sure that the statesman would do all within his power to implement those principles. Politicians, on the other hand, are an entirely different and malignant group of "public servants."

---

377 Lytle quoted in Wilson, Clyde, *From Union to Empire*, (The Foundation for American Education, Columbia, SC: 2003), 117.

Politicians, indeed, are a pernicious breed that was succinctly described by John C. Calhoun in the 1840s. He predicted the future state of America when politicians would rule:

> *When it comes to be once understood that politics is a game; that those who are engaged in it but act a part; that they make this or that profession, not from honest conviction or intent to fulfill it, but as a means of deluding the people, and through that delusion to acquire power; when such professions are to be entirely forgotten, the people will lose all confidence in public men. All will be regarded as mere jugglers—the honest and patriotic as well the cunning and the profligate—and the people will become indifferent and passive to the grossest abuses of power, on the ground that those whom they may elevate, under whatever pledges, instead of reforming, will but imitate the example of those whom they have expelled.*[378]

No better description of modern American politicians has been written. Recall these famous political pledges: "Read my lips, no new taxes." "If you like your doctor, you can keep your doctor." And add to these examples generations of Southern politicians who swore to "we the people" of Dixie that they fervently embraced the political theory of states' rights but never did anything to reclaim *real* states' rights—all the while they were busy ingratiating themselves to the ruling elite of the federal empire's national political parties.

Thomas Jefferson (Photo courtesy Wikimedia Commons)

The Good—1776 to 1865

Southern statesmen, such as Thomas Jefferson, looked to create and maintain a system of government strong enough to protect the borders from foreign invasion while maintaining a free trade zone within the geographical territory composed of the sovereign states that created the federal government. Volumes have been written about the Southern anti-federalists and federalists who labored to create a government large enough to protect the new country but small enough not to infringe upon the civil liberties of we the people of the sovereign states. The primary goal of Southern statesmanship was to prevent the

378 Calhoun quoted in Wilson, *From Union to Empire*, 213-214.

development of a large central government—similar to the one in London from which the Thirteen Colonies had seceded in 1776. The sovereign and independent states were the creators of their federal government. The States designed their agent, the federal government, in a manner that would hopefully prevent the development of anti-liberty tendencies. Their labors produced the new federal government under the constitution proposed in 1787. A constitution that was hotly debated—not in Congress —but in the various independent and sovereign states that eventually ratified the constitution. The states created the federal government and the states retained the right to be the ultimate judge as to whether or not their agent, the federal government, was acting according to the limitations imposed upon it by its creators—sovereign and independent states. Note that each sovereign state acted independently of all other states. [379]

President Thomas Jefferson made this point clear in his first inaugural address when he declared:

> What I deem the essential principles of our government…the support of state
> governments in all their rights, as the most competent administrations for our
> domestic concerns and the surest bulwarks against anti-republican tendencies….[380]

Jefferson also noted that the federal government should be "frugal" to the point that the people would hardly notice it and its taxing policies would "not take from the mouth of labor the bread it has earned." The potential of a centralized federal government to use its taxing powers to exploit the people of certain states for the benefit of a ruling elite and their cronies was a major concern of Southern statesmen. This was a point that was hotly debated in the state conventions that decided whether or not their specific state would ratify the proposed constitution and thereby voluntarily accede to the new union of sovereign states.

Patrick Henry, an outspoken Anti-federalist, warned his fellow Southerners that Virginia and the South would be the minority in the federal government created by the proposed constitution of 1787. Although it did not make him popular, he nonetheless issued his militant warning:

> The [proposed] government subjects everything to the Northern majority….How
> can the Southern members prevent the adoption of the most oppressive mode of

---

379 See Article VII, U.S. Constitution.

380 Jefferson quoted in, Wilson, *From Union to Empire*, 156.

taxation in the Southern states, as there is a majority in favor of the Northern
States? Sir, this is a picture so horrid, so wretched, so dreadful, that I need no longer
dwell upon it.[381]

Statesmen, such as George Mason, added their voices to Henry's warning, declaring: "The eight Northern States have an interest different from the five Southern States....The Southern States had therefore grounds for their suspicions."[382] Hugh Williamson of North Carolina warned: "The Southern interest must be extremely endangered by the present arrangement. The Northern States are to have a majority in the first instance, with means of perpetuating it."[383] General Charles Cotesworth Pinckney of South Carolina declared that if the Southern States were to form no more than a mere minority in the new government under the proposed constitution, "and the regulation of trade is to be given to the General Government, they will be nothing more than overseers for the Northern States."

It did not take long before the Federal government used unconstitutional power to oppress the rights of "we the people" who were supposedly protected by the Constitution. In 1798 the Federal Congress passed, Federalist President John Adams signed, and Justices of the Federal Supreme Court aggressively enforced the Alien and Sedition Acts. These Acts were a flagrant violation of the rights of free speech and a free press. Yet, the supposed protection guaranteed by the Constitution's "Bill of Rights" proved to be no more than a mere parchment barricade. The Constitution was no real impediment to the aggressive acts of power-hungry ruling elite who controlled the Federal government. It became clear that the Federal government could not be relied upon to police or control itself. The old Roman adage of "Who shall guard the guards?" comes to mind. By 1798 it was clear that the ultimate barricade between the rights and liberties of "we the people" and an aggressive Federal government was NOT the Constitution but the sovereign state. The era from 1798 to 1865[384] was the era of real states' rights. It is not an accident that 1798 to 1865 were also the years that gave us the era of "good" Southern statesmen.

Southern Statesmen Thomas Jefferson and James Madison would become leaders of the States' Rights movement by writing the Kentucky and Virginia Resolves of

---

381 Patrick Henry as cited in Kennedy & Kennedy, *Was Jefferson Davis Right?*, 198-199.

382 *Ibid.*

383 *Ibid.*

384 The era of real states' rights died in April, 1865, at Appomattox.

1798-1800. Southern statesmen, unlike their Northern counterparts, were not engaged in setting up political, commercial or financial empires, but were leaders in the effort to preserve liberty for we the people of the sovereign states. They exemplify the "good" because they were intent upon establishing and maintaining a limited government that would protect individual liberty from enemies both foreign and domestic. While politicians of the North were busy encouraging the development of a centralized, "energetic" national government, a government that would help the North to develop a worldwide commercial and financial empire, Southern statesmen labored to maintain the liberty of we the people of the sovereign states—to protect the liberties of a people who only asked government to simply leave them alone.

Southern statesmen were "good" because they did not seek power in order to exploit that power for personal gain but they sought to preserve liberty and local self-government. As representatives of their people (their kith and kin) they knew that solutions to complex social issues would be best served by those close to the problem—problems such as how to abolish the system of African-American slavery that had been imposed upon the South by British and New England shipping interests. [385]

Northern-Imposed Cultural Distortion—Prerequisite to Bad and Ugly Politicians

The question that should come to mind at this point is "What caused the South to shift from the "good" to the "bad" and eventually the "ugly"—from statesmen to politicians? This question is never asked by national scholars. The reason is that national academics[386] (political scientists and historians) serve as the Federal Empire's propagandists. Their job is to maintain the false narrative that the "Civil War" was fought by an evil, hate-filled South to keep their slaves, while the North unselfishly offered its blood to free their black brothers and sisters from cruel Southern slavery. In reality the War for Southern Independence was fought by the South in an attempt to prevent Southerners (black and white) from becoming the

---

385 Kennedy & Kennedy, *The South Was Right!*, 59-80.

386 "National scholars" refers to those in academia who slavishly parrot the Northern (national) party line regarding their leftist justification for the invasion, conquest and occupation of the sovereign nation—the Confederate States of America. Those few brave men and women who refuse to do so are punished by severe criticism that results in career- limiting notoriety among the rulers of politically correct academia. Those scholars who bravely challenge the Northern pc narrative are modern day heroes and freedom fighters.

tax serfs and political/economic slaves to Lincoln's newly emerging federal empire. [387]

The invasion, conquest and occupation of the Confederate States of America by the United States of America not only imposed poverty upon we the people of the South but it distorted the South's culture in a manner that *prevented* the continuation of statesmanship. Northern imposed *cultural distortion* destroyed the Southern culture that had created America's finest statesmen and replaced it with a distorted culture that could only create a bad and ugly social order ruled over by bad and ugly politicians—politicians who were and are the lackeys of the Federal Empire's ruling elite.

Understanding the creation of contemporary Southern society ruled over by self-serving politicians is much easier if one understands the impact of cultural distortion that results from foreign invasion, conquest and occupation of any people. Southern cultural distortion explains why the post-Appomattox South was compelled to abandon statesmanship and embrace crass politics that produced a "bad" and "ugly" social order in the once free and prosperous states of Dixie. It was and is a social order imposed upon the people of the South—a social order that relied upon racial hatred in order to assure first (during Reconstruction) Republican domination of the South; then (during the era of Jim Crow white supremacy) Democratic domination of the South. Today it provides the Democratic Party with an endless supply of obedient black Southern voters, while the Republican Party can take the white conservative Southerner for granted. In the meantime, both political parties cater to the whims of the national party's donor class and the ruling elite in Washington, D.C.[388]   Again, all of this would not have happened absent Northern- imposed cultural distortion that arose as a result of invasion, conquest, and continuing occupation of we the people of Dixie.

Vidkun Quisling of Norway, who betrayed his people by cooperating with Nazi invaders. (Courtesy LOC)

Social scientists attempt to explain how individuals rationalize otherwise immoral or unethical behavior—

---

387 See "Sharecropping: Northern- Imposed Post-War Slavery" herein for a discussion of how the victorious North impoverished the South and turned it into a colonial appendage of the North, and how Southern resources and people were used to enrich the Federal Empire's ruling elite and their crony capitalist allies.

388 See "Last vote" theory as described in Kennedy & Kennedy, *Why Not Freedom!* , 51-2.

such as post-War Southern politicians who abandoned the *legitimate* idea of a constitutionally limited federal government enforced by real states' rights and embraced of the *illegitimate* concept of a supreme federal government that is the final judge of its powers.[389] Social scientists have attempted to explain the unethical acts of individuals such

as collaborating with the invading and occupying forces of one's nation. World War II provides a number of examples of individuals who willingly betrayed their own people by cooperating with the Nazis. In France they were known as Vichymen. They were willing to betray their nation's honor in the hope of improving their material standing, and

Native Americans Scouts serving U.S. Army during Indian Wars. Note white officer on right. (Courtesy LOC)

they most likely rationalized their action by declaring that "someone had to run the new government." The same thing happened in Norway when Vidkun Quisling became the puppet leader of Nazi-occupied Norway. Those who cooperated with the Nazi occupiers were disparagingly referred to as "Quislings." Even some Jews in Nazi concentration camps were willing to cooperate with their Nazi captors—the kapo or Jewish guards were organized by the Nazi SS and given special treatment in exchange for their service. In America there were a large number of Native Americans who sold their service to the United States cavalry during the "Indian Wars." Their "service" as trackers and knowledge of their homelands were essential in the eventual victory over and removal of Native Americans from their ancestral lands. In the post-War South, we had native Southerners known as Scalawags who, for "filthy lucre's sake," willingly served the federal empire's occupying forces. What takes place in an individual's mind that would allow him to

---

389 Kennedy, *Nullification: Why and How*, 53-65. Provides a detailed account of the type of Federal government the Founding Fathers specifically *rejected* but which is very similar to the illegitimate one Lincoln and the Republicans created—the one we live under today.

betray his native country and help those who are actively oppressing his "kith and kin?"[390]

Whenever powerful external pressures are brought to bear in an attempt to influence a citizen of an occupied nation to carry out activities detrimental to the best interests of the occupied nation, the decision-maker (the Scalawag in post-war South) can seize upon these external social/political/military pressures as a basis or rationale to mentally justify his treasonous actions. He denies his own personal responsibility for making the choice to betray his people. He attributes his treason to the external pressures and denies that he is personally responsible, claiming that his choice is forced upon him by external circumstances.[391] Southern politicians who attempt to gain favor with the ruling elite of both national political parties are constantly using this technique to rationalize their inability to protect Southern interests in the Federal Empire's Congress.[392]

Eventually the reality of the new political order will become firmly fixed upon the rank and file subjects of the occupied nation. At that point the people of the former free and prosperous nation begin to accept their nation's new position as a colonial appendage of the conquering Empire. Their new social status as *subjects* of an all-powerful empire as opposed to *citizens* in their own country becomes the new "normal." This new "normal" cannot occur except in the total absence of resistance to occupation. This lack of resistance to the occupying powers betrays a perception of hopelessness on the part of the subjugated people; the occupied people no longer believe that they will ever live in a country of their own, ordered upon their free and unfettered consent. The people of the occupied nation no longer expect to be the master in their own home. The conquering Empire allows local self-government only if the locals pay their tribute to the Empire (taxes) and do not transgress the Empire's rules and regulations. In the post-war South this was the case as the traditional Southern political philosophy of states' rights was replaced with the new reality of states' privileges—privileges exercised at the discretion of the ruling elite of the supreme Federal Empire. After a generation of such rule, the people of the South no longer remembered the promise of freedom and passively accepted their second class

---

390 "Kith and Kin" is a Scottish-Irish term, of Middle English origin, used in the South to denote more than just blood relationship. It included friends and neighbors. Therefore, in the South the term does not recognize racial barriers.

391 Janis & Mann, *Decision Making: A Psychological Analysis of Conflict, Choice, and Commitment* (The Free Press, NY: 1977), 93.

392 For contemporary examples of Southern Congressmen's inability and possible desire not to protect specific Southern interests in the Federal Empire's Congress see Kennedy & Kennedy, *Was Jefferson Davis Right?*, 274-5, and Kennedy & Kennedy," *Our Re-United Country?," To Live and Die In Dixie*, 497.

status in this "one nation indivisible." It is similar to the way a docile and submissive slave accepts his enforced servitude and tries to make the best out of a bad situation.

This has been and still is the *modus operandi* of Southern political leaders since the end of Reconstruction. External forces (the Federal Empire and its cronies on Wall Street and K-Street) prevent them from doing what they should be doing to free their people (the voters who elected them) from an oppressive and unconstitutional misrule. Instead of working to reclaim the South's lost inheritance of constitutionally-limited federalism via a return to *real* states' rights,[393] they make hot speeches for home consumption and then work to ingratiate themselves with the Federal Empire's ruling elite of both national political parties. After all, just like the Vichymen and Quislings, they tell themselves that "somebody has to run the existing government."

Post- Appomattox "bad" politicians in the South worked tirelessly to claim their share of political power in Lincoln's evolving federal empire. They never challenged the legitimacy of the newly created supreme federal government and only gave lip service to the concept of states' rights—which amounted to no more than mere states' privileges exercised only with the permission of the Federal Empire. But from a social point of view Northern-imposed cultural distortion was even worse than its effect on the political environment because it encouraged racial hatred and the development of Jim Crow white supremacy. Today there remains, among black Southerners, an extreme political hatred and mistrust of conservative white Southerners—much to the benefit of the national Democratic Party. The post-Reconstruction rise of white supremacy benefited both national political parties. It provided a "Solid South" to the Democratic Party and drove the Reconstruction Republican-initiated wedge of racial hatred even deeper into Southern society. After 1965 this racial bitterness assured obedient black votes for the Democratic Party and subservient white conservative votes to the Republican Party. It was a win-win for the Federal Empire's political elites of both parties, but it was a lose-lose for black and white Southerners. But what is never acknowledged is that the system of white supremacy was a social system that was imposed upon black and white Southerners via Northern-created Southern cultural distortion.

Today white supremacy/Jim Crow segregation is viewed as a *natural* part of Southern history. But white supremacy was much closer to race relations as practiced in the pre-

---

393 *Real* states' rights is the first step in establishing a prosperous society based on low taxes, individual responsibility, and a government that will leave the people alone. See discussion of liberty-based society in Kennedy, *Reclaiming* Liberty.

War North than to the racial attitudes and practices of the pre-War South.[394] Thus "bad" politicians created "bad" social policy. The Federal Empire's sycophants and defenders ignore the fact that it was the United States of America's Supreme Court that made racial segregation the legal and therefore the official policy of the United States in its infamous 1896 Plessy decision.[395] The Federal Supreme Court based its decision in support of segregation on an 1848 Massachusetts law. The majority opinion was written by the Chief Justice who was from Michigan. All but one of the Northern Justices voted in favor of racial segregation—one brave fellow merely abstained from voting. The only dissenting vote was from Justice Harlan who was a Southerner whose family owned slaves prior to the war!

This bad social policy (racial hatred and white supremacy) imposed on the South by the Federal government was then expertly used by both national political parties as they struggled to see which would use black or white Southern voters to help them gain the reins of power in the Federal Empire's national capitol. The *cultural distortion* of Southern society caused by the Federal Empire's invasion, conquest, and occupation of the Confederate States of America created a social environment that not only allowed but encouraged the development of bad political order centered around racial fear and hatred. But this new and unnatural hate-filled social order was a boon to national politicians of both Republican and Democratic parties. This Northern-imposed hate-filled social order was used first by Republicans during Reconstruction, then by the Democrats during the era of white supremacy/Jim Crow, and today it provides both national political parties with reliable and obedient voters to help these parties maintain control of their Federal Empire.

All made possible by the *cultural distortion* of Southern society created by the invasion of the Confederate States of America by the United States of America. The U.S.A. under Lincoln and Radical Republicans became a country that morphed into an industrial, financial, political and military empire.

Huey Long (Courtesy LOC)

The Bad—1865-1965

Huey Long, Democratic Governor and then U.S. Senator from Louisiana, 1928 to

394 Livingston, "Confederate Emancipation" *To Live and Die In Dixie*, 455-89.

395 *Plessy v. Ferguson*, 163 U.S. 537 (1896).

1935, is typical of the Bad Southern politicians produced by Northern-imposed cultural distortion of Southern society. Huey Long held harsh racial attitudes that were an accepted part of the progressive movement. His tactics and economics were more in line with Fascism than classical Southern conservative thought. As governor he raided gambling establishments[396] to gain support and votes from Christian fundamentalists, while using such raids to gain protection money from the remaining gambling establishments. He appointed a censor for the Louisiana State University's student newspaper *Reveille*. When students protested, the Dean chastised the students, telling them "you students value your principles too much."[397] Race-baiting was not his strong point but Long used the technique when necessary. He would often accuse his opponents of working with "niggers."[398] While in Congress he opposed anti-lynching laws, declaring such laws were not necessary because "we just lynch an occasional nigger."[399] Such was the type of politician produced post-Appomattox in a culturally distorted South. Compare Long's views to those of former Confederate General Nathan Bedford Forrest when, well after the war, he was invited to speak to a group of black Southerners and he told them:

> *we were born on the same soil, we breathe the same air, live in the same land, and why should we not be brothers and sisters….I want you to do as I do—go to the polls and select the best men to vote for….Although we differ in color, we should not differ in sentiment.*[400]

Compare other post-Reconstruction Southern politicians such as "The Great White Chief" James K. Vardaman of Mississippi, who was an outspoken white supremacist, to another former Confederate officer, P.G.T. Beauregard, who advocated civil rights for the freed slaves, including the right to vote, and declared:

> *The Negro is Southern born; with a little education and some property qualifications he can be made to take sufficient interest in the affairs and prosperity of the South to insure an intelligent vote.*[401]

396 Jeansonne, Glen, *Messiah of the Masses*, (Addison-Wesley Educational Publishers Inc., NY: 1993), 69.

397 *Ibid.*, 98.

398 Williams, T. Harry, *Huey Long*, (Alfred A. Knopf, Inc., NY: 1969), 538.

399 *Ibid.*, 705.

400 Seabrook, *A Rebel Born; A Defense of Nathan Bedford Forrest*, 483-485.

401 Williams, *P.G.T. Beauregard: Napoleon in Gray*, 269.

From the end of Reconstruction to 1965 the South was beset with a continuing stream of bad politicians. The progressive era gave us men such as Huey Long, James K. Vardaman, and eventually Lyndon Banes Johnson. What caused this change from Southern statesmen to unprincipled politicians who used black and white Southerners for their own benefit? Yankee-imposed cultural distortion is the only legitimate explanation for the radical change in the way Southern political leaders approached black voting and civil rights post-Reconstruction.

Nothing distorts a people's natural or native culture (its society as opposed to its government) more than invasion, conquest and occupation. An alien invasion will quickly turn a peaceful and trusting social order into an oppressive, suspicious, and unnatural society. For example, who today would blame modern Frenchmen or Norwegians for the deaths of French or Norwegian Jews that resulted from the actual or tacit cooperation of the French Vichy or Norwegian Quisling governments during Nazi occupation? Overnight old friendships and neighborly social relations that had lasted for generations prior were corrupted and destroyed. This was not the natural order of French or Norwegian society, but it was the new, culturally distorted, society that resulted from Nazi invasion, conquest, and occupation. The same type of *cultural distortion* occurred in the states of the invaded, conquered and occupied Confederate States of America. To be clear, the destruction of good Southern statesmanship, the development of bad social order by bad post-Reconstruction Southern politicians, and the continuation and exploitation of the current ugly political system by current Southern politicians is due to Northern-imposed *cultural distortion* that arose from the invasion, conquest, and continuing occupation of the Confederate States of America by the evil forces of the Federal Empire. This evil Empire bears the name, symbols, and flag of the old United States of America, but it is void of the substance of that original republic of republics. *It has become an empire that bears the name and flag but none of the attributes of America's original constitutionally- limited Republic of Republics.*

Subsequent to Lincoln's death, the control of the newly created Federal Empire passed to the Radical Republicans who controlled Congress. Representative Thaddeus Stevens, Republican of Pennsylvania, was the leading actor in the charade of government in the post-War United States. During the War, while the United States of America was busy invading the Confederate States of America, Congressman Stevens proudly proclaimed that the military forces of the United

States of America had "a sword in one hand and shackles in the other."[402]   Empires'
use the sword to conquer free people and shackles to enslave the people of the
conquered and occupied nation. His plan for the South was as simple as it was brutal:

> *The future condition of the conquered power [the Confederate States of America]*
> *depends on the will of the conqueror [the United States of America, i.e., Federal*
> *Empire]. [The Southern States are] conquered provinces they must...eat the fruit*
> *of foul rebellion.*

His plan was to keep the South under Republican domination until the Republicans had
amended the Constitution (the Fourteenth and Fifteenth Amendments) so "as to secure
perpetual ascendancy to the party of the Union"—that is the Republican Party.   His
chosen method was to disenfranchise a large portion of the South's leadership as well as
rank and file white voters, to mobilize battalions of newly enfranchised, mostly illiterate,
freedmen under strict Republican control, and thereby create a harsh and angry division
between black and white Southerners. Republicans would then use hatred to energize
their battalions of angry, mostly illiterate black Southern voters, who would march
faithfully to the polls and cast their vote for anti-white (white Southern) candidates. He
declared: "I think there would always be Union men enough in the South, aided by the
blacks, to divide the representation and thus continue Republican ascendancy."[403] And
what were the results of this "Republican ascendancy" for we the people of the conquered
and occupied states of the formerly free and prosperous Confederate States of America?

The military conquest of the Confederate States of America ended early in 1865
but by 1866 it was clear to the *London Telegraph* what had actually happened. In a report
to their readers, the *Telegraph* noted that the United States of America "may remain
a republic in name, but some eight million of the people are subjects, not citizens."
[404]The "shackles" promised by Republican Thaddeus Stevens were now firmly placed
upon we the people of Dixie, and from that moment forward those "shackles" would
never be removed—at times they would be loosened but *never* removed. Empires do
not voluntarily release their captive nations, and never forget that the Confederate
States of America was the Federal Empire's first but not its last captive nation. Added

---

402 *Congressional Globe*, January 22, 1862, cited in Bowers, *The Tragic Era; The Revolution After Lincoln*,
(Halcyon House, NY: 1929), 72.

403 *Ibid.*

404 *Ibid.*, 146-147.

to this unspoken truth is that when people of a conquered nation are led by "bad" and "ugly" politicians even the hope of true local self-government is prevented from emerging. The reason is that if hope of freedom to emerge it would spell the end of the careers of those "bad" and "ugly" politicians. We the people of the South are held captive by our political rulers who enjoy the perks, privileges and power granted to them by the Empire's ruling elite. The perks, privileges and power thus granted are the compensation paid by the Federal government to Southern politicians for keeping "we the people of the South" in line. A Judas payment Southern politicians eagerly accept and a burden we the people of Dixie have become accustomed to enduring— like the dog that licks the boot of his master moments after the master kicks the poor trembling dog. We keep re-electing politicians who enlarge their fortunes but do nothing to reclaim our inherent right to be the masters in our own homes. Local self-government via real states' rights is the first step in the process of exchanging Southern poverty for a prosperous Southern economy.[405] Restoring local self-government is also the first step in reclaiming a moral society in which we order our social relations on the Christian principle of "do unto others as ye would have them do unto you."[406]

In order for the post-war Republicans to maintain their control of Congress and the Electoral College they had to devise a method to prevent the conquered Southern States from joining forces with the national Democratic Party. The Republicans did this by (1) dissolving legitimate,[407] post-War, Southern State governments and thereby making the states of the former Confederate States of America (less Tennessee which the Republicans firmly controlled) into conquered and occupied provinces; and (2) by destroying the friendly working relationship between black and white Southerners— which was a source of great surprise and embarrassment to the Yankees during their invasion of the Confederacy. The Radical Republicans would thereby create an unnatural social environment in which black and white Southerners feared and hated each other. After creating this fear and hatred, the Republicans then used black votes to further Republican political ambitions on the national level. Republican-instituted

---

405 See "Creating Wealth" in Kennedy & Kennedy, *Nullifying Tyranny*, 85-91.

406 The Golden Rule based upon the words of Jesus in Matthew 7:12 in the *Holy Bible*.

407 Legitimate only in the sense that these post-Appomattox state governments comported to the requirements forced upon the people of the South by Lincoln and Republican-controlled Congress. As governments established by an alien, occupying power and imposed upon a previously free and prosperous people (similar to Vichy France after Nazi invasion & occupation), these state governments can *never* be viewed as legitimate.

Reconstruction in Dixie became the vehicle to establish the false premise that black and white Southerners are natural enemies. Even the German socialist and former Union military officer Carl Schurz recognized the natural friendly relations between white and black Southerners—even though as an outsider he did not understand it:

> *Instances of the most touching attachment of freedmen to their old masters*
> *and mistresses have come to my notice. To a white man whom they believe*
> *to be sincerely their friend they cling with greater affection even than to one of*
> *their own race.... Centuries of slavery have not been sufficient to make them the*
> *enemies of the white race.* [408]

What centuries of slavery could not do (create hatred and mistrust between white and black Southerners) Republicans accomplished in a few years of Republican-imposed Reconstruction.

Review for a moment the conditions in Republican-imposed Reconstruction state legislatures that white Southern taxpayers were forced to subsidize: Often in Mississippi pistols and knives were used to settle "points of order;" in Virginia, disagreements were often settled with fists; in Florida, legislators puffed cigars while watching fistfights that would determine issues before the legislature. A large percentage of the members of Dixie's Reconstruction legislatures had no property to speak of and therefore little if any taxes to pay. Free from the personal burden of taxation, they spent taxpayers' money with lavish prodigality. Each Southern state suffered under the tyranny of the Federal Empire's minions who controlled the North's conquered Southern provinces. Mississippi prior to the War had been a rich and prosperous state, but post-War and even today she is the poorest state in "our" gloriously reunited nation—a new nation "with liberty and justice for all" except Southerners.

Taxes established by Mississippi's Reconstruction legislature exemplify what was happening across the South. In 1871 taxes were four time greater than in 1869; in 1872 taxes were eight- and- a -half times greater than in 1869; in 1873 twelve- and-a-half times greater; and in 1874 taxes were fourteen times as great as they had been in 1869. [409] Such was the gift given by the "one nation indivisible" to the people of Mississippi and the South.

---

408 Schurz, 140.

409 Bowers, 452.

State legislatures became scenes of vulgar comedy and engines of fraud and corruption. The white people of Northern states would never have allowed such a lawmaking body to rule their states but these same Northerners were more than willing—actually eager—to impose such rule upon the conquered people of Dixie. Ohio's *Cincinnati Commercial* was forced to declare: "My God! The whites have borne and borne until forbearance ceased to be a virtue and almost became a crime."[410] White Southerners' fear of black rule was produced by Republicans in Congress. It was the genesis of the current black/white political divide in Dixie. This is a culturally unnatural divide that greatly benefited first the white Republican Party (during Reconstruction), then the white Democratic party (during the era of white supremacy). Today both national political parties rely on black or white Southern votes to maintain the ruling elite's control of the Federal Empire as the elite in Washington dispense perks, privileges and power to their crony capitalist allies.

Origins of White Fear of Black Rule

During Reconstruction white Southerners learned to fear black rule. This fear was purposely generated by the Republican Party to promote an unnatural divide between black and white Southerners. The Republicans in Washington knew that if black and white Southerners worked together to control their own states, the Democrats would take over Congress. Something had to be done and racial hatred was the Republican solution to their political problem. By convincing black Southerners that white Southerners were their enemy and the Federal government under Republican Party control was their friend, the Republicans were able to drive an unnatural wedge between the Southern people and use one side against the other, thereby maintaining Republican control of elected Southern representatives in Congress.[411] Post-war Republicans used Reconstruction to set up a situation in which armed black militias roamed the streets and roads of the conquered South. The only "legal" system available for white Southerners was the one established by the United States Army and it was controlled by Republican political operatives. Barn burnings, theft, rape, and murder became

---

410 *Ibid.*

411 Dividing the people of an occupied nation into warring camps and using the ensuing antagonism as a means to maintain control of the occupied nation has been an effective technique used by empires. The British referred to it as "divide and rule." For example, the British Empire divided the Hindu and Muslim population in India; they exploited and used the division between the Clans of occupied Scotland; and, they used Protestant Celts from Scotland against Catholics Celts in Northern Ireland. Also see Johnson, Chalmers, 131.

common across occupied Dixie. The Republican Party taught white Southerners that they could no longer trust their black neighbors—folks who had been trustworthy during Yankee invasion. Judge Garnett Andrews described the fear that pervaded the white people of the South during Reconstruction. He described that time thusly:

> I have never suffered such an amount of anguish and alarm in all my life…
> [as] the fear and alarm and sense of danger which I felt that time. And it was a
> universal feeling among the population, among the white people.…It showed on the
> countenance of the people.…Men looked haggard and pale.…I have felt when I
> laid down that neither myself, nor my wife and children were in safety. I expected,
> and honestly anticipated, and thought it highly probable, that I might be assassinated
> and my house set on fire at any time.[412]

This situation was imposed upon we the people of the South by an arrogant and self-admiring people of the North, who used their control of the Federal Empire to punish Southerners. We the people of the South were being punished for claiming the right to live under a government based upon the consent of the governed as declared in the United States' Declaration of Independence. Desire to punish the South was often openly declared:

> Every secessionist risked his all upon secession, and has received as the **penalty**
> of defeat only **poverty**. It is the mildest **punishment** ever inflicted after an
> unsuccessful civil war, and it proves in this case a blessing in disguise.[413]

Even if one could consider Southern "poverty" as a mild "punishment" (ignoring how Yankees obtained a legitimate right to "punish" Southerners), how could a rational Northerner justify the poverty of black Southerners who suffered even more than their white Southern kith and kin?

The Republican Party created the situation that produced such white fear and then reaped a large political reward from black Southern voters. In exchange for their votes black Southerners were given many promises but few if any were ever truly fulfilled. The more things change, the more they remain the same!

One of the many problems facing the newly freed slaves was that they were landless. Add the fact that many of them were innocently ignorant about how

---

412 Fleming, *Sequel of Appomattox*, 278.

413 Higginson, Thomas Wentworth, "Some War Scenes Revisited," (July 1878), *A Just and Lasting Peace*, 527; Higginson was a Harvard-trained Unitarian minister from Rhode Island.

they were to gain their living post-slavery. The Yankee propagandists had promised them freedom from slavery. Many of the former slaves took this to mean no more labors—the Day of Jubilee! Thus vagrancy became a major issue, especially in counties where blacks outnumbered whites. Carl Schurz (German Socialist, Union Army Officer and later Senator and Cabinet member under Republican Rutherford B. Hayes) admitted as much in his December 19, 1865, report to President Grant:

> *Other emancipatory movements, for instance the abolition of serfdom in Russia, have resulted in little or no vagrancy; but it must not be forgotten that the emancipated serfs were speedily endowed with the ownership of land.*[414]

The United States of America—now the Federal Empire—had at its disposal millions upon millions of acres of land in the western territories that could have been provided to the newly freed slaves, but such an offer was never seriously considered by the Federal Empire.[415] The reason is very simple—Northern racism!

The Yankee had already declared that the western territories would be reserved for the white man. Lincoln boldly advocated "our new Territories being in such a condition that white men may find a home." He reinforced this white only concept by declaring that these western territories would be "an outlet for free white people everywhere, the world over."[416] In 1862 Lincoln's friend and supporter, Republican Senator Lyman Trumbull from Illinois, stated: "There is a very great aversion… against having free negroes come among us. Our people want nothing to do with the negro."[417] Yankee abolitionist Shepherd Pike, a correspondent for the *Atlantic Monthly*, demonstrated his racist views in an article in the February 1861 issue, declaring:

> *We say the Free States should say, confine the Negro to the smallest possible area. Hem him in. Coop him up. Slough him off. Preserve just so much of North America as is possible for the white man….*[418]

Numerous influential Northerners openly declared that they did not want blacks in their current or future states. Before the War most Northern states had enacted exclusion laws

---

414 Schurz, 137.

415 Wilson, Clyde, "Defeat and Occupation: The Cold War Known as "Reconstruction," *To Live and Die In Dixie*, 448.

416 Walters, Ryan S., "The Powers of a Usurper," in *To Live and Die In Dixie*, 309.

417 Wilson, "Defeat and Occupation," 448.

418 Livingston, "Confederate Emancipation" *To Live and Die In Dixie*, 463-464.

to prevent the migration of free blacks into their states. Racist Northerners did not want blacks among them and refused to give any of the "free" land out west to the newly freed slaves. The Yankee attitude toward black Southerners was simple "coop him up" and let them "root hog or die," as Lincoln said when asked what was to become of the newly freed slaves.[419] Joseph Henry Allen, a New England clergyman, wrote in a Unitarian journal (April 1862) that black Southerners should be herded into reservations in the South and that the rest of the South should be "cleansed" of white Southerners, thereby allowing for a re-populating of the South with white Northerners.[420] It should be noted that the racist hatred of the North was not just toward blacks but also toward white Southerners—in other words, their hatred was toward all Southerners regardless of color. They felt that white Southerners were no longer pure whites because of the prolonged close social contact with blacks. They even referred to Thomas Jefferson as America's first black President. They did this because of what Northerners perceived as Southerners

being too closely associated with black Southerners—too close for Northern comfort! In addition, the South gained political influence from the mere presence of blacks in Southern society due to the three-fifths rule for computing representation in Congress.[421] Republican Thaddeus Stevens of Pennsylvania wanted to confiscate land owned by Southerners and give it to the freed slaves.[422] Of course this would serve two purposes: (1) it would help to cleanse the South of whites and (2)

Dr. Leonard Haynes & Ron Kennedy. Dr. Haynes accepting a gift after his address to the LA Div. Sons of Confederate Veterans, 1992, Baton Rouge, Louisiana.

---

419 This came from one of Lincoln's "stories" told at the Hampton Roads Conference in 1865. See Stephens, Alexander, *The War Between the States*, Vol. II, 615; also see https://democraticthinker.word-press.com/2009/09/05/weekly-story-root-hog-or-die (Accessed 4/20/2016) and http://civilwartalk.com/threads/root-hog-or-die.71206 (Accessed 4/20/2016).

420 Wilson, "Defeat and Occupation," 464.

421 Livingston, "Confederate Emancipation," 6, 9.

422 Stevens, Thaddeus, "Reconstruction," *A Just and Lasting Peace*, 71, 77.

it would help to drive a wedge of racial bitterness between white and black Southerners, thereby gaining black Southerners as a reliable Republican voting bloc. The conquered and defenseless white South faced an enemy (the Republican Party controlling the Federal Empire) that was determined to complete the work of extermination they had begun when Lincoln first invaded the Confederate States of America. Post-war, the Republicans who controlled the Federal Empire used black Southerners as their primary weapon against a defenseless and occupied South. The fear arising from the Republican use of black Southerners against white Southerners "poisoned the well of friendship between our peoples and today black and white Southerners are still drinking the bitter water from those wells."[423] It created a mindset among white Southerners of fear and mistrust of black *political* power that would be exploited for political gain by bad Southern politicians. This unnatural psychology[424] of fear and mistrust (cultural distortion) would eventually be used by "bad" white politicians to establish the era of white supremacy. During the era of white supremacy, the Democratic Party gained the benefit of the reliable Solid South during national elections. The ruling elite in the national political parties that controlled Washington reaped the benefits while black and white Southerners continued to languish in poverty. Black Southerners had been abandoned by the Republican Party, while the Democratic Party ignored impoverished white Southerners. And while those "bitter waters" continue to poison the relationship between black and white people in our Southern society—the ruling elite of both national political parties grow ever more powerful, rich, and oppressive of the Southern people's unalienable right to be the masters of their own society, the masters in their own home.

The Modern South Ruled by Ugly Politicians

The era of bad politicians ended in 1965. From that point forward, the South fell under the leadership of ugly politicians. Recall that the definition of "ugly" Southern politicians (Southern politicians post-1965) describes them as being "ugly," not in reference to their

---

423 This quote is from a personal conversation between the authors and the late Dr. Leonard Haynes, African-American Professor at Southern University, Baton Rouge, Louisiana. At my (RK) invitation, as Division Commander, Louisiana Sons of Confederate Veterans, Dr. Haynes became the first African-American to address the Louisiana Division of the SCV.

424 The post-war psychology of Southerners was noted in passing by one scholar, "Louisianans were victims of the psychological retrogression into which the South lapsed after the Civil War: the South was poor, and in certain areas, such as education, Southerners simply had to be content with second or third place." Williams, T. Harry, *Huey Long* (Louisiana University Press, Baton Rouge, LA: 1969), 493. As a typical Northern-born scholar, Williams never questioned what made the South poor or why the people of Dixie were *compelled* to accept second or third place in this newly created "one nation indivisible" or what were the origins of the South's "psychological retrogression."

physical appearance but to their willingness to use black or white votes to advance their personal political careers—careers that would financially benefit themselves and their crony capitalist donors. The state and national donor class are necessary to provide the huge finances required to win political office (national or state) in the Federal Empire.

Black Southerners regained access to the ballot in 1965 and the Democratic Party was determined to have black Southerners voting as a reliable Democratic bloc for the next 300 years.[425] The Republican Party then inherited the white Southern vote. Both national political parties benefited, but once again the rank and file people of the South were left out. Both black and white Southerners have been used (exploited) by their respective political parties. The following is a review of how the Republican Party exploited white Southern voters, and then a review of how the Democratic Party exploited black Southern voters.

Nikki Haley is typical of the ugly Republicans who have greatly benefited from white Southern votes but who have zealously denounced those voters when it was politically expedient. The removal of the Confederate flag at South Carolina's state capitol and her endorsement of the Republican establishment's candidate (Marco Rubio) were rewarded with a nationwide address in reply to President Obama's State of the Union speech in 2016. In her response she viciously attacked the character of those who opposed Obama's policies—that is those who were supporting Republican presidential primary candidates who were opposed to the Republican establishment and its donor class. This is but a continuation of the betrayal of the white South by the Republican Party that has been going on since 1965. Republican President Nixon sent word to the NAACP and other left-wing groups to not worry

Nikki Haley, scalawag Gov. of S.C., whose actions initiated the current round of slanderous anti-South cultural genocide. Nikki Haley proudly displays her pagan heritage but viciously attacks Southerners who bravely defend their Southern heritage. Like most Republicans her desire to climb the national GOP political corporate-ladder is more important than honor. (Photo courtesy Times Examiner Greenville, SC)

---

425 It has often been stated that this is what President Lyndon Baines Johnson told white Democratic supporters while in New Orleans, Louisiana, seeking support for the 1965 Voting Rights Act. Although it was reported that he used another word other than "black" to describe the new voters.

about his so-called "Southern Strategy." His spokesmen told them, "Watch what we do, not what we say." The Republican Party establishment viewed the white South as captive to the GOP because there was no other place for Southern conservative voters to go. [426]

In the rare occasions in which a true candidate emerges at the local level, someone who represents the concerns of the people and thereby is a danger to the donor class and the ruling elite—when that occurs the ruling elite will do whatever is necessary to defeat said candidate, even if it means allowing the election of a liberal Democrat. If such candidate, against all odds, happens to get elected, then the establishment will either convert him with bribes or marginalize him to the point that he will not be re-elected. In the 2014 Senatorial elections in both Mississippi and Louisiana the national Republican Party dumped millions of dollars into the campaign to defeat popular senatorial candidates who represented a threat to the state and national Republican establishment. The sad truth is that both national political parties are ardent defenders of the political status quo—a system of government (the Federal Empire) that provides them with unlimited perks, privileges and power.[427] The goal of Southern Republican politicians is not to improve the lot of the Southern people by reclaiming our right to local self-government via *real* states' rights but to climb the political ladder and eventually end up as part of the Republican Party's ruling elite. They may make hot speeches for home consumption or issue news releases designed to tickle the ears of local conservative activists but they never do anything to jeopardize their climb up the corporate political ladder.

As bad as the betrayal of the white South by the Republican Party has been, the betrayal of the black South by the Democratic Party is far worse. Black Southerners have been the recipients of more lies (unfulfilled promises) from politicians than any other group in America. From the false Republican promises of emancipation and forty acres and a mule, to the modern day Democratic promises of economic improvement (War on Poverty) and an improved social environment (affirmative action, busing, etc.)—all have been promises unfulfilled. Unfulfilled in the sense that the end result has not been a marked improvement in black economic or social environment. In short the black South has been lied to by national politicians of both political parties. What has been the actual result of the Civil Rights movement once it became captive

---

426 Kennedy & Kennedy *Why Not Freedom*, 51. Also see "Last vote theory," 51-53, 92, 113, & 272.

427 See, Kennedy, *Nullification: Why and How*, 75 (Available as free e-book at: http://www.kennedytwins.com/Nullification_Book_2012.pdf) ff.

of and an intricate part of the Democratic Party? No one can deny the benefits of civil liberties that were won by black Southerners in the mid-1960s. The South is a better place today as it relates to free exercise of civil liberties but not socially, economically or politically. The Democratic Party has used black Southern votes to gain elected positions, but this advantage to the Democratic Party has not evolved into an economic and social advantage to black Southerners. The Federal Empire's propagandists, especially the ones in Hollywood—and, make no mistake about it, Hollywood is the most effective left- wing propaganda center in human history—are constantly blaming poor black performance on educational tests, and high black incarceration and unemployment rates as a "legacy of slavery and racism." The intent is twofold: (1) to draw attention away from the progressive left's abject failure to improve black society since 1965 and (2) to fan the anger of blacks and keep it directed toward white Southerners. The emotions of anger, revenge, and hatred are easy for leftist propagandists to enflame. Emotions overrule rational thought and therefore emotional arguments do not require evidence and are not subject to close inspection. In fact, when a rational individual tries to communicate with an emotional individual using indisputable facts, the reaction is most likely to be an increase in anger, hatred and a desire to seek revenge on the part of the emotional person. The revenge can be as mild as calling the rational speaker a racist or as harsh as threats or actual physical violence. But facts do matter!

Several black scholars have compared the deterioration of black society in the fifty years after 1965—the era that saw an explosive growth in the liberal/socialist welfare state programs directed toward black Americans— to the fifty years before 1965. According to Dr. Thomas Sowell, murder rates among black males were declining in the 1950s during the height of Jim Crow segregation. After the mid-1960s the murder rate for black males more than doubled![428] In the 1950s the majority of black children were raised in a two-parent home, but today over 85% are raised in a single parent home. It should be apparent by now that the interests being served by Democratic politicians are not the same as the interests of the black community that provides them with their votes. Dr. Sowell noted that politicians need a "dependent voting constituency" and that a "paranoid ...resentful" group is of the greatest value to liberal politicians. Liberals can rely on left -wing social justice warriors (propagandists) in the media, Hollywood and education to maintain a high level of hate and resentfulness in certain voting blocs. These angry voting blocs will then obediently cast their votes for the liberal candidate

428 Sowell, Thomas, *Wealth, Poverty, and Politics*, (Basic Books, NY: 2015), 159.

who promises to represent these angry, resentful voters. The "down-trodden" exchange their votes for liberal promises—all the while social and economic conditions grow worse for the dependent voting bloc. Both black and white Southerners have been exploited for their votes by both national political parties—political parties whose existence depends upon maintaining black and white Southerners in a condition of political slavery reinforced by the Federal Empire's propaganda of racial hatred.

The South's transition from the most prosperous to the poorest section of the United States of America was paralleled by the South's transition from a region of America's constitutionally limited Republic of Republics to part of the Federal Empire governed first by bad (1866-1965) and now ugly politicians (1965-today). These two parallel tracks represent the demise of Southern society. These two tracks were shaped by the envious, money-grubbing capitalists and politicians of the North in general and of New England particularly. Other nations, like Ireland and the Baltic states, have been overrun and occupied for an extensive length of time by foreign empires, yet they managed to keep the dream of freeing their country alive over generations. As a reward they eventually re-gained their countries' independence. But the South has spent a century-and-a-half meekly obeying the dictates of the ruling elites in Washington, D.C. The primary difference between the people of Ireland or the Baltic states and the South is that the peoples of Ireland and the Baltic states never surrendered their dream of freedom; they never gave up on the idea, the dream, the vision that one day they too would be the masters in their own homes. They never allowed their children to become docile and obedient slaves to the ruling empire. In fact, they never allowed their society (as opposed to the government) to accept the idea of *Vae Victis*—Woe to the Vanquished.

Chapter 12

TWO NATIONS, ONE EMPIRE

Tyranny is wonderfully ingenious in the art of inventing specious
phrases to spread over its nefarious designs.[429]

United States of America

States with the lowest income, common accent, highest church attendance, highest charitable giving, most conservative voting record.

Evidence of the South as a distinct nation within the Federal Empire

Map Illustration by Brian McClure

In January of 1821 a report was released from the United States House of Representatives Committee on Manufactures supporting the call for high protective tariffs. Like so many other efforts by the Northern majority, this tariff would protect and promote Northern industry at the expense of the Southern consumer and Southern agriculture. In response to the call for more protective tariffs, John Taylor of Caroline County, Virginia, wrote and published *Tyranny Unmasked*. His chief aim was to demonstrate

---

429 Taylor, John, *Tyranny Unmasked*, F. Thornton Miller, ed., (Liberty Fund Press, Indianapolis, IN: 1992), 78. John Taylor was known as "John Taylor of Caroline."

how in the name of doing "good" tyrants are successful in destroying liberty—as he noted, tyranny is "artful in inventing specious phrases to spread over its nefarious designs."[430]

Only 33 years after the establishment of the new government under the Constitution, Southerners were already realizing the adverse consequence of being a minority segment of a government run by the Northern majority. John Taylor of Caroline is pointing out that not only is the South under the control of the Northern majority but there is a large difference between the people of the North and the people of the South. In *Tyranny Unmasked*, Taylor, an American Founding Father and veteran of the War for American Independence, points out that not only is the economic life of the South at risk of being trampled upon, but, even worse, the hard-won liberties of Southerners were being threatened.

Many Americans, including Southerners, often repeat the fable that the "Civil War" was a war of "brother against brother." Nothing could be more removed from reality than the "brother against brother" myth of the War for Southern Independence. The War was actually a war between two different people, two different cultures, two different economies, two different types of government, and two different nations. In the foreword of Richard Weaver's, *The Southern Tradition at Bay*, Donald Davidson[431] noted that Weaver explains for his reader that the South is so filled with rich traditions and cultural values as to distinguish the "South from the North."[432] As explained in chapter 3, both McWhiney and Owsley boldly announced that the South and the North are two distinct societies. This should not be a surprising announcement. Even non-Southern historians have pointed to the various and different waves of English-speaking immigrants that settled what were to become the Thirteen Original Colonies. In *Albion's Seed: Four British Folkways in America*, David H. Fischer demonstrates that the English speaking people who settled the American Colonies for the first 150 years were mostly drawn from four different and distinct regions of Great Britain.

---

430 *Ibid.*

431 Davidson, Donald, one of the famous Nashville Agrarian writers and poets based at Vanderbilt University, Nashville, TN, during the 1920s and 30s, and contributor to *I'll Take My Stand*. Like the other Agrarians, Davidson questioned the exchange of a society based upon "repose, *noblesse oblige*, romantic love, beauty, good manners, and a belief in God for an industrial dollar worshiping Yankee style society." The Agrarians did not question change as much as they were opposed to rapid uncontrolled change. See, Conkin, Paul K, *The Southern Agrarians* (The University of Tennessee Press, Knoxville, TN: 1988), 35.

432 Donald Davidson as cited in Richard Weaver, *The Southern Tradition at Bay* (Arlington House, New Rochelle, NY: 1968), 23.

Basically, two waves settled in the North and two waves settled in the South. These four different waves of immigrants brought four different cultures with them as they settled in their respective regions of the New World. These different cultures had different "dialects of English," different ways of home construction, and different ways of addressing work and life. But most importantly they had different ideas of what freedom meant and how government should be organized. According to Fischer, these differences were the most important factor in the formation of the government and its citizens' relationship, not only to the government but to each other.[433]

As these scholars point out, the different background, culture, and history of the people who populated the North and the South created two different societies (actually two new nations). By pointing out the sharp differences between these two societies, these scholars affirm the truth in the warnings of Southern Revolutionary patriots who feared a government controlled by a Northern majority. It was more than simply economics and/or slavery that separated Northerners from Southerners. They were simply different peoples. The truth is these United States has always been two different nations, one in the North and one in the South. The major source of friction between these two different and divergent "nations" was control of the national government. With its numerical majority the North began to act more like the ruler of an empire rather than an equal partner with the South in governing the common republic—empires always act differently than republics.

An empire exists for the benefit of its ruling elite, not for the benefit of the whole as is true in a free republic. As the North gained greater control of the Federal government, the government began to view the states as mere provinces of the empire. Upon the floor of the United States Senate in 1861, Oregon Senator Joseph Lane pointed out that the "Union," that is, the Federal government, was treating the states as if they were provinces of

Sen. Joseph Lane, of Oregon, in 1861 warned Congress about the danger in making sovereign states mere provinces of an empire. (Courtesy LOC)

433 Fischer, David H., *Albion's Seed: Four British Folkways In America* (Oxford University Press, NY: 1989), 7.

an empire. He then noted that, "A province of an empire…is held by the oppressor as an integral part of his dominions."[434] Regardless of how heavy the yoke of oppression may be, the subjects of the empire's province will be compelled to yield to the empire's rule. According to Senator Lane, "This is the theory of despotism."[435] As Senator Lane points out, to recognize the right of secession would deal a fatal blow to the tyrannical rule of an empire, therefore no empire would ever allow its subjects to go in peace.

Senator Lane's speech on the floor of the United States Senate at the outbreak of the war, warning Americans of the danger of losing their republic and having it replaced with an empire, fell on deaf ears. The empire was determined to maintain its power over its "milch cow" and continue the lucrative exploitation of the South—a South that was now viewed more as a colonial province than an equal partner in a common union. At that point in American history, profits, revenue, and filthy lucre trumped government by the consent of the governed. What the North hoped to gain was the ability to continue looting the South's wealth, but the South saw it was losing both wealth and liberty. Yet, this scenario had been played out earlier when the colonies seceded from their union with Great Britain. Fortunately for Americans, American liberty was won and Great Britain lost it wealth- producing colonies. Great Britain was to retrace these steps in India and Ireland as those peoples struggled to gain their right to rule themselves—to regain the right to be the master in their own home.

Empires seldom freely relinquish control of a profitable province. The history of the nations of Eastern Europe during the Cold War is another example of how empires will fight to maintain control of their provinces. Noteworthy is the use of language and slogans by the empire as it tries to hide the real reason for the subjugation of its provinces. In 1776 Great Britain claimed it was only defending the King's loyal American subjects from "rebels," just as in Ireland it was protecting the good citizens from Irish brigands and thugs. In India, it had to protect Muslims and Hindus from hurting each other, since the British, after all, were just acting the part of good police officers. In the Soviet Union the Russians were not invading and oppressing the citizens of Eastern Europe, they were bringing freedom from capitalist exploitation and abuse. Remember the words of John Taylor, "Tyranny is wonderfully ingenious in the art of inventing specious phrases to spread over its nefarious designs."

---

434 Joseph Lane cited in Kennedy, *Rekilling Lincoln*, 288.

435 *Ibid.*

Saving the union and *freeing the slaves* were the "ingenious…specious phrases to spread over its nefarious designs" that the North used to protect its Federal empire, an empire of filthy lucre—all the while impoverishing black and white Southerners.

There is one great question that must be asked, "Is the current Federal government 'one nation,' or is it really two nations in one—one nation composing the empire and the other nation composing the conquered province?" Without a doubt there are great differences between the people of the South and the rest of the people of America. Even foreign visitors comment on the different style of language, food, social customs, and levels of wealth between the two areas of the United States. If one would take a map and color the states which most often vote for conservative candidates as opposed to liberal candidates, a near perfect map of the Confederate States of America is displayed. Next color a map of the states with the highest church attendance and a near perfect map of the Confederate States of America is displayed. Next color a map with people who speak a distinct type of Southern dialect/accent and one will see a near perfect map of the Confederate States of America. Now color a map with those states with the highest per capita charitable donations and again we see a near perfect map of the Confederate States of America. Then color a map where the poorest people in America live, and a near perfect map of the Confederate States of America is displayed. Now color a map where children have a much lower expectation of lifetime earning power and a near perfect map of the Confederate States of America is displayed. And now overlay these maps— what do we see but *The Confederate States of America!* [See maps in center section.]

This difference of life- style, customs, and even politics is displayed in many ways, not the least in the voting records of Southern senators and representatives as compared to Northern senators and representatives. These marked differences in voting records demonstrate the fulfillment of the ominous warnings of men like Patrick Henry, as they predicted how the South would be out- voted in the Federal Congress. These votes are the "still quite voice" of a conquered nation pleading for justice for its children. When looking at the voting patterns of the senators and representatives in the Federal Congress, it becomes exceedingly obvious that the Southern votes are more often cast in the affirmative on conservative issues than those of Northern senators and representatives. But, as Patrick Henry warned, when an issue is near and dear to the South, the South is too often out- voted by the North. For examples, in a vote to increase immigration in 1990 the majority of Southerners voted "no" but they were overruled by the North. In 1994 in an effort to ban so-called "assault weapons," Southern delegates in Congress voted 68% against the ban, whereas the North voted in favor of the ban, and the South's defense of the Second Amendment was overruled. In response to the Federal government prohibition on school prayer, the South sought to pass a bill to protect the right to pray in public schools; the South's delegates in Congress voted 72% in favor of limiting the Federal government's role in school prayer but were overruled by Northern votes. In the now infamous Obama Care Nationalization of healthcare, the South voted overwhelmingly against Obama Care but once again, as one would expect when in the minority, the South's votes were overruled by the North.

The preceding are examples of what Patrick Henry warned the South about while debating whether to join the union as a minority section with the North back in 1788! Henry states:

> When oppressions may take place, our representatives may tell us, We contended for your interest, but we could not carry our point, because the representatives from Massachusetts, New Hampshire, Connecticut, etc., were against us. Thus, sir, you may see there is no real responsibility.[436]

This warning to Southerners is just as true today as it was when Patrick Henry first enunciated it. Clearly, just as Ireland had a vote in the British Parliament, yet she was always out- voted, i.e., overruled by the majority in Parliament, in the Federal Empire's Congress the South is overruled by the North's majority in Congress. Yet, we are assured that it is all fair and square for, after all, "you got to vote on the issue." Southerners need to recall that John C. Calhoun warned that tyrants can come to power using "majority rule" and with all done in a neat, clean "democratic" fashion.[437]

Now, as gay rights and the use of a public bathroom by anyone regardless of gender comes before the Federal Empire's Congress, the South will again get a chance to be out-voted and told to "shut up" and "act right" because, after all, "you got to vote on the issue"— and ,after all, "majority rules." Northern majority that is![438] Just like the

---

436 *Patrick Henry: Life, Correspondence and Speeches*, Vol. III, 519.

437 Calhoun, John C., "A Disquisition on Government," *The Complete Works of John C. Calhoun*, (D. Appleton & Co., New York: 1854), I, 14-5.

438 In the Congress of the Confederate States of America, Southern interests were, and could still be, the majority interest.

Irish under British rule or the nations of Eastern Europe under Soviet Communist rule, the South's vote counts for little or nothing—we are simply used as a parent would use a pacifier to keep a child quiet and under control. The Federal Empire uses the South's votes in elections and in Congress as a pacifier to keep we the people of the South quiet and under control. But just as in the example of the child's pacifier, regardless how dedicated the child is to the pacifier, the child receives no nutritional value for his labor.

In May of 2016 the South's woeful position as a minority in Congress was once again demonstrated. One can imagine Patrick Henry looking down from the portals of Heaven—no doubt thinking, "I told you so." By a vote of 265 to 159, the House of Representatives banned display of the Confederate flag at national Veterans monuments and cemeteries. The Republican-controlled House of Representatives thus created a national prohibition preventing descendants of Confederate Veterans from appropriately honoring their deceased family members. These Confederate Veterans honorably served the South during the War for Southern Independence. Paul Ryan (Wisconsin), Republican Speaker of the House, noted that "tough votes happen"[439] and "people have to get use to that fact."[440] Southerners need to understand that this is not just a flag issue. Every issue that is near and dear to the people of the South is held in contempt by the Northern majority. The Northern majority will at their preference ban, bar, or prohibit any Southern value for which they have no love or respect. This can range from public display of traditional Christian symbols, the Ten Commandants, male and female bathroom signage, etc., and the list will go on. Just as Patrick Henry, George Mason, Rawlins Lowndes, and a whole host of other Southern patriots warned the South more than two centuries ago, the South's vote counts for nothing in the Federal Empire's Congress—in other words, the rights, liberties, and interests of we the people of the South count for nothing. The Federal Empire's Congress is controlled by those who have been taught to "hate and despise"[441] the South; therefore, Southern culture, values, and freedom are always at risk of being trampled on.

The South is being treated no differently than any other conquered and occupied nation. Is this to be the lot of each successive generation of Southerners? At the

439 Paul Ryan as cited in *The Hill*, "House votes to restrict Confederate Flag at national cemeteries," Christina Marcos, 5/19/16 http://thehill.com/blogs/floor-action/house/247171-house-votes-to-ban-confederate-flags-at-federal-cemeteries (Accessed 5/20/2016).

440 *Ibid.*

441 Vallandigham, 71.

death of the current generation of Southerners, shall that miserable old Southern corpse be removed only to be replaced by its children? Is poverty, subjugation, insults, and tyranny the only future for the children of the South—children whom Yankees hoped to *"see privation in the anxious eyes of mothers and the rags of children"?*[442]

If one resolves neither to live the life of poverty and subjugation, nor to allow his descendants to be forcefully seated upon the "stools of everlasting repentance,"[443] then something far different must be done than what has been done since 1865. Southern scholar Dr. Donald Livingston described the opportunity and dilemma we the people of America are facing:

Division of the Union in the direction of a more human scale is a genuine political possibility open to Americans. [444]

Dr. Livingston explains the absurdity of allowing as few as 135 Congressmen or five unelected Judges to rule 305 million Americans. He notes that such power in the hands of a few elites in Washington "is something no free people whose souls are attuned to the republican tradition would tolerate."[445]

Every conquered and subjugated people have the right to hope for a brighter future where freedom and prosperity are the common birthright of each new generation. The people of the conquered and subjugated Confederate States of America have the same rights as the people of Ireland, India, and the former republics of the old Soviet Union. We the people of Dixie have the right to be masters of our own homes and our own country. Understanding this logic and therefore desiring these things is just the beginning. Next we must plan and work for that which is rightfully ours.

---

442 Simkins, 219.

443 Owsley, "The Irrepressible Conflict," *I'll Take My Stand*, 63.

444 Livingston, Donald, "American Republicanism and the Forgotten Question of Size," *Rethinking the American Union for the Twenty-First Century*, 158.

445 *Ibid.*

Chapter 13

CSA Today: North – South Income Inequality

"One nation indivisible with liberty and justice for all" except for Southerners.

As was pointed out in chapter 1, Southerners are "patriotic" and loyal Americans and have proven it in every American war since 1865 by an outpouring of volunteers in the U.S. military. No section of the U.S.A. has a larger portion of its population who are

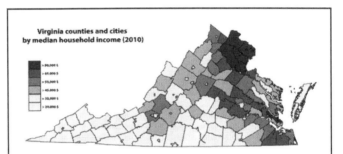

Virginia counties and cities by median household income (2010)

Note: The darkest counties on the map above represent wealthy, liberal counties populated by the rich bureaucrats who are employed by the Federal Empire in Washington, D.C. (Map created by Ali Zifan, Creative Commons https://creativecommons.org/licenses/by-sa/4.0/deed.en).

ardent advocates for constitutional principles and who proudly display the Federal Empire's flag. But the sad fact is that the Federal Empire punished the South with poverty and that punishment did **not** end with the close of active reconstruction.[446] The punishment of poverty was accepted and given the *appearance* of legitimacy by the South's "bad" and "ugly" politicians.[447] These Scalawags were willing to

---

446 Active reconstruction was the time when United States military occupied Southern states; passive reconstruction followed the removal of U.S. military from Southern states, but the threat is always present that if the South (or any other state) refuses to follow the Federal Empire's orders then active reconstruction will be re-applied.

447 "Bad" politicians ruled from end of Reconstruction to 1965; "ugly" politicians' rule began in 1965 and continues today.

accept Southern impoverishment rather than risk the loss of their status within the Federal Empire's ruling elite by demanding equal treatment for Southerners and a return to real states' rights. Today, the South's ugly politicians refuse to acknowledge the fact that the South's punishment continues! Relative to the rest of the U.S.A., the states of the former C.S.A. are poorer and Southern workers have less opportunity to increase their income to the same level as Northern workers. The harsh reality is that the South's ugly politicians are more concerned with enriching themselves and climbing the political ladder than they are in taking radical action to reclaim the South's economic and political parity with the rest of the U.S.A.

The War is Over—You Lost—Get Over It!

Often, while the authors are doing interviews on radio or TV, the interviewer or a call-in guest attempts to shut down the discussion about the War for Southern Independence by boastfully proclaiming, "The war is over, you lost, get over it!" Our typical reply is something to the effect that the boastful sentiment the caller expressed is the same sentiment that the British Empire's sycophants would tell the Irish each time one of their "risings" failed. But the Irish did not heed the British Empire's boastful admonitions, and eventually one of their "risings" was successful and Ireland became a free and prosperous nation. Over? It's not over until freedom is won!

Top Five U.S. States Median Household Income
(Income data rounded to nearest thousand)
1. Maryland--------- $70,000
2. Alaska--------------- 70,000
3. California----------- 67,000
4. Connecticut-------- 66,000
5. Massachusetts---- 65,000
   Washington, D.C.- 65,000

Bottom Five U.S. States Median Household Income
46. Alabama------------- $41,000
47. Kentucky----------- 41,000
48. Arkansas------------ 39,000
49. West Virginia------- 37,000
50. Mississippi---------- 35,000

U.S.A. national household income = $51,000

Nine of the ten lowest income states are Southern

The only Southern states above national median household income are Maryland and Virginia; states that are adjacent to the Empire's capital and have been re-populated with the Empire's highly paid, liberal- voting lackeys. See footnote 449 for data source.

Unfortunately, too many Southerners have become docile and pacified worshipers of the Federal Empire! They have never questioned their assigned position as the United States of America's poorest people; they have never questioned why Southern children have a lifetime earning expectation 33% below the average for children born in New England; they have meekly accepted their assigned position on the "stools of everlasting repentance." Too many Southerners have accepted the North's narrative about the War for Southern Independence and the implied suggestion that after the South surrendered everything went back to "normal" except that slavery (a purely Southern problem according to the Northern narrative) was abolished. Most Southerners seem to think that after Lee surrendered the North and South had a "Kum Ba Yah" moment—one large group hug and everything was forgiven and forgotten.[448] The "Kum Ba Yah" moment never happened! Not only did the "group hug" never occur, but things never went back to normal. Remember, "normal" would have meant a very prosperous and free South where cordial race relationships existed. Rather than normal, the South became a colonial appendage of the Federal Empire and the once free and prosperous people of Dixie became an impoverished embarrassment in an otherwise prosperous United States. While the Federal Empire's ruling elite and their crony capitalist allies were eager to exploit cheap Southern labor and the South's abundant natural resources—neither crony capitalists nor national politicians were concerned about the impoverished people of Dixie. We the people of the formerly free and prosperous Confederate States of America were intentionally impoverished by the Federal Empire. This impoverishment continues even today! (See table for Median Household Income.)

While the Baltic States (Lithuania, Latvia, and Estonia) were struggling to secede from the Soviet Union (1991), high-ranking officials of the Soviet Union denied the right of secession. Denial of the right of secession was based upon the premise that a large number of voters in those countries were opposed to secession. That was true! The reason that there were a large number of voters in the Baltic states who were against secession was because the Soviet Union had "repopulated" (sound familiar?) those states with native Russians who were enriching themselves as part of the Soviet Union's highly- paid bureaucracy. The re-populating of a conquered nation is a tried and true method of maintaining control of an occupied people. A review of the map at the beginning of this chapter will demonstrate that the Federal Empire is doing the same thing to the once solidly conservative Southern state of Virginia. The same can be said of Maryland. With the exception of Virginia and Maryland, every Southern state's median household income is below the *national* median household

---

448 See, Kennedy & Kennedy, "Our Re-United Country?," *To Live and Die In Dixie*, 491-510.

income.[449] Think about that simple statement. At one time the South was the richest section of America. But today it is the poorest! Where did all these poor folks come from? Did the sky open-up one day and rain down poor folks on Dixie?

Maryland and Virginia.[450] "enjoy" a better median household income than their sister Southern states due to the invasion of rich, liberal bureaucrats (government parasites) who are well paid to do the Empire's work in Washington. and who maintain expensive homes in surrounding counties. Virginia, once a solid conservative state, has been transformed into to an almost solid liberal state as a result of "repopulating" it with foreign workers and Federal bureaucrats who have a vested interest in big government. Recall that during Obama's Great Recession, while most folks were suffering during the economic downturn—Washington, D.C., Wall Street and the counties of Virginia and Maryland close to the Empire's capitol were booming![451] An Empire and its cronies can always prosper by extracting resources *from* its enslaved provinces, [452] but we the people of the invaded, conquered and occupied provinces have no option but to accept the status quo—at least that is what the South's ugly politicians would like for Southerners to believe.

It is not enough to merely honor Southern heritage; just being "good" citizens and dutifully going to the polls to elect "good" conservatives will not restore Southerners to their rightful status as a free and prosperous people. Hoping that the next Federal President will restore constitutional government will never bring about the radical restoration needed if we are to regain a constitutionally- limited republic of republics. And never forget that a Federal Republic *cannot* be *controlled* and kept within its constitutional bounds without *real* states rights', inclusive of the unalienable American rights of nullification and secession. The spiritual, political, and economic impoverishment of the Southern people will continue until we the people act to reclaim

---

449 Median household income data from: https://www.huduser.gov/portal/datasets/il/il07/index.html (Accessed 6/5/2016).

450 It is important to remember that the high incomes in Washington, D.C. and surrounding counties of Maryland and Virginia DO NOT represent wealth created due to productive activity. It represents the exact opposite. It represents wealth extracted from the free market by parasitic government exploitation of taxpayers. See, Kennedy & Kennedy, Nullifying Tyranny, 61-66.

451 As cited in, Kennedy & Kennedy, "Our Re-United Country?," *To Live and Die In Dixie*, 499, footnote 16.

452 The warning of Senator Joseph Lane of Oregon rings more true today than in 1861 when he warned Americans that the Republican Party and Lincoln were turning these United States into an empire rather than a republic. Lane noted, "A province of an empire is held by the oppressor as an integral part of his dominions." He further stated that a province existed for the benefit of the empire.

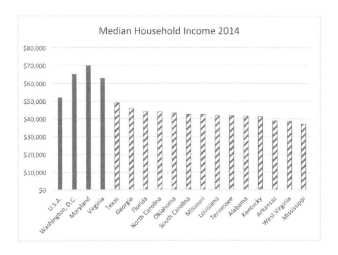

Median Household Income 2014

liberty. This impoverishment is a direct result of the post-War South's failure to take the initiative in the struggle to dethrone the illegitimate Federal Empire and to restore legitimate constitutional government—reclaiming America's Republic of Republics.

The graph[453] showing the 2014 median household income for the U.S.A., Washington, D.C., and the Southern states demonstrates the plight of the modern-day South. Even "rich" Southern states such as Texas, Georgia, and Florida are still below the national median for household income. A similar graph using 2002 data for per capita income was published in *Reclaiming Liberty* in 2005, and it shows almost identical results for Southern states vs. Washington and national averages.[454] In other words, "the punishment continues!"

Take a good look at the graph of Median Household Income. No Southern state other than the two repopulated states adjacent to the Empire's capital (Maryland and Virginia) are above the national median household income. Another (2016) study reveals that the five states where children are living in the lowest income homes were from Southern states (80%); children living in the five highest income homes were all from Northern States.[455] Yes, the Federal Empire is still punishing Southerners!

The increased income in Maryland and Virginia comes at the cost of the displacement of native Southern population by liberal, politically correct sycophants

453 "SELECTED ECONOMIC CHARACTERISTICS, 2010-2014 American Community Survey 1-Year Estimates". U.S. Census Bureau. Retrieved 2016-02-12. As listed at: https://en.wikipedia.org/wiki/List_of_U.S._states_by_income (Accessed 6/20/2016).

454 Kennedy, *Reclaiming Liberty*, 83.

455 https://wallethub.com/edu/best-worst-states-underprivileged-children/5403/ (Accessed 8/15/2016).

of the Federal Empire's bloated bureaucracy. These "repopulated" Federal citizens of Maryland and Virginia have a vested interest in voting for candidates who promise to increase the size of big government—and therefore their paychecks. These Federal voters in Maryland and Virginia have a built-in liberal conflict of interest when voting. They would never vote to decrease their potential earning power or potential career advancement. It would be like expecting a life-long welfare recipient to vote for a candidate who plans to reduce welfare payments! What the Federal Empire has done via "re-population" in Maryland and Virginia it is now doing via "re-population" of other conservative states with foreign immigrants. It is only a matter of time. Empires, whether the Soviet Union or the Federal Union, use "re-population" as a tool to dispossess the native population of their country and turn a once free and prosperous people into obedient subjects of the Empire.

We the people of the once free and prosperous states of the Confederate States of America can remain docile subjects of the unconstitutional (illegitimate) Federal Empire, or we can initiate bold action to reclaim the right to be the masters in our own homes—the right to live under a constitutionally- limited republic of republics preserved by real states' rights. Only the brave deserve freedom.

Chapter 14

REPARATION FOR SOUTHERN SLAVERY— ABOLISHING SOUTHERN POVERTY

Even "good" conservatives once elected must work within the current political
system; a system that is <u>designed </u>to favor the ruling elite; a system in which
elected officials have a vested interest in maintaining the status quo; a corrupt and
corrupting system that quickly converts "good" conservatives
into loyal Democrats or Republicans.[456]

There is little use in listing and documenting the numerous ways in which the Federal Empire has impoverished the South, if after learning the truth Southerners do nothing to overcome Southern poverty. A vibrant free market that by definition does not tolerate crony capitalism is the only way in which Southern poverty can be exchanged for Southern prosperity.[457] But we the people of Dixie must not lose sight of the fact that Southern society lost more than just dollars. Due to Northern- imposed cultural distortion the South lost a friendly, moral, and prosperous society that was governed by statesmen. The South lost the opportunity to peacefully integrate freed slaves into a mutually shared society. The dollar amount owed to we the people is important, but it is not the only factor in resurrecting a free, moral and prosperous South. But first— look at examples of the dollars the United States owes we the people of the South.

How Much Does the U.S.A. Owe the Southern People?

The South has been the political, social, and economic slave to the Federal Empire since the end of the War for Southern Independence. Money alone will not resolve all the problems our Southern society has—problems that arose as a result of

---

456 Kennedy & Kennedy, *Nullifying Tyranny,* 163-164.

457 *Ibid.,* 85-91; Chapter 10, "Creating Wealth that Benefits Everyone."

Northern invasion, conquest and occupation of the Confederate States of America. But in some manner it should be a part of the solution. The adjacent list gives a small indication of the money the Federal Empire owes we the people of the South. But the listing is merely an *example* of the dollars that were directly exploited from an invaded, conquered, and occupied South. Other costs must also be calculated and added to the total amount—in current dollars—owed by the United States of America to we the people of the Confederate States

> ### Examples of
> ### Southern Dollars Exploited
> ### By Federal Empire
>
> 1. Slave Capital_____$2,000,000,000
> 2. Cotton Tax_____68,000,000
> 3. Northern supplies____80,000,000
> 4. Homelessness_____750,000,000
>
> Total for this example alone in 1865 dollars is $2,898,000,000
>
> Converted from 1865 dollars to 2010 dollars it would be equal to approximately **$32,490,000,000.00**
>
> [See footnote 508 for method used to approximate current dollars; also explanation of cost for Northern purchased supplies & homelessness on page 180.]

of America. Again it is impossible herein to make a complete list but the following will demonstrate the enormous economic loss Southern society suffered due to Lincoln's invasion and enslavement of we the people of the Confederate States of America.

Other examples of losses suffered by the Confederate States of America as a result of the war initiated[458] by the Federal Empire—also known as the United States of America—would include:

- Cost of Reconstruction debts; South Carolina, for example, did not completely pay off its Reconstruction debt until 1955[459]

- Cost of state pensions for Confederate veterans; while the South paid Federal taxes and the Federal government paid unusually generous pensions to Union veterans, it refused to use any Federal money to pay Confederate veterans' pensions

- Costs associated with the loss of international cotton market due

---

458 For a time-line of Lincoln's secret efforts to invade the South and thereby force the South to "fire on the flag" see, Kennedy, *Uncle Seth*, 341-351.

459 Wilson, "Defeat and Occupation," *To Live and Die in Dixie*, 444.

to foreign countries developing alternative markets during wartime Federal blockade of Southern ports

- Cost of private businesses destroyed during the invasion of the Confederacy

- Cost of private homes, contents, and out buildings destroyed or looted during Federal invasion

- Cost of public buildings destroyed by Federal armies during invasion

- Cost of public infrastructure such as roads, bridges, and levees destroyed by or as a result of the invading Federal armies

- Cost of churches destroyed by the invading Federal armies

- Cost of private educational institutions destroyed by Federal invaders

- Cost of railroad tracks, trestles, rolling stock, stations, and locomotives destroyed by or as a result of Federal invasion of the South

- Cost of draft animals, hogs, and cattle destroyed or stolen by the U.S. army during invasion

Added to these costs would be the tremendous costs inflicted upon each successive generation of black and white Southerners arising from the "opportunity cost" suffered due to the direct financial losses inflicted upon the South by the Federal Empire during the war and Reconstruction. Post-war Northern manufacturing, commerce and financial institutions flourished, creating vast wealth in the hands of Northern crony capitalists— often referred to as Robber Barons. The opportunity to develop a true, flourishing, and sustainable free market economy was denied the South. Thus, post- Appomattox, the South became an economic backwater in an otherwise flourishing United States. President Grant acknowledged the South's impoverishment but offered no help to the defeated and occupied South.[460] The sad truth is that no one cared about the impoverished people down South—not even the South's "bad" politicians. Sharecropping and the destruction of vast areas of Southern virgin forest became the alternative to starvation and utter poverty. Opportunity costs are unseen costs but they often have a greater impact than direct, visible, costs—costs that continue generation after generation.

---

460 Grant, Ulysses S. "Inaugural Address" (March 4, 1869), in *A Just and Lasting Peace*, 364. President Grant in his Inaugural Address, March 4, 1869, recognized "ten states in poverty from the effects of war," but he offered no plan to remove said poverty.

An Equitable Distribution of Reparation Dollars

The United States could give each living Southerner his/her "share" of reparation dollars, but would that result in a prosperous and sustainable Southern economy? Would a one-time cash payment erase generations of North-South income inequality? Would it create an economic base that future generations of Southerners would enjoy? The answer to all these questions is "no." Reparation should not be a windfall for one generation but it should be something that would radically alter (fundamentally change) for the better the South's economic status. This could be done by altering current Federal corporate tax regulation to reduce corporate taxes for existing Southern companies for the next twenty years by 25%, and any new corporation would have a 50% initial reduction for ten years and then 25% for the remainder of the twenty-year period. "Southern" corporations would include only companies that have their headquarters in one of the 16 Southern states,[461] with a majority of their governing boards being native-born Southerners. Southern workers would be given priority over foreign job applicants and, for industry, the majority of the manufacturing would be done in the South, utilizing, as much as economically feasible, Southern resources. This would incentivize initial investment and reinvestment of profits earned into an expanding Southern economy. The major beneficiaries of this plan would NOT be corporations but black and white Southern workers who would be able to secure sustainable income for themselves and their families in a flourishing Southern economy. The point of reparations would be to remove poverty from the South. The only way to remove poverty is to produce wealth. The only non-violent way to gain wealth is through free and voluntary exchange in the free market.[462] But never lose sight of the fact that the Southern people lost more than money and that too must be regained. Reparations must be a part of restoring a Southern society (as distinguished from government) in which civility, equality before the law and a flourishing economy allows

---

461 The 11 traditional Confederates states plus, West Virginia, Kentucky, Maryland, Oklahoma, and Missouri.

462 See, Kennedy & Kennedy, *Nullifying Tyranny*, 85-91. Explaination of how the free market is the only way to create wealth that benefits all of society and doing so without using compulsion or force. In a true free market, exchange between consumer and producer occurs only if the producer pleases the customer—which includes consideration of both price and quality. The producer must consider price and quality because he has competitors who also want the customer's business. In a true free market both parties gain as a result of the exchange—the producer gains money from the customer and the customer gains a desired product that he values more than the money he offered in exchange. In a true free market, the consumer is king. Crony capitalism, on the other hand, is **not** a function of the free market but is in fact a form of national socialism or fascism.

individuals to fully develop their talents as they engage in the "pursuit of happiness."

The Current Government Hates Traditional Southern Values

The Federal Empire's recent attack on traditional Christian values such as the definition of marriage and the enforcement of "gender neutral" rules should convince black and white Southerners that the South and the Federal Empire are two different peoples and should, therefore, be two different nations. For example, one of the authors recently took a trip across the State of Washington, from Pasco to Seattle and back, a drive of around 460 miles. The author decided to count the number of churches visible from the highway both going to Seattle and returning to Pasco. During each trip the number of churches was counted to produce an average of 13 churches per 230 miles. Back in Louisiana the following week the author drove from his home to church, a distant of 30 miles, and counted 12 churches visible from the highway. According to these observations there is one church per 17.5 miles in Washington State, whereas in Louisiana there is one church every 2.5 miles. This should come as no surprise. In 2014 Gallop International's survey of weekly church attendance demonstrated that the State of Washington ranked 46th in weekly church attendance. The same survey showed that Louisiana ranked 4th in weekly church attendance.[463] This is not just a peculiarity with Washington and Louisiana. The same survey demonstrated that with the exception of Utah, the States with the highest weekly church attendance were Southern States. Depending on which survey is studied, Mississippi and Utah are always vying for first place for weekly church attendance. All states with the lowest weekly church attendance were Northern states, particularly the New England states—Massachusetts, number 47, Maine number 48, New Hampshire number 49, and Vermont number 50. As noted in chapter 3, Dr. McWhiney observed that, "The values of Southerners and Yankees...were not just different—they were antagonistic."[464]

The preceding data should call to mind the Biblical warning to Christians in 2 Corinthians 6:14: "Be ye not unequally yoked together with unbelievers." We the people of the South are yoked together with radical leftist, secular humanists who are waging aggressive war against Christian values that Southerners hold dear. Yet,

---

463 "Culture of the United States of America; Weekly Church Attendance." https://en.wikipedia.org/wiki/Religion_in_the_United_States Also see, Megan Gannon, "The Least and Most Religious U. S. States," February 3, 2014, http://www.livescience.com/43064-most-least-religious-us.html#sthash.Fhmh-dTNQ.dpuf (Accessed 5/7/2016).

464 McWhiney, Grady, *Cracker Culture*, 245.

churches have been reluctant to engage the enemy in the battle for soul of the South. Perhaps Southern priests and ministers do not believe that there is an active war being waged by leftist secular humanists against the South and its traditional values.

Even 150 years after Appomattox there are still calls for the total destruction of the conservative Bible-Belt South. Yankee cultural bigotry was openly displayed in a slanderous anti-South article, "How the South Skews America," published in the July 03, 2015, issue of *Politico Magazine*, by staff writer Michael Lind. This secular humanist advocated the total removal of Southern influence in the United States because "Jesusland" has always held the United States back, and with the conservative Bible-Belt South removed, "We'd be less violent, more mobile and in general more normal if not for Dixie."[465] And of course, as a conquered nation we the people of Dixie have no defender and no way to appropriately respond to such slander.

In an article titled "Dems, It's Time to Dump Dixie" another secular humanist columnist, Michael Tomasky, writing for *The Daily Beast*, December 14, 2014, declared that Southerners who reject liberal Democratic candidates do so because they live in a "reactionary, prejudice-infested place." Tomasky was smarting from the decisive loss administered to Louisiana's liberal Senator Landrieu. He declared that Louisiana and "almost the entire South" had "rejected nearly everything that's good" and had become "just one big nuclear waste site of choleric, and extremely racialized, resentment." [466]

Secular humanist/leftists such as Tomasky and Lind declare the South to be a place populated by racist, evil, hateful, folks totally lacking the intellectual capacity of progressive Northerners. They do so while ignoring available evidence that disproves the slanderous, hate-filled, anti-South propaganda they so zealously spew forth. For instance; a recent study demonstrated that of the twenty-five most segregated cites in the U.S. seventeen were in the North—including such bastions of civility as New York City and Chicago![467] Another study noted that four of the five friendliest cities in the U.S. were in the South. It also noted that all five of the most unfriendly cities were all outside of the

465 Lind, Michael, *Politico Magazine*, http://www.politico.com/magazine/story/2015/07/how-the-south-skews-america-119725_Page2.html#.VaKVN_IVhBd (Accessed July 12, 2015).

466 Tomasky, Michael, "Dems, It's Time to Dump Dixie," http://www.thedailybeast.com/articles/2014/12/08/dems-it-s-time-to-dump-dixie.html (Accessed 12/14/2014).

467 McClanahan, Brion, "Please, "Dump Dixie", http://www.abbevilleinstitute.org/blog/please-dump-dixie/ (Accessed 12/12/2014).

South.[468] Perhaps this is the reason the Christian Science Monitor reported that black Americans were moving back to the South, primarily due to "economic and cultural" reasons.[469] Dixie's strong Christian faith is one of the reasons that the leftists hate the South. Because the South is America's "Bible Belt," the left's loathing of Christianity is displayed against all American Christians in general but against Southerners in particular.

In May of 2016 a professor from Harvard declared that they (secular humanists, progressives, liberals) have already won the cultural war and now it is time to deal with the defeated Christians. His recommendation is to treat evangelical Christians like Nazis. He declared that it is time to mop up the mess and deal with the "losers" of the culture wars. And how did the intellectually superior Harvard professor recommend dealing with the "losers?" In his own words, "taking a hard line seemed to work well in Germany and Japan after 1945." In other words, he views evangelicals as no better than or as bad as Nazis.[470] This Harvard Professor is merely following the example set by numerous racists and South-hating Northern professors of the nineteenth century. For instance, Charles Bancroft in 1875 justified the horrors of the so-called "Civil War" on the grounds that to let the South go would have caused grave economic damage to the North;[471] Charles Eliot Norton, a professor at Harvard, declared that he wanted to keep the western territories "free soil" and to "confine the Negro within the South."[472] And let us never forget that the first "scientific" theory of black racial inferiority came from the New Englander Josiah Nott, whose family was one of Connecticut's oldest and most respected. [473]

The South, with its traditional Christian values, its honored Confederate heritage, and its love of limited government, is detested by the Federal Empire's radical-leftist ruling elite. This hatred of the Southern people and their values is also shared by the radical leftists who now control or have dominant influence on education, Hollywood, and the media. One is much more likely to find a supporter of same sex marriage in the mainline media, educational systems, Hollywood, the

468 *Ibid.*

469 *Ibid.*

470 "Harvard Prof Urges Liberals to Treat Evangelical Christians Like Nazis," http://www.breitbart.com/big-government/2016/05/10/harvard-prof-urges-liberals-treat-evangelical-christians-like-nazis/ (Accessed 5/10/2016).

471 Livingston, "Confederate Emancipation" *To Live and Die in Dixie*, 485.

472 Livingston, "Why The War Was Not About Slavery," *To Live and Die in Dixie*, 17.

473 *Ibid*, 6-7.

donor class, and the ruling elite than an open believer in traditional Christian values.

The fact that the people of the North and South are two different peoples (nations) is clearly seen in data regarding the number of conservatives who self-identified as "evangelical" per 100 conservatives surveyed. The results demonstrated a radical difference between conservatives from Southern states vs conservatives from non-Southern (Federal Empire) states. Even among "conservatives" the South's religious faith separates us from "those people" of the North—we are two different peoples. A study by Pew Research Center, *Trends in Political Values*, published in 2007, looked at the number of conservatives per 100 who self-identified themselves as evangelical Christians. The survey demonstrated that the average number of conservative evangelicals for the United States was 21 per 100, whereas the average for the South was 36 per 100. Every Southern state had a larger number of "conservatives" who self-identified as evangelicals than the Northern average! This includes "repopulated" Southern states that are occupied by a large number on non-Southerners—states such as Maryland, Virginia, and Florida.[474]

This trend of strong religious values in the South runs deep in Dixie's history. During the War for Southern Independence there were many religious "revivals" that swept through Southern camps. Devastation and rank poverty in the post-war South forced Southerners to rely upon their kith and kin and place their faith in God. Religion has always been more important in the "spiritual" South than in the "materialistic" North. But the Federal Empire and their lackeys of the left are determined to remake the conservative South with its traditional Christian values into an impoverished reflection of their secular humanist, immoral nation.

Dr. Grady McWhiney noted that Confederate President Jefferson Davis understood that if the North destroyed the South's independence it would then attempt to destroy the South's spiritual foundation. McWhiney noted:

> *Jefferson Davis did not mistake the intentions of Yankees when he expressed his fear that they would overrun a defeated South, bringing with them what he called "New England's grasping avarice and evil passions"; scarcely had the war ended when the Nation announced that Northerners must "colonize and Yankeeize the South,…in short to turn the slothful, shiftless Southern world upside down.[475]*

---

474 Kennedy & Kennedy, "Dixie's Unwelcomed Presence in Rosie O'Donnell's America," *Nullifying Tyranny*, 189.

475 McWhiney, Grady, *Cracker Culture*, 259-60.

Prior to the War the South was able to maintain its cultural values but subsequent to Yankee invasion, conquest and continuing occupation, Southern values are slowly dying as a result of constant attacks from the Federal Empire's lackeys, sycophants, and running dogs[476] in the media, education, and Hollywood.

The Federal Empire uses its unlimited power to suppress the will of the people at the local level when the will of the people conflicts with the Empire's policy. This harsh fact is true for all Americans, especially Christians. For example, when the people of California voted to define marriage as between one man and one women, the Federal Empire voided the voice of the people and ordered the vote of the people to be ignored. As long as the Federal Empire remains supreme, then the values held dear by Christians will be held at the pleasure of the secular humanists who control the Federal Empire—in other words Christian values are no longer accepted in the United States of America. But there is a solution.

A Liberty Based Society—Key to Effective Reparations

What is meant by effective reparations? Effective reparations would be reparations that include not merely dollars but *a fundamental change in governance*. A fundamental change that would destroy the system that produced bad and ugly politicians and restore a government that would allow for the development of statesmen. In other places this type of government has been referred to as a liberty based society.[477] The essence of a liberty based society is that it has a limited government, sound money, and low taxes. Taxes under such a government would be no more than 10% for local, state, *and* federal governments.[478] The Federal Empire today extorts up to 60% of income via direct and indirect taxation.[479] In a liberty based society government borrowing would not be allowed except in a national emergency and inflation would not exist due to the use of sound money—no federal reserve creating money/credit out of thin air.[480] In a liberty based

---

476 "Running dog" is a Chinese expression of derision indicating the individual(s) would run to do his master's bidding just like a cur dog running to his master to receive scraps of food left over from his master's table.

477 Kennedy, *Reclaiming Liberty*, see "Liberty Based Society" in index.

478 Economic historian Carlo Cipolla noted that absolute monarchs never drew more than 5-8% of their nation's income in taxes. As cited by Hoppe, Hans-Hermann, *Democracy The God That Failed* (Transaction Publishers, New Brunswick, London: 2005), 54. Today the Federal Empire extracts between 40 to 60% in direct & indirect taxes.

479 Kennedy, *Reclaiming Liberty*, 163-83.

480 *Ibid.*, 127-45.

society the federal government would be accountable to we the people of the sovereign state via the unalienable rights of state nullification and secession. The current Federal Empire would be replaced with the type of government created by the founding fathers in 1787—a constitutionally limited Republic of Republics enforced by *real* states' rights.

How to Enforce the South's Claim for Reparations

As noted throughout this work, the poverty inflicted upon black and white Southerners is not merely economic poverty but it is also a poverty of the spirit. The destruction of the natural friendship between black and white Southerners, the attack upon our most dearly held religious convictions, the banishment of God from the public sphere, the emergence of inner city crime, drugs, unwed mothers, and disease, all are part of Southern impoverishment. This impoverishment was inflicted upon the people of the South by the Federal Empire. This spiritual and economic impoverishment will not be resolved by money alone. Economic reparation is useless without first regaining the right to be the master in our own home—the right of self-government via real states' rights, where nullification and secession are options to we the people of any state threatened with federal abuse and tyranny.

Before Southerners can even make their claim for Southern reparations they must first educate the people of the South about their legitimate right to make the claim for reparations. Southern activists must inform their fellow Southerners about their right to be the masters in their own homes by reclaiming *real* states' rights; and they must explain how this can be done.

First thing is to make sure the Southern people understand that they cannot win by playing business-as-usual politics. Business-as-usual politics is the chosen game of the ruling elite. They wrote the rules and their judges are the referees of the game—there is no way the South can win playing their game! This is explained in *Nullification: Why and How*[481] but in short it is a plan to engage in *political* irregular warfare by doing an end run around the political establishment. It would NOT be a campaign to elect "good" conservatives—a monumentally expensive undertaking that has a very low probability of victory. Instead, we the people of Dixie should concentrate on getting state legislation passed establishing a ballot initiative giving the people a vote on a Federal constitutional amendment acknowledging the unalienable rights of state nullification and secession.

---

481 Kennedy, Nullification: Why and How. (Available as free pdf download at: http://www.kennedytwins.com/main.htm)

The grass roots effort to get the state legislation passed in each Southern state will provide the opportunity to "educate" the rank and file people of the South. Convincing Southerners that they have been and are being exploited by the Federal Empire is actually more important than getting the legislation passed. Once a people in bondage no longer accept their rulers as being legitimate, then they are already free—all that remains is for the people to stay committed to freedom while the circumstances necessary to obtain their freedom are worked out. Once this is accomplished the Southern states would be in a position to demand reparations. Each Southern state's plebiscite calling for a constitutional amendment acknowledging the states' rights of nullification and secession will send shock waves through the Federal Empire. Each vote, win or lose, will send the message that the *South's sons and daughters are yours no longer*—the South will no longer sit submissively upon stools of everlasting repentance. Each vote will encourage another state to take up the effort. It will announce to the people of the South and the world that the people of Dixie have awoken from their self-imposed hibernation. It will demonstrate that we the people of the once free and prosperous South are beginning to realize that as Americans descended of the men who wrote the Declaration of Independence, we the people do indeed have an unalienable right to be free! The constitutional amendment acknowledging the states' rights principle of nullification and secession will become the tool needed to initiate the movement to reclaim liberty. The proposed constitutional amendment is discussed in *Reclaiming Liberty; Why Not Freedom; and Nullification: Why and How.*

In 1868 Confederate Vice President Alexander Stephens declared that due to the massive concentration of power in Washington, D.C., and the subsequent loss of liberty for all Americans, "the cause of the South is now the cause of all."[482] The South's demand for reparations, inclusive of the right of local self-government via *real* states' rights, should be viewed by all liberty loving Americans as a golden opportunity to restore constitutional liberty to an American society that has been raped by anti-Christian, leftist, secular humanists. Therefore, the majority of non-Southern Americans should support our efforts. *But what if they do not support the South's call for reparations and return to a constitutionally- limited Republic of Republics?* What if they actually want to keep the South as a conquered province in *their* Federal Empire? In 1994 the Kennedy Twins answered that question in their first book, *The South Was Right!*:

---

482 Stephens *The War Between the States*, Vol. II, 666.

There must be a radical reformation in the current, overgrown, unresponsive, tax-and-spend federal government. If those who are in control of the government in Washington reject the demands of the people for a government more respectful of our rights, then it will be faced with the prospect of the Southern people following the lead of Lithuania as we demand the right of self-determination.[483]

We the people can accept our current status as *subjects* of an illegitimate, all-powerful, supreme federal government or we can organize and begin the movement to allow the people to vote to change our status to that of *citizens* in a constitutionally limited Republic of Republics. We the people do not need to win major elections to become once again free and prosperous citizens—we need to engage the ruling elite with a battle that they have never fought, one in which the advantage is to the audacious, the brave, the dedicated, and ultimately the free! No longer *Vae Victis*, Woe to the Vanquished, but now *Deo Vindice*, God shall vindicate.

"Promoters of 10th Amendment resolutions," observes Dr. Clyde Wilson, "need to understand that the 10th Amendment does not enforce itself. Nor will it ever be recognized by any of the three branches of the central apparatus or existing political parties. It will have to be enforced by the people of the States whose freedom it was intended to protect."[484]

[For a detailed description and guide for initiating and conducting a campaign of irregular *political warfare* to replace the Federal Empire with a constitutionally- limited republic of republics enforced by we the people of the sovereign stages via *real* states' rights, see *Dixie Rising— Rules for Rebels* by James Ronald Kennedy. (Forthcoming from Shotwell Publishing)]

The contest is not over; the strife is not ended. It has only entered on a new and enlarged arena. The champions of constitutional liberty must spring to the struggle...until the Government of the United States in brought back to its constitutional limits, and the tyrant's plea of "necessity" is bound in chains...

President Jefferson Davis, CSA
Rise and Fall of the
Confederate Government,
Vol. II, (William Mayes Coats,
Nashville, TN: 1881), 294.

---

483 Kennedy & Kennedy, *The South Was Right!*

484 Wilson, Clyde N., *Nullification: Reclaiming Consent of the Governed*, (Columbia, SC: Shotwell Publishing LLC, 2016), 8.

Addendum I

SHARECROPPING: NORTHERN IMPOSED POST WAR SLAVERY[485]

James Ronald Kennedy

His was a grueling existence working the cotton fields of the Deep South. It was a back-breaking existence of daily labors in a field that he did not own—doing the work of a landowner who would soon reap the rewards from his labors. His survival depended upon staying in the "good graces" of the landowner—a stern business man who did not continence anything other than complete submission to his instructions to make a good crop or else! His work garments consisted of three or four changes of work cloths in various stages of wear and repeated mending. Although only in his mid-forties, his physical condition had been broken by grueling years of working in the field under the hot Southern sun. He could no longer stoop over to pick the mature cotton come harvest time. In order to meet the landowner's demand to make and harvest a good crop he would crawl on all fours, pulling the heavy cotton sack down endless rows of white puffy cotton. He was bound to this miserable existence with shackles forged by America's ruling elite in faraway Washington. These inhumane shackles were fastened, without care or concern, upon him and his impoverished people. The ruling elite's crony capitalist friends grew rich while he and his people grew exceedingly hopeless of ever freeing themselves from this new form of slavery. Fate had dealt him a miserable life and no one seemed to care. What great crime had he and his people committed that they were to be so thoughtlessly punished by an indifferent nation? Such was the life of this typical white Southern sharecropper of the 1930s.[486]

"If it were not for the Civil War, we would have never gotten rid of slavery." This or similar Yankee truisms are typical of the excuses used by those who try to justify the death of upwards of one million black and white Southern men, women and children during and after the War for Southern Independence. Our Southern kith and kin died as a result of Yankee invasion, conquest and occupation of a sovereign nation—the Confederate States of America. The Federal Empire's apologists use their

---

485 Originally published in *Confederate Veteran*, Vol. 74, No. 1, January/February 2016, 16, *et seq.*

486 This universal description is based upon James Agee's description of Floyd Burroughs a 1930s, relatively successful, white Alabama sharecropper; see, Agee, James, *Cotton Tenants: Three Families* (Melville House Publishing, Brooklyn, NY: 2013—from 1939 original manuscript), 148.

Sharecroppers circa 1938
(Courtesy LOC)

moralistic verbal smoke-screen to hide the fact that the War was *not* a moral crusade to end slavery and to obscure the fact that the War did *not* end slavery—it merely changed its form. The victorious North successfully replaced chattel slavery with tenant farming or the furnishing system—more popularly known as sharecropping. Prior to the War the average plantation had five slave families working the plantation; after the War and Reconstruction the average large landowner had five white and black families working his land.[487] Under chattel slavery the slave holder was legally responsible for the wellbeing of the slave in sickness and old age—under sharecropping the landowner had no obligation to the worker—the worker was on his own. Chattel slavery in the Old South was similar to the system of slavery practiced by Old Testament patriarchs in which servants were treated as part of an extended family. But in post-Appomattox Dixie landowners using tenant farming or sharecropping treated their workers similar to the way Yankee industrialists treated their workers—they had no responsibility for the worker after paying his wages. And of course it was the worker's responsibility to take care of himself and his family. Slavery in the antebellum South, despite violating the principle of personal liberty, was a much lighter cross to bear than was the peonage of sharecropping. Sharecropping was foisted upon the South by our conquering Yankee masters. It was a system of peonage[488] that was far more evil and destructive than antebellum chattel slavery as practiced in the pre-War South.[489]

---

487 McWhiney & McDonald, "The South from Self-Sufficiency to Peonage: An Interpretation," *The American Historical Review*, Vol. 85, No. 5, Dec., 1980, 1113; by 1900 Louisiana had more "plantations" than it had in 1860, Hair, William Ivy, *Bourbonism and Agrarian Protest* (LSU Press, Baton Rouge, LA: 1969), 53.

488 Clark & Kirwan, 92, 93, 98.

489 The politically correct apologists for the Federal Empire will attempt to censor anyone making such a statement by branding him/her as a racist or a neo-Confederate attempting to justify slavery as a good institution. I am pointing out that the Federal Empire's invasion, conquest, and continuing occupation of the sovereign nation—the Confederate States of America—left black and white Southerners impoverished. If "we the people" of the Confederate States of America had been left alone, we would have resolved the issue of chattel slavery. It would have been resolved in a manner that would have benefited the slave, slave holder, and the 75% of the white Southern population who were non-slave holders. See, Livingston, Donald W., "Confederate Emancipation Without War," *Confederate Veteran*, July/August, 2014, 16 et seq.

The Origins of Post Appomattox Southern Poverty

There was no mass poverty in the South prior to the War for Southern Independence. Yet after the War poverty became the norm for Southerners and even today Southern per capita income still lags behind the other sections of the U.S.A.[490] For example, no one seems to think it unusual that Mississippi, once one of the nation's richest states, is now and has been since the War the U.S.A.'s poorest state. National[491] historians, social scientists or politicians have never asked "Where did all of these poor Southerners come from?" Poverty did not rain down from the sky on Dixie like burning brimstone flung from the hands of an angry God! It was and is the byproduct of Yankee invasion, conquest and continuing occupation of the Confederate States of America.

A Northern visitor shortly after the War celebrated the destruction of the white South he witnessed during his visit when he wrote "The whites are talking of selling their houses or lands to get bread. The fresh tide of Northern enterprise will soon sweep rudely enough against these broken remnants of the *ancient regime,*

and wash them under." [492] The massive destruction of Southern wealth and human resources was the direct cause for the development of tenant farming.[493] Sharecropping became the only alternative to starvation for upwards of eight and a half million[494] black and white Southerners in "our" reunited country. Remember, sharecropping was not a choice freely made by our people but it was the only alternative left

Pre-war Plenty replaced with Post-war Poverty.
People of a conquered nation.
(Courtesy LOC)

---

490 Kennedy & Kennedy, *Nullifying Tyranny*, 196-197.

491 "National" meaning the Federal Empire of which the South is not an equal partner but merely a conquered province that is allowed certain state privileges as opposed to being sovereign states exercising *real* states' rights as established under the original constitution of 1787.

492 Johnson, 190.

493 Tenant farming was also referred to as sharecropping or the furnishing system.

494 Agee, James, *Cotton Tenants: Three Families*, (1939, Melville House Publishing, Brooklyn, NY: 2013), 30. Clark & Kirwan, noted that as late as 1938 there were almost 2 million sharecropper *families*, 104.

to them by our conquering Northern (i.e. Republican) masters!

Sharecropping is similar to the old western system of "grub staking" for prospectors. A Western "grub staking" merchant would provide the prospector with food and supplies and the prospector would then share a portion of the gold or other precious metals found by the prospector. But grub staking was intended for solitary individuals whereas sharecropping involved entire families. Another important difference was the fact that the western prospector was not bound to the merchant by debt contracts. If he failed to find precious metals he would simply move to another area and the grub staking merchant would lose his investment. The Southern sharecropper was bound to the land via a system of legal debt contracts.[495] The interest rate on these debt contracts has been estimated to have been between 50 to 125%.[496] At one point in the early 1930s there were upwards of eight and a half million sharecroppers in the South. Of this number 66% were white.[497] An efficient sharecropper in 1930s Alabama would clear around $140 dollars in a good year but if the crops failed or if market price for cotton bottomed out, then the sharecropper would end the year owing the "company store," large landowner, or banker around $80.00.[498] Sharecropping was a system that destroyed people, families, the land and much of our Southern society. But from the Northern point-of-view this was acceptable because Southerners were merely paying for the sins of slavery and secession, that is, treason—a "debt" that will never be paid-in-full in this "our" reunited country.

The vast majority of pre-War white Southerners were not a part of the plantation system. Indeed, slaveholders were a minority in the South.[499] Most of the plain folk were not even heavily engaged in farming. The primary economic enterprise of the "plain folk" of the old South was as herdsmen with large herds of cattle and hogs roaming the South's open range.[500] They had a healthy life style that stressed out doors activities such as hunting and fishing. Their cattle and hogs provided food and the little cash they

---

495 Clark & Kirwan, 91.

496 *Ibid.*; Hummel, sets the interest rate at 30 to 70% and notes "The combination of exorbitant interest and crop liens kept some tenant farmers perpetually in debt." Hummel, *Emancipating Slaves, Enslaving Free Men*, 324; interest in Louisiana was as high as 500%, Hair, William Ivy, *Bourbonism and Agrarian Protest*, (LSU Press, Baton Rouge, LA: 1969), 51.

497 Agee, 30-31. Also see, Clark & Kirwan, 92.

498 Agee, 41.

499 Hummel, 22.

500 Owsley, *Plain Folk of the Old South*, 1-22. Also see, Clark & Kirwan, 104.

needed. Low intensity farming provided vegetables and corn for cattle, the making of bread or liquid adult refreshment. They were a clannish people who relied on family, extended family, friends and neighbors—often referred to collectively as their "kith and kin." They enjoyed a healthy and relatively care free life style.[501] They were often incorrectly and *intentionally* referred to by Northern writers as "poor white trash." They were rugged individualists who had little need for local government and even less for one in faraway Washington. Their main demand of government was simply to leave them alone! Thus, when the Federal Empire marched its armies into the South these hardy and self-reliant "plain folk" rallied to the defense of their Southern homeland.[502]

Yankee Destruction of Southern Financial Resources

During the War the Yankee invader intentionally destroyed much of the South's livestock in an effort to exterminate through starvation their Southern enemy. Shortly after Appomattox a U.S. Congressional Committee toured the area between Washington and Richmond. They were assured that General Sheridan had the foresight to remove all cattle and horses. The lack of draft animals to pull plows forced the surviving population to use primitive methods of cultivation. [503] One historian observed that from 1865 to 1895 "most cotton farmers worked with implements that were as primitive as those in use in the Balkans and India."[504] The intentional destruction of Southern wealth (capital that should have been used to re-create the post-war Southern economy) has been conveniently ignored or glossed over by the Federal Empire's apologists (aka, national historians). [505]

The loss of the capital investment in slaves is overlooked by politically correct historians but its impact on both black and white Southerners post-War should not be ignored. It should also be remembered that Yankees establish, for themselves, a system of gradual emancipation that allowed the Yankee slave master to maintain his slave's service until a given point in the future and then he would sell his slaves south of the Mason Dixon Line. This allowed the Yankee slave master to recover his capital

---

501 McWhiney, *Cracker Culture*, 51-79.

502 Clark & Kirwan, 2.

503 *Ibid.*, 22.

504 *Ibid.*, 85.

505 Of course these national historians are handsomely rewarded for their work as the Federal Empire's propagandists. On the other hand, any historian who dares to challenge the Empire's party line will be professionally ostracized and punished by a politically correct lynch mob.

investment as well as to remove from his white society a people with whom the Yankee did not wish to associate.[506] What was felt to be necessary for the thrifty Yankee (reclaiming their capital investment in slaves) was denied—at the point of bloody bayonets—to Southerners. In 1860 Louisiana's per capita wealth was ranked as first in the South and second in the entire United States but after Yankee "liberation" she joined the ranks of the intentionally impoverished. In Louisiana alone over $170,000,000 of capital investment in slave property disappeared overnight.[507] That would be in excess of $4,063,000,000 in 2015 dollars![508] Louisiana did not suffer alone—every one of her sister states were equally punished by a calloused and arrogant conqueror. No civilized nation had abolished slavery in such an economically disastrous manner—a manner that guaranteed the impoverishment of both former slave, former slave master, white Southerners who had not been a part of the plantation system and all future generations of Southerners. The Yankee slave master had used his recouped capital investment in his slaves to establish industries such as textile mills thereby allowing the Yankee to remain prosperous by milling slave grown cotton purchased from the South.

Even exclusive of the destruction of the South's vast investment in slaves, the property destruction resulting from the Federal Empire's invasion of the South was on a level not exceeded until the total war on Japan and German in the 1940s. But even though Germany and Japan suffered greater material loss, they none-the-less recovered much faster than did Dixie. Within five years these foreign nations were well into economic recovery.[509] But five years after Appomattox the South had not begun a recovery—in fact "we the people" of the once sovereign and prosperous South were sinking deeper into poverty. Yet, no one dare ask "Why?" The reason they dare not ask is that the correct answer would bring damnation upon the "exceptional" nation so loved by America's "conservative" talking heads and make void the left's claim to being the advocate and protector of black and white working people.

After the War the South was ruled by Northern controlled scallywags and carpet

---

506 Hair, 34.

507 Winters, *Civil War In Louisiana*, 428. Fleming estimates a loss of $2 Billion dollars for the entire South, see Fleming, *The Sequel of Appomattox*, 2.

508 This is an estimate using inflation calculator that only goes back to 1913. http://data.bls.gov/cgi-bin/cpicalc.pl?cost1=170&year1=1913&year2=2015 (Accessed 05/26/2016).

509 Hummel, 322; Observing that within *"five years"* after the close of World War II (1950) both Germany and Japan were well on the road to economic recovery. This paper makes the contrast that *One Hundred & Fifty years* later the South still has not achieved economic parity with the victorious Northern states.

baggers. Northern controlled Reconstruction state legislatures enacted enclosure laws which closed off much of the South's open range on which the plain folk had freely grazed their hogs and cattle prior to the War.[510] Indeed many of the plain folk were "landless" prior to the War but were rich due to their ownership of large numbers of hogs and cattle roaming on the South's open range.[511] Post Appomattox a large portion of the Southern population was reduced to poor whites and even poorer blacks. In order to make a crop the farmer had to borrow money (similar to grub staking of prospectors out west) and hope that he made enough on his crop to repay the debt and carry him and his family through the winter months. The winter months were referred to as "the lean times" when they often had virtually nothing to eat.[512] In spring the endless cycle of borrowing, planting and hoping for a fair harvest began again. This debt bondage was unheard of prior to Appomattox but debt peonage[513] became the norm for millions of black and white Southerners after Yankee victory and occupation. The War created a situation in which cash (capital) became almost nonexistent[514] in the Yankee occupied Confederate States of America. This had not been an issue before Yankee conquest and occupation! Southern banking capital in 1860 was $61 million but in 1870—*five years* after Appomattox—it was only $17 million and currency in circulation had crashed from $51 million in 1860 to $15 million in 1870.[515] In addition to destroying or stealing Southern resources, after Appomattox the Yankee victors began to systematically exploit the meager Southern resources that remained in Dixie. Northern politicians, businessmen and financiers viewed the conquered and occupied South as an opportunity for personal gain and exploitation.[516] This Northern exploitation of the South was done with no concern for what they were doing to the occupied people of the Confederate States of America. The *New England Loyal Publication Society* celebrated this opportunity for profit by publishing a series of articles titled "The Resources of the

---

510 McWhiney & McDonald, 1116; much of the open range was acquired by Northern land speculators, Hair, 48.

511 Owsley, 24-35.

512 Agee, 46.

513 Clark & Kirwan, 92, 93, 98; Hair, 52, 78; Also see McWhiney & McDonald, generally.

514 Clark & Kirwan, 85, 87, 103, 137, 157, 161-2, 270, 273; also see, Johnson, 189; & Fleming, 3.

515 Johnson, 189.

516 Clark & Kirwan, 32, 61,91-2, 152, 160; also see Hummel, 331; Johnson, 110, 114-5, 190, 193, 194, 206, 211, 249, 257-8; Hair, 48.

South." [517] After Yankee conquest and occupation the South became in many ways "a colonial appendage to industrial and grain-growing sections of the country."[518] All were beholding to our Yankee masters. Most of the profit gained by landlords and merchants ended up in Northern hands. [519] The Republican Party, now in complete control of the Federal Empire's Congress, passed taxes on Southern cotton that extracted from the defenseless and cash strapped Southern people $68 million by 1868.[520] These monies were "legally" looted from starving and struggling Southerners and flowed into the pockets of Northern politicians and their crony capitalist allies.

Due to the lack of capital Southern industries and food production could not develop but this too was also turned into a windfall for Northern commercial interests. Because the South did not have the capital to develop local industries and food production it was forced to purchase over $80M of food and agricultural supplies from Northern sources.[521] This represented Southern capital flowing into Northern pockets that should have been used to recover and develop a sustainable Southern economy.

In 1938 almost two million nomadic tenant *families* fed a constant stream of migrants moving across the South from one landowner's farm to another's— the cost of this constant moving was estimated to be $25M annually.[522] Post Appomattox, poverty, malnutrition, and disease became epidemic across the South. Bound to his miserable existence of debt peonage the poor Southern sharecropper became gist for the mills of Northern propagandists eager to promote their leftist/progressive political agenda. These Northern wordsmiths interpreted the Southern sharecropper's existence using the Northerner's Marxist, socialist, and/or progressive mindset.[523] Northern ideologues were eager to use the sharecropper's pathetic existence to further their Northern ideological agenda while ignoring the North's responsibility for the very existence of debt peonage in the post-War/Reconstruction

---

517 Johnson,194.

518 Clark & Kirwan, 91.

519 Hair, 87.

520 Fleming, op. cit., 8.

521 Clark & Kirwan, 97.

522 *Ibid.*, 104. If you assume only 30 years of sharecropping that would equal $750,000,000 costs of moving suffered by homeless sharecroppers during Federally imposed sharecropping slavery.

523 For examples of Northern progressive/liberal/socialist frame of reference when viewing the economic condition foisted upon the South by the Northern invader, see, Agee, 13-26, 222.

South. Northern ideologues in the 1930s and thereafter treated sharecropping, and the South in general, with the same intellectual dishonesty as their abolitionist forefathers had treated slavery in the 1800s—both have had disastrous results for "we the people" of the once free, sovereign and prosperous states of Dixie.

Eight and a Half Million Homeless Southerners

The cultural distortion[524] foisted upon the South as a result of Yankee invasion and continuing occupation resulted in not only the establishment of sharecropping peonage but the destruction of many family and community ties that had supported and held Southerners together during the harrowing years of war. Prior to the War the plain folk of the Old South held to their clannish ways that stressed family and community (kith and kin) relations. These relations served as an insurance against "bad times," sickness, or tragedies such as house fire or storm damage to homes. But sharecropping required millions of families to move each year—up-rooting communities and putting distance between kith and kin. The invader's destruction of Southern resources during the War combined with the colonial exploitation of the South's remaining resources by the occupying Yankee nation resulted in millions of homeless white and black Southerners in post-War Dixie. Toward the end of the War there were approximately 200,000 homeless Southerners in the unconquered portions of the Confederacy.[525] But Yankee imposed "peace" in post-War Dixie *created* over eight million homeless Southerners! With respect to creating a population with no permanent home—that is a homeless population in the South—it could be argued that Yankee imposed peace was forty times worse (or more effective when viewed from the invader's point of view) than Yankee invasion of the Confederate States of America. This nationally unlamented homelessness

Evicted Sharecroppers in MO circa 1935 (Courtesy LOC)

---

524 For an explanation of cultural distortion see, Kennedy & Kennedy, "Our Re-United Country? The sad reality of reconciliation," Confederate Veteran, Sept./Oct. 2014, Vol. 72, No. 5, 56-8.

525 Hummel, 279.

continued for almost a hundred years after Appomattox—glory, glory, hallelujah!

In addition to the social cost there was also a financial cost to moving large numbers of Southern families each year. As previously noted it has been estimated that the cost of sharecropper migration across the South as late as 1938 was $25,000,000 annually and of course this cost had to be paid by individual sharecropping families. Under chattel slavery the cost of moving (which happened rarely) was paid by the plantation owner—but under sharecropping slavery the cost was born by black and white sharecroppers. This is yet again another example of how the system of sharecropping slavery prevented the accumulation of capital by millions of white and black Southern farmers. It represents millions of dollars that were wasted—not saved and invested but wasted in order for the family to merely survive in this "one nation indivisible with liberty and justice for all." Of course "liberty and justice for all" excludes people of the defeated and occupied Confederate States of America.

Malnutrition and Pellagra—an Exclusively Southern Disease

Malnutrition became endemic across the South post-war. Sharecroppers suffered especially because they were homeless[526] and were therefore forced to depend upon making a "good crop" to supply the cash necessary to pay off the landlord and hopefully have a little cash left to get them through the lean times after harvest and before the next planting season. "Making a crop" required the majority of the family's labor in the cotton field with very little left to tend gardens or raising livestock—even if they were the lucky ones who had the money to purchase these animals. The vegetables harvested from their small garden would be "put-up" or canned but it would often spoil because many families could not afford the fifty cents needed to purchase new canning lids.[527] The combination of malnutrition and exhausting working conditions post-war gave rise to a disease that, in America, was almost exclusively a "Southern" disease—pellagra.[528]

The dramatic decline in agricultural productivity under sharecropping slavery is another factor in sharecropper malnutrition. For example, in six counties, three in Mississippi and three in Alabama, all six had been self-sufficient in food production before the War but after the War all six counties became net importers of food.

---

526 Homeless in the sense of not owning their home and being forced to rely on the good graces of the landlord to keep a roof over their heads.

527 Agee, 96.

528 McWhiney & McDonald, 1117. Pellagra is an illness caused by a diet with severe deficiency in certain essential nutriments—specifically having too little niacin or tryptophan in the diet.

Prior to the War hog ownership was 2.1 per person but sixty-five years after the War (1930) it had fallen to 0.4 hog per person. In a similar manner corn production had fallen from a pre-War high of 48.5 bushels per person to 22.8 bushels per person in 1930. This represents an 80% and 50% reduction in two key Southern food products. Prior to the War farms in these counties were privately owned and operated but in 1930 71% were operating under the new form of slavery, sharecropping.[529]

The malnutrition of the South's post-War sharecropper slaves is testimony supporting the allegation that post-War sharecropping slavery[530] was harsher than antebellum chattel slavery. Slaves in antebellum Dixie were provided with a healthy diet drawn from the plantation storeroom and smokehouse. Whether out of humanity or plain good business sense, the plantation owner made sure his slaves were well fed. The caloric intake of pre-War slaves exceeded the caloric intake of the U.S. population in 1879![531] The pre-War slave's diet even exceeded the U.S. recommended "daily levels of chief nutriments" for 1964.[532] A typical daily food allotment for pre-War slaves was "two pounds of corn and one-half pound of pork per adult."[533] Compare the pre-War slave's diet with the post-War sharecropper slave's diet: The midday meal consists of cornbread, peas, and molasses. The cornbread is made without milk or eggs as "appetizing and as heavy as wet concrete"[534] and typically no meat[535] or if meat is available it is pork "fat almost untainted by any hint of pink fiber."[536] A Northern observer noted that some sharecroppers have no midday meal and those who do their meal cannot compare with the "heartiness and variety to the proud enormous dinners cooked up for harvest hands in the wheat country."[537] All-in-all, the situation in Yankee occupied Dixie was not that dissimilar from the Irish in subjugated Ireland who were starving during the potato famine while their English colonial masters were enjoying

529 *Ibid.*, 1114.

530 Bishop Anthony Durier specifically referred to sharecropping as "a new form of slavery" in his Pastoral Letter. Hair, 52.

531 Fogel & Engerman, 112.

532 *Ibid.*, 115

533 *Ibid.*, 110.

534 Agee, 90.

535 *Ibid.*, 91.

536 *Ibid.*, 85.

537 *Ibid.*, 143.

hearty meals three times a day. Whether looking at Old England or New England there is not that much difference—except the Irish kept their dream of self-government alive during their "lean times" and eventfully became a free and prosperous people.

Exploitation and Destruction of the South's Natural Resources

Perhaps the creation of post-War slavery was the unintended consequence of Yankee invasion, conquest and occupation of the Confederate States of America. While the profit driven Yankee[538] may not have set out to recreate slavery in the South; he was, none-the-less, completely indifferent to its creation while he was busy profiting from War, Reconstruction, and his post-War colonial exploitation of occupied Dixie. The profit driven character of the Yankee was noted in the 1830s by Alexis de Tocqueville thusly "the commercial fervor which seems to devour the whole of society, the thirst for gain, the respect for money, and the bad faith in business which appears on every side...[all have been] absorbed in just one: the love of wealth."[539] Profit was and remains the Yankee's only enduring principle—all else must bow to the supreme principle of profit regardless of the unethical methods employed in its gain.

Prior to the War the South had stood in the way of Northern politicians using the Federal government to enlarge Northern commercial profits but after the extermination of their mortal enemy down South they were free to place their hand in the Federal treasury for any purpose they could label as advancing the "general welfare." In the ten years prior to the War they were able to extract only $370,000 from the Federal treasury for "internal improvements." But with the *extermination* of their Southern enemy the Republicans in Congress increased such expenditures in the ten years ending in 1870 to $1,272,300.00 and in the ten years ending 1880 to $8,080,000.00.[540] And of course today we speak not in billions but trillions of dollars!

Self-proclaimed Northern elites still have a burning desire to *exterminate* the South. Even 150 years after Appomattox there are still calls for the total destruction of the conservative, Bible Belt, South. Yankee cultural bigotry was openly displayed in a slanderous anti-South article published in the July 03, 2015 issue of Politico Magazine authored by staff writer Michael Lind. This secular humanist

---

538 Semmes, 481-482.

539 Tocqueville as cited in Johnson, Ludwell H., "The Plundering Generation," *Southern Partisan*, 1987-88, Republished at http://www.abbevilleinstitute.org/blog/the-plundering-generation/ (Accessed 07/14/2015).

540 Johnson, 111.

advocated the total removal of Southern influence in the United States because "Jesusland" has always held the United States back and with the conservative/ Bible-Belt South removed "We'd be less violent, more mobile and in general more normal if not for Dixie."[541] And of course, as a conquered nation "we the people" of Dixie have no defender and no way to appropriately respond to such slander.

In desperate situations men will invariably turn to short term solutions even if it means greater long term problems. When the choice is death today or death tomorrow men will invariably select whatever means are available to survive today. This was the situation that was foisted upon the people of the South by our conquering Northern masters post-War. The circumstances during Reconstruction was described thusly "Perhaps you know that with us of the young generation of the South, since the war, pretty much the whole of life has been merely not dying."[542] The situation had not improved for the sharecropper slave some sixty-five years later in the 1930s. One observer noted that the sharecropper's "life so continuously and entirely consumed into the effort merely and barely to sustain itself; so profoundly deprived and harmed and atrophied in the courses of that effort, that it can be called life at all only by biological courtesy."[543] The struggle to survive not only destroyed human beings but it destroyed the very land of the South—a land that had been sanctified by the effusion of Southern patriots' blood defending their people from a cruel and evil invader's sword and shackles. [544]

Each planting season the sharecropper's primary concern was to bring in the best harvest possible. Plowing the fields in contour rows to prevent soil erosion and crop rotation to prevent soil depletion was part of modern agriculture that the sharecropper could not afford. His primary concern was to plant as much land as possible which meant plowing rows as straight as possible. While this method of cultivation was faster it encouraged soil erosion. In addition to needing to cultivate using the fastest

---

541 Lind, Michael, "How the South Skews America," *Politico* Magazine, http://www.politico.com/maga-zine/story/2015/07/how-the-south-skews-america-119725_Page2.html#.VaKVN_lVhBd (Accessed July 12, 2015).

542 Sidney Lanier as quoted in Fleming, 279-80.

543 Agee, 36.

544 "Our Generals have a sword in one hand and shackles in the other." Republican Congressman Thad-deus Stevens January 22, 1862. Cited in James Albert Woodburn's "The Attitude of Thaddeus Stevens Towards the Conduct of the Civil War" *Annual Report of the Southern Historical Association for the year 1906*, vol. I, 220.

method possible, the sharecropper had no permanent attachment to the soil.[545] Unlike his pre-War predecessors his was a nomadic existence—if the land was "used up" he would move on to work other landowner's farms. This disconnection to the soil was part of the cultural distortion that arose as a result of Yankee conquest and occupation. It resulted in a post-War agriculture system that caused the destruction of billions of dollars' worth of Southern top soil.[546] Erosion of Southern farming land became so bad that a Presidential committee declared in 1938 that "Sixty-one percent of all the Nation's land badly damaged by erosion in the Southern States…at least 22 million acres of once-fertile soil has been ruined beyond repair…And other area the size of Oklahoma and Alabama combined has been seriously damaged by erosion."[547] In addition to erosion damage to the soil, millions of acres of land that had been productive pre-War had been farmed to exhaustion post-War. It was said that "Erosion and soil wastage were high crimes which robbed the region of more wealth than a half-dozen Yankee armies marching to the sea."[548] What happened to cause a people who pre-War were expert agriculturalists to suddenly become destructive farmers? The answer is simple but one politically correct historians avoid like the plague—the answer is: cultural distortion caused by Yankee invasion, conquest, and occupation of the once free and prosperous people of the Confederate States of America.

While the South's sharecropper slaves' short sighted agricultural methods were destroying much of the South's valuable top soil due to erosion and farming its soil to exhaustion, others were busy destroying the South's virgin forest. All of this was done in an effort to stave off poverty—poverty foisted upon the people of the South by a cruel and evil invader. Such short sighted methods in agriculture and industry were done out of economic necessity—an economic necessity imposed on the South via cultural distortion arising from invasion, conquest and occupation. This cultural distortion foisted upon the Southern people created and sustained sharecropping slavery for almost 100 years post-Appomattox. In addition to sharecropping slavery, cultural distortion produced other negative results in post-Appomattox Dixie.

---

545 Clark & Kirwan, 100.

546 Clark & Kirwan, 100.

547 *Ibid.,* 101.

548 *Ibid.,* 90.

By 1933 Mississippi's once vast virgin forest was gone[549] but Yankee imposed poverty remained. This was done all across the South with no thought of future needs[550] or with any thought of saving tracks of virgin forest for the admiration of future generations. In less than sixty-five years post-War, Southerners had butchered their inheritance of vast tracks of virgin forest[551] all in an effort to stave off poverty. This vast natural resource was destroyed but Yankee imposed poverty remained.

Railroads and telegraphs were the 19th century's equivalent of twenty-first century interstate highways, jet travel and the internet. Railroad development in the South was initially slowed by two realities: (1) much of the South was undeveloped with low population density, especially the lower South; and (2) nature had supplied the South with a wealth of navigable rivers and stream that, unlike those in the North, would not freeze over during the winter months. But by 1860 Southern owned railroads were on the verge of completing construction of their main lines.[552] These Southern own railroads would have prevented Northern railroads from expanding into the South and would have become a major competitor of the Northern railroads—especially in the competition for the beginning point (Southern vs. Northern) for the much talked about transcontinental railroad connecting the East coast with the West coast. The War ended the era of Southern owned railroads being constructed for the purpose of developing Southern commerce. As a result of Yankee invasion approximately 10,000 miles of Southern railroads were destroyed.[553] Unlike the Southern railroads built before Yankee invasion and occupation; Southern railroads built post-war served an entirely different purpose. They were built by Northern investors to "haul heavy goods long distances, and away from the South; they were *not* thought of as adjuncts to a rising manufacturing industry in the region".[554] These Northern own railroads have been criticized as being "The worst of all trusts."[555]

By 1860 the South had begun to develop its own cotton mills. These Southern

---

549 Clark & Kirwan, 282.

550 *Ibid.*, 138; Hair, 48.

551 Clark & Kirwan, 139.

552 *Ibid.*, 269.

553 *Ibid.*

554 *Ibid.*, 270.

555 *Ibid.*, 61.

textile mills had the advantage of location, being close to the source of cotton gins, and were therefore a source of real national competition to the cotton mills in New England. In 1860 it appeared that these mills would become a major part of the South's industrial development. Northern industrialists had always faced foreign competition but had minimized it by forcing protective tariffs through Congress. But the rise of Southern mills would have put the New England mill owners (i.e. crony capitalists) at a distinct market disadvantage—meaning loss of profits. As we have already noted, profit is the only enduring principle for "those people." The destruction of these emerging competitors became a major goal during Yankee invasion of the Confederate States of America. By 1880 New England had a virtual monopoly in the manufacture of textiles.[556] Fighting to survive economically the South by the 1920s had developed mills of its own. But a comparison between the wages of the Southern mill worker and the Northern mill worker demonstrates that the Southerner was working longer hours for much less wages than his Northern counterpart. The Southerner's yearly earnings were $659.35, while the Northerner earned $945.83.[557] The South had become the North's colonial[558] possession—a source of raw natural resources and cheap labor to feed the Federal Empire's commercial and financial interests. While Northern and self-hating Southern historians refer to the period from 1861 to 1865 as the "Civil War" and the period from 1866 to 1876 as Reconstruction; it was actually a time of revolution[559] in which a former free, happy and prosperous people, living in a constitutionally limited republic of republics were turned into impoverished colonial subjects at best or at worst sharecropper slaves in Lincoln's newly created Federal Empire.

Northern Post War Prosperity vs. Southern Impoverishment

Empires do not invade, conquer, and occupy foreign nations to improve the lot of the conquered people. Empires act aggressively against other people to expand the territory from which the Empire can extract cheap resources and tribute—generally in the form of raw natural resources, cheap labor and taxes. If one understands this simple truth, then it is easy to understand why the North grew rich post-war and the South became improvised. It also explains why the United States of America invaded

---

556 *Ibid.*, 148.

557 *Ibid.*, 152.

558 *Ibid.*, 91.

559 *Ibid*, 92.

and occupied its smaller Southern neighbor—the Confederate States of America.

In 1910, almost half a century after the War, the property value of land and buildings in the 46 states then in the Union equaled $16,082,267,689 giving an average of approximately $35 million per state. In the same period the property value of land and buildings in twelve Southern states equaled $2,193,774,898[560] giving an average of approximately $18 million per Southern state. After a half century of enjoying life in our "re-united" nation Southern property value was only 51% of the national average—"with liberty and justice for all?"

The impact of the South's colonial existence within the United States can also be demonstrated by comparing the property value of Virginia and Ohio in 1860, 1870 and 1900. In 1860 Virginia's property value (rounded) was $793 million and Ohio's was $1 billion; 1870 Virginia's was $404 million and Ohio's was $2 billion; and in 1900 Virginia's was $707 million and Ohio's was $3 billion.[561] Over the same time period the victor's state (Ohio) had increased its property value by a factor of three while the vanquished state (Virginia) had lost 11% of its pre-War property value. Remember, in an Empire, the function of colonial possessions is to feed resources and wealth to the Empire. Today the South remains the poorest section within our gloriously re-united country. And yet one can still hear deluded Southerners proudly proclaiming "You know we are so much better off as a result of losing the War!" This and similar declarations by

Black and White Sharecropper children circa 1938

Do these young Southerners have more in common with each other or with the ruling elite in Washington, D.C & crony capitalists on Wall St.? Who benefits from the post-War, Northern created racial divide in Dixie? (Courtesy LOC)

---

560 Computed from data at *Ibid.*, 93, fn.

561 *Ibid.*, 176, fn.

Yankee educated Southerners is evidence of just how effective the invader's propaganda system has been. If Herr Gobbles, the Nazi Party's chief propagandists, had possessed an equally effective system of public indoctrination we all would be goose-stepping today!

Racial Hatred as Tool of Northern Control

The fact that supposedly abused, whipped and otherwise mistreated Southern slaves did *not* rise up and slaughter their white Southern masters as soon as Yankee troops invaded the Confederate States of America was no doubt a surprise to most Northerners. Many Northern "intellectuals" had supported the abolitionist terrorist John Brown[562] and eagerly looked forward to a Haiti type massacre of white Southerners—but it did not happen. Northern troops were not only surprised but were astonished to find black Southerners actively serving in the Confederate Army. A Yankee Lieutenant Colonel noted "There were quite a number of Negroes attached to the Texas and Georgia troops, who were armed and equipped, and took part in the several engagements with my forces during the day."[563] Northerners could not comprehend the basic truth that although black Southern slaves prior to the War may have hated slavery, they did not hate white Southerners. Even in modern days of the 1960s Civil Rights movement in the South the same could be said of racial segregation—while black Southerners hated racial discrimination, they did not hate their white Southern neighbors. It is only when politics is mixed into the social setting that hatred begins to emerge—this was true during active Reconstruction and remains true today in passive Reconstruction.[564]

Radical Northern politicians and abolitionists were leaders in the effort to portray all Southerners as evil and therefore worthy of extermination—via a South-wide slave uprising or via the point of massed Yankee bayonets.[565] William Lloyd Garrison, a leading Radical Abolitionist, was described by an associate thusly, "He is a Robespierre with ...the same absolute incapacity of tolerating those who differ

---

562 Scott, *The Secret Six*, 3-4; Republican Thaddeus Stevens sought to encourage such uprisings claiming that it "was not so abhorrent as a rebellion" of Southerners. *Annual Report of the American Historical Association* for the Year 1906, Vol. I, 219.

563 Lieutenant Colonel John G. Parkhurst as cited in, Seabrook, *A Rebel Born*, 276-277.

564 For distinction between active and passive Reconstruction see, Kennedy & Kennedy, "Our Re-United Country? The Sad Reality of Reconciliation."

565 Republican Thaddeus Stevens as cited in Fleming, 59, urging Congress to adopt measures to "de-populate" the South and "plant a new race" in the South. See *Annual Report of the American Historical Association for the Year 1906*, Vol. I, 218.

from himself."[566]   Robespierre is the French Revolutionary who callously declared "There are only two parties in France: the people and its enemies....We must exterminate all our enemies."[567]   When black Southerners failed to rise up subsequent to Yankee invasion they (black Southerners) became an enemy that suffered the same fate as white Southerners. In many respects the fate of black Southerners during the War and post-War has been worse than the fate of the white South.[568]

By the end of the War Republicans in Congress understood that there was a high likelihood that the newly freed slaves would remain friendly with their white neighbors[569] and may even become politically associated with their former masters! The infamous three fifths rule had limited the South's power in Congress by only allowing each slave to count as three fifths of a person with respect to representation in Congress. Remember, the three-fifths rule had been inserted into the U.S. Constitution at the insistence of New England to *limit* Southern political power. Now that slavery had been abolished the three fifths rule no longer applied therefore, black Southerners now counted the same as white Southerners with respect to Congressional representation! The Republican Party had initiated a war that resulted in increasing Southern representation in a Congress that they had heretofore controlled! Something had to be done—Reconstruction and racial hatred was the Republican Party's answer.

After Appomattox many former Confederate leaders were willing to work politically with the newly freed slaves. General Beauregard and business men in New Orleans formed the Unification movement to encourage mutual political efforts by black and white Southerners. Businessmen openly stated that they would cooperate with black Southerners, recognize their political rights and civil equality. The political philosophy espoused by this group stressed political efforts to maintain low taxes[570] and thereby allow the Southern economy to recover. These men were not adversely concerned about allowing black Southerners the right to vote because as Beauregard declared "The Negro is Southern born; with a little education and some property

566 Floan, *The South in Northern Eyes 1831-1861*, 18, fn.

567 Robespierre as cited in Goldberg, *Liberal Fascism*, 12.

568 For example; Governor Allen of Louisiana issued a statement in 1864 noting that more blacks had died as a result of Yankee invasion than the total of all deaths in both Union and Confederate armies; Pollard, E.A., *Southern History of the War*, (1866, The Fairfax Press, New York: 1977), Vol. II, 198.

569 *A Just and Lasting Peace*, 140.

570 Williams, *P. G. T. Beauregard: Napoleon in Gray*, 269.

qualifications he can be made to take sufficient interest in the affairs and prosperity of the South to insure an intelligent vote."[571]   General Beauregard understood this and make no mistake the Republicans in Congress understood it as well.

This willingness to work politically with black Southerners remained even after Republican imposed Reconstruction. In 1872 General Forrest was asked if he opposed allowing black Southerners to vote. The General replied "I do not think I would favor their disenfranchisement. We will stand by those who help us...I would sooner trust him than the white scalawag or carpet-bagger."[572]   And again in 1875 General Forrest addressing a gathering of black Southerners declared "I am here as the representative of the Southern people—one that has been more maligned than any other...We were born on the same soil, breathe the same air, live in the same land, and why should we not be brothers and sisters...I want you to do as I do—go to the polls and select the best men to vote for...Although we differ in color, we should not differ in sentiment...Do your duty as citizens, and if any are oppressed, I will be your friend."[573] The continued friendship between black and white Southerners posed a threat to continued Republican domination of Lincoln's newly created Federal Empire. It was a threat that had to be eliminated.

It has been noted by other authors, that race hatred arose more in Yankee freedom than in Southern slavery.[574] Toqueville, in the late 1830s, noted that "The prejudice of the race appears to be stronger in the States which have abolished slavery, than in those where it still exists."[575] Fear and racial hatred were used by the Republican Congress via Reconstruction legislation to drive a wedge of bitterness, fear, and hatred between former friends and allow the Republicans to use black Southerners to maintain control of Congress.[576]   Black Southerners were unscrupulously used by Republicans to the point that a major black Mississippi Republican, Hiram Rhodes Revels, the first African American to serve in the United States Senate, abandoned the Republican Party and issued a scathing denunciation

571 *Ibid.*, 266.

572 Seabrook, 480-1.

573 *Ibid*, 483-5

574 Johnson, 182.

575 Tocqueville, 343.

576 Clark & Kirwan, 67.

of the Republican Party's bad faith as it related to policies that would have benefitted black and white Southerners.[577] It was well known that the Republicans had no particular love for black Southerners but were only using them to maintain control of Congress.[578] A number of New England investors etc. were concerned that if too many black Southerners gained title to the land it would drive down property values.[579] Toward the end of Reconstruction Republicans began to abandon their black Southern "friends" and attempted to gain more white participation in the party down South—a clear demonstration of just how calloused Republicans were relative to black Southerners as well as white Southerners.[580] But the wedge of racial bitterness between natural friends in the South remained and continues even today.

The Abolition of Sharecropping Slavery

Sharecropping slavery that was imposed upon a destroyed and occupied South died a natural though belated death. The abolition of sharecropping slavery did not require threats of Northern financed slave uprising nor did it require Northern invasion and the death of a million Southerners to rid the South of sharecropping slavery. It died the same way chattel slavery would have died even if there would have been no Southern efforts to abolish it. It died due to agricultural mechanization. This mechanization came to the South very slowly—much slower than the mechanization in the grain fields of the North and West. Why? Mechanization was slow in the South because, even in the 1930s, the South still had very little capital to invest in updated farming methods. Debt was still a major problem for Southern farmers even after the heyday of sharecropping.[581] And when the Wall Street generated economic crash came in the late 1920s many Southern farmers could not repay their bank loans causing them to lose their land and return to sharecropping— glory, glory, hallelujah, Yankee justice just keeps running amuck through Dixie.

---

577 McClanahan, Brion, "Harmony, Friendship, and Mutual Confidence Would Have Taken the Place of the Bayonet," January 2, 2015; http://www.abbevilleinstitute.org/blog/harmony-friendship-and-mutual-confidence-would-have-taken-the-place-of-the-bayonet/ (Accessed 06/30/2015).

578 Clark & Kirwan, 67.

579 Johnson, 206.

580 Ibid.

581 Clark & Kirwan, 106.

Summary

The inherent evil of slavery lies not only in the fact that it commands and exploits the fruits of another man's labor but also that it perverts and destroys the human spirit. Thus, the evil of sharecropping slavery extended into and destroyed the spirit of those black and white Southerners bound by its shackles. The

"We were born on the same soil, breathe the same air, live in the same land, and why should we not be brothers and sisters," Gen. Nathan B. Forrest. (Courtesy LOC)

spiritual vacuum created by Northern imposed cultural distortion was too often filled with racial bitterness and hatred by both black and white Southerners—to the benefit of the Republican Party that controlled Congress. Yankee invasion, conquest, and occupation were responsible for this cultural distortion. The Federal Empire's ruling elite and their crony capitalist allies benefited from this unnatural divide between black and white Southerners. In reality black and white Southerners had (and still have) far more in common with each other than they did with the ruling elite in Washington or crony capitalists on Wall Street.

While the North grew wealthy and prosperous after the so called "Civil War;" the majority of black and white people of the impoverished and subjugated South struggled to merely survive. Meanwhile the nation demanded that Southerners joyfully join them in taking the modern equivalent of the loyalty oath by pledging allegiance to a nation that supposedly promised "liberty and justice for all" except, of course, for Southerners.

Southern author Frank Lawrence Owsley noted that the South was impoverished by war and peace. We the people of the South were then assigned to our permanent position upon the "stools of everlasting repentance." Today, in the United States of America, the traditional Bible believing, conservative, constitution loving Southerner serves one primary purpose—we the people of the conquered and occupied Confederate

States of America are the nation's scapegoat. Any time this politically correct, secular humanist nation feels a need to placate leftist pressure groups, p.c. America pulls out the Southern "redneck" and thoroughly and publicly flogs him for his supposed sin of treason, slavery, racism and hatred. The Southerner is then firmly replaced on his assigned position upon the stool of everlasting repentance. Even though New England was the first to institute slavery and became rich plying the nefarious slave trade—it is the South that must bear the nation's burden of guilt for slavery. Even though it was the United States Supreme Court that legalized racial segregation in 1896; based on an 1849 Massachusetts (not Mississippi) law; the majority opinion was written by a Justice from Michigan (not Mississippi) and voted for by seven of the eight Northern judges (one Yankee Judge abstained from voting—brave fellow); & the one dissenting vote came from the only Southerner on the bench—whose family owned slaves prior to the War—it is, none-the-less, the South that must pay for the nation's sin of racism. As a conquered and occupied province within the Federal Empire we the people of the once sovereign and prosperous states of Dixie have no advocate to defend our heritage, our honor, or desire to live in a constitutionally limited republic of republics as delivered to us by our Colonial ancestors. We are the only people in America who are not allowed to celebrate our heritage or express our desire to be truly free! "With liberty and justice for all?" Not if you are Southern!

Addendum II

THE YANKEE SLAVER

James Whelan

While we makes the journey many weak ones die,

We pitch their bodies over the side.

If we get low on darkies we'll raise the price,

I am the Yankee Slaver!

I am a sailor for New England,

I deal in the blood of the African,

And I sail from Boston to the Dark Congo,

I am the Yankee Slaver!

When I get tired of slaving I'll make money still,

I'll buy myself a textile mill;

I'll make more profit from the slaves I sold,

And by starving the immigrant Irish laborers.

I trade cheap rum to the native Chief

For a hole full of black ones with healthy teeth.

Only the choicest bodies in the barracoon,

Will survive the Middle Passage.

Oh the devil smiles with favor

Upon the Yankee Slaver,

Getting rich from selling black labor,

To farm the lands below.

Oh the devil smiles with favor

Upon the Yankee Slaver,

Getting rich from selling black labor,

To farm the lands below.

Our Yankee Bankers will get the price,

Of the Southern produce 'till our profits are just right;

And the tariff will make them pay with all their might,

For the goods we make them buy.

When the South asserts her Constitutional rights,

We'll invade the Southland like a locust's blight;

And we'll defeat them using the industrial might,

We built with our slave blood money.

Oh the devil smiles with favor

Upon the Yankee Slaver,

Getting rich from selling black labor,

To farm the lands below.

We will rob, rape, pillage and burn the South,

And lies of "abolition" will pour forth from our mouths;

And our Carpetbagger brothers will make more money still,

On the backs of the slaves we sold them.

The truth about our dealing will be mystery,

'Cause we will write the history;

To be not from old New England will be misery,

And we'll make a god of Abe Lincoln!

And Abe Lincoln smiles with favor,

Upon the Yankee Slaver,

Getting rich from selling black labor,

To farm the lands below.

Come on me laddies,

Come on and pack that hole,

For the tighter we pack 'em,

We'll make more Yankee gold.

Don't worry with your conscience,

The truth will never be told,

By the children of the Yankee Slavers.

Yes, Abe Lincoln's Empire similes with favor.

Upon the decedents of Yankee slavers.

I'll make more money still

I'll buy myself a textile mill!

POSTSCRIPT: POST RECONSTRUCTION POLITICIANS & LAND OWNERS

In a short book it is impossible to go into great detail regarding many of the topics discussed and great sweeping generalizations often cause unintended conclusions by readers. In the text we refer to post-Reconstruction politicians as "bad" leaders of the South. Due to the general refusal of Southern leadership to take up the call for real states' rights, inclusive of nullification and secession, we the people of the South were left defenseless against an ever more aggressive and oppressive Federal Empire. This resulted in a "bad" political environment that gave the South a system of racial hatred similar to the racial hatred exhibited by Northerners prior to and after the so called "Civil War." This generalization is not meant to deny the fact that there were honorable Southern politicians who tried to work within the system to better the lives of the Southern people. But the problem remained that regardless of the good intentions of honorable Southern leaders, the Federal Empire continued to punish the South with enduring slander and poverty. Regardless of their efforts, the strategic defeat of Constitutional liberty and Southern freedom remained and continues today.

The discussion of sharecropping slavery may seem to imply that Southern land owners were intentionally cruel to white and black sharecroppers. But, as documented, the major profits earned by the land owner ended up in the pockets of Northern crony capitalists. Just like post-War Southern politicians, the land owners were working within the culturally distorted system foisted upon we the people of the South by the Federal Empire.

Honorable political leaders, land owners, sharecroppers, and all other Southerners were victims of Northern-created cultural distortion of Southern society. The point made by this book is that had Southerners not accepted the fact of surrender at Appomattox as the final decision regarding the right of Southerners to live under a government based upon their free and unfettered consent, the pernicious consequences of Northern-imposed cultural distortion would not have become an accepted fact of Southern existence. By surrendering the right of local self-government, home rule, via real states' rights, the South became a docile and pacified colonial appendage of Lincoln's newly created Federal Empire. Freedom belongs to only those who are willing to call evil by its true name and to resist tyranny!

BIBLIOGRAPHY

Books

Agee, James, *Cotton Tenants* (1936). New York: Melville House Publishing, 2013

Alexander, Edward Porter, *Fighting for the Confederacy*. Chapel Hill: University of North Carolina Press, 1989

Allen, James S., *Reconstruction: The Battle for Democracy*. New York: International Publisher, 1937

Benson, Al and Walter Donald Kennedy, *Lincoln's Marxists*. Gretna, LA: Pelican Publishing Co., 2011

Bettersworth, John K., *Mississippi: A History*. Austin: The Steck Co., 1959

Bledsoe, Albert T., *Is Davis a Traitor?* (1866). Advocate Publishing House, 1879

Bowers, Claude G., *The Tragic Era*. New York: Halcyon House, 1929

Bradford, M. E., *Against the Barbarians*. Columbia, MO: University of Missouri Press, 1992

_____, *Founding Fathers*. Lawrence: University of Kansas Press, 1994

_____, *Original Intentions: On the Making and Ratification of the United States Constitution*. Athens: University of Georgia Press, 1993

Buckingham, J. S., *The Slave States of America*. New York: Negro University Press, 1968

Calhoun, John C., "A Disquisition on Government," *The Works of John C. Calhoun*. New York: D. Appleton & Co., 1854

Centz, P. C., *The Republic of Republics*. Boston: Little, Brown, and Co., 1881

Cisco, Walter Brian, *War Crimes Against Southern Civilians*. Gretna. LA: Pelican Publishing Co., 2008

Clark, Thomas D., and Albert Kirwan, *The South Since Appomattox*. New York: Oxford University Press, 1967

Conkin, Paul K., *The Southern Agrarians*. Knoxville: University of Tennessee Press, 1988

Cooper, William J., *Jefferson Davis*, American. New York: Alfred A. Knopf, 2000

Dabney, Robert Lewis, *A Defense of Virginia and the South* (1867). Harrisonburg VA: Sprinkle Publications, 1977

Davis, Nicholas A., *The Campaign from Texas to Maryland, with the Battle of Fredericksburg*. Baton Rouge: Louisiana State University Press, 1999

Davis, Jefferson, *Rise and Fall of the Confederate Government*, Vol. II. Nashville: William Mayes Coats, 1881

Debates in the Several State Conventions on the Adoption of the Federal Constitution,, Jonathan Elliot, ed. New York: J. B. Lippincott, 1876

Downs, Jim, *Sick from Freedom; African-American Illness and Suffering during the Civil War and Reconstruction*. New York: Oxford University Press, 2012

Edmonds, David C., ed., *Conduct of Federal Troops in Louisiana*. Lafayette, LA: Acadiana Press, 1988

Fischer, David H., *Albion's Seed: Four British Folkways In America*. New York: Oxford University Press, 1989

Fleming, Walter Lynwood, *The Sequel of Appomattox*. Toronto: Glasgow, Brook & Co., 1970

Floan, Howard R., *The South in Northern Eyes 1831-1861*. New York: McGraw-Hill Book, 1958

Fogel, Robert W., and Stanley Engerman, *Time on the Cross*. Boston: Little, Brown, and Co., 1974

Garner, James, *Reconstruction in Mississippi*. New York: Macmillan Co., 1901

Goldberg, Jonah, *Liberal Fascism*. New York: Random House, 2007

Graham, John Remington, *A Constitutional History of Secession*. Gretna, LA: Pelican Publishing Co., 2002

Greene, Lorenzo, Jr., *The Negro in Colonial New England, 1620-1776*. Port Washington, NY: Kennikat Press, 1966)

Hair, William Ivy, *Bourbonism and Agrarian Protest*. Baton Rouge: LSU Press, 1969

Henry, William Wirt, *Patrick Henry: Life, Correspondence and Speeches*. Harrisonburg, VA: Sprinkle Publishing, 1993

Hopkins, John Henry, *A Scriptural, Ecclesiastical, and Historical View of Slavery*. New York: W. I. Pooley and Co., 1861

Hoppe, Hans-Hermann, *Democracy: The God That Failed*. New Brunswick, NJ and London: Transaction Publishers, 2005

Hummel, Jeffery R., *Emancipating Slaves, and Enslaving Free Men*. Chicago: Open Court, 1996

I'll Take My Stand (1930). Baton Rouge: LSU Press, 1983

Ingraham, Joseph Holt, *The South-West By A Yankee*. New York: Harper & Brothers, 1835

Janis, Irving L. and Leon Mann, *Decision Making: A Psychological Analysis of Conflict, Choice, and Commitment*. New York: The Free Press, 1977

Jeansonne, Glen, *Messiah of the Masses*. New York: Addison-Wesley Educational Publishers, 1993

Johnson, Chalmers, The Sorrows of Empire. New York: Henry Holt and Co., 2004

Johnson, Ludwell H., *North Against South: The American Iliad, 1848-1877*. Columbia, SC: Foundation for American Education, 1978

Kennedy, Doris L. C., *The Kennedy Family of Copiah County, Mississippi and Their Kinfolks.* Jackson, MS: Self-Publishing, 2002

Kennedy, *Nullification: Why and How,* (The Scuppernong Press, Wake Forest, NC: 2014), available as free download at: http://www.kennedytwins.com/main.htm

Kennedy, James Ronald, *Reclaiming Liberty.* Gretna, LA: Pelican Publishing Co., 2005

_____, *Uncle Seth Fought the Yankees.* Gretna, LA: Pelican Publishing Co., 2015

Kennedy, James Ronald and Walter D. Kennedy, *Nullification: Why and How.* Wake Forest, NC: Scuppernong Press, 2014). Available as free download at: http://www.kennedytwins.com/main.htm

_____, *Nullifying Tyranny.* Gretna, LA: Pelican Publishing Co., 2010

_____, *The South Was Right!.* Gretna, La.: Pelican Publishing Co., 1994

_____, *Was Jefferson Davis Right?.* Gretna, LA: Pelican Publishing Co., 1998

_____, *Why Not Freedom!* Gretna, LA: Pelican Publishing Co., 1995

Kennedy, Walter D., *Myths of American Slavery.* Gretna, LA: Pelican Publishing Co., 2003

_____, *Rekilling Lincoln.* Gretna, LA: Pelican Publishing Co., 2015

Kent, James, *Commentaries on American Law* (1826). New York: DeCapo Press, 1971

Keys, Thomas Bland, ed., *The Uncivil War: Union Army and Navy Excesses in the Official Records.* Biloxi, MS: Beauvoir Press, 1991

Livingston, Donald, ed., *Rethinking the American Union for the Twenty-First Century.* Gretna, LA: Pelican Publishing Co., 2012

McCubbin, Robert G., ed., *The Life of John Wesley Hardin.* Norman, OK: University of Oklahoma Press, 1961

McDonald, Forrest, *A Constitutional History of the United States.* Malabar, FL: Robert E. Krieger, 1982

McManus, Edgar J., *Black Bondage in the North.* Syracuse, NY: Syracuse University Press, 1973

McWhiney, Grady, *Cracker Culture: Celtic Ways in the Old South.* Tuscaloosa, AL: University of Alabama Press, 1988

Melish, Joanne Pope, *Disowning Slavery: Gradual Emancipation and "Race" in New England, 1780-1860.* Ithaca, NY and London: 1998

Mises, Ludwig von, *Human Action; A Treatise on Economics,* (1947). Auburn, AL: Ludwig von Mises Institute, 1998

Mitcham, Samuel W., Jr., *Bust Hell Wide Open: The Life of Nathan Bedford Forrest.* Washington: Regnery History, 2016

Northup, Solomon, *Twelve Years a Slave* (1853), edited by Sue Eakin and Joseph Logsdon. Baton Rouge: Louisiana State University Press, 1968

Official Records War of the Rebellion, XXXIX

Olmsted, Frederick Law, *A Journey in the Back Country*. New York: 1860

Owsley, Frank L., *Plain Folk of the Old South* (1949). Baton, Rouge, LA: LSU Press, 1982

Phillips, Ulrich B., *Life and Labor in the Old South*. New York: Grosset & Dunlap, 1929

Pollard, Edward A., *Southern History of the War* (1866). New York: Fairfax Press, 1977

Popkin, Jeremy D., ed., *Facing Racial Revolution: Eyewitness Accounts of the Haitian Insurrection*. Chicago: University of Chicago Press, 2010

Powell, III, Frank, ed., *To Live and Die in Dixie*. Columbia, TN: Sons of Confederate Veterans, 2014

Rawle, William, *A View of the Constitution* (1825). Baton Rouge, LA: Land & Land, 1993

Record of Hon. C. L. Vallandigham on Abolition, the Union, and The Civil War. Columbus, OH: J. Walter and Co., 1863

Roper, Gary L., *Antebellum Slavery An Orthodox Christian View*. Gary L. Roper: 2008

Rothbard, Murray, *America's Great Depression* (1963). Auburn, AL: Ludwig von Mises Institute, 2000

Scott, Otto, *The Secret Six*. Murphys, CA: Uncommon Books, 1993

Seabrook, Lochlainn, *A Rebel Born; A Defense of Nathan Bedford Forrest*. Franklin, TN: Sea Raven Press, 2010

Semmes, Raphael, *Memoirs of Service Afloat* (1868). Secaucus, NJ: Blue and Gray Press, 1987

Simkins, Francis Butler, *A History of The South*. New York: Alfred A. Knopf, 1959

Smith, John David, ed., *A Just and Lasting Peace*. New York: Signet Classics, 2013

Smith, Mark M., *Debating Slavery: Economy and Society in the Antebellum American South*. Cambridge, UK: Cambridge University Press, 1998

Sowell, Thomas, *Wealth, Poverty, and Politics*. New York: Basic Books, 2015

Stephens, Alexander H., *The War Between the States* (1870). Harrisonburg, VA: Sprinkle Publications, 1994

Stokes, Karen, *South Carolina Civilians in Sherman's Path: Stories of Courage amid Civil War Destruction*. Charleston, SC: The History Press, 2012

Sullivan, Walter, ed., *The War the Women Lived: Female Voices from the Confederate South*. Nashville, TN: J. S. Sanders & Co., 1995

Taylor, John, *Tyranny Unmasked*. Indianapolis: Liberty Fund Press, 1992

Tocqueville, Alexis de, *Democracy in America*. New York: Adlard and Saunders, 1838

Tourgee, Albion W., *A Fool's Errand*, (1879, The Belknap Press, Cambridge, MA: 1961)

Weaver, Richard M., *The Southern Tradition at Bay*. New Rochelle, NY: Arlington House, 1968

Williams, T. Harry, *Huey Long*. New York: Alfred A. Knopf, 1969

_____, *Napoleon in Gray*. Baton Rouge: Louisiana State University Press, 1995

Wilson, Clyde N., *From Union to Empire*. Columbia, SC: Foundation for American Education, 2003

_____, *Nullification: Reclaiming Consent of the Governed*. Columbia, SC: Shotwell Publishing, 2016

Winters, John D., *Civil War in Louisiana*. Baton Rouge: Louisiana University Press, 1963

Woodward, C. Vann, *The Burden of Southern History*. Baton Rouge: Louisiana State University Press, 1960

Articles

Annual Report of the American Historical Association for the Year 1906, Vol. I,

"Black Lives Matter: The Schott 50 State Report on Public Education and Black Males," as cited in Superville, Denisa R., "Graduation Rates Rise; Gap Between Black and White Males Grows, Report Says," February 11, 2016, http://blogs.edweek.org/edweek/District_Dossier/2015/02/as_nation_graduation_rate_grew.html (Accessed 03/12/2016)

Bloodhound Dogtime.com, http://dogtime.com/dog-breeds/bloodhound

Brown, Richard, "Literacy—Looking at History," http://richardjohnbr.blogspot.com/2011/01/literacy-revised-version.html (Accessed 04/14/2016)

"Culture of the United States of America; Weekly Church Attendance" https://en.wikipedia.org/wiki/Religion_in_the_United_States (Accessed 05/07/2016)

Gannon, Megan, *Live Science*, "The Least and Most Religious U. S. States," February 3, 2014, http://www.livescience.com/43064-most-least-religious-us-states.html#sthash.FhmhdTNQ.dpuf (Accessed 05/07/2016)

"Harvard Prof Urges Liberals to Treat Evangelical Christians Like Nazis," http://www.breitbart.com/big-government/2016/05/10/harvard-prof-urges-liberals-treat-evangelical-christians-like-nazis/ (Accessed 05/10/2016)

"Hiram Revels Letter to President Grant," November 6, 1875 as cited in NCPedia, http://ncpedia.org/biography/revelsletter

Institute for Historical Review, "Abraham Lincoln's Program for Resettlement," http://www.ihr.org/jhr/v13/v13n5p-4_Morgan.html accessed 4/17/16

Jefferson, Thomas, letter to John Holmes, April 22, 1820, in Thomas Jefferson Foundation, Inc., https://www.monticello.org/site/jefferson/wolf-ear-quotation

Johnson, Ludwell H., "The Plundering Generation," Southern Partisan, 1987-88, republished at http://www.abbevilleinstitute.org/blog/the-plundering-generation/

Lind, Michael, "How the South Skews America," *Politico Magazine*, http://www.politico.com/magazine/story/2015/07/how-the-south-skews-america-119725_Page2.html#.VaKVN_lVhBd (Accessed 07/12/2015)

Lindert, Peter H., (University of California—Davis) and Jeffery G .Williamson (Harvard University and the University of Wisconsin), "American Incomes 1774-1860," 14, http://eml.berkeley.edu/~webfac/cromer/e211_f12/LindertWilliamson.pdf accessed 3/21/2016

Malvasi, Mark, "Philosopher-Poet of the Rednecks: Donald Davidson and the Defense of the Agrarian South," http://www.theimaginativeconservative.org/2013/06/philosopher-poet-donald-davidson-agrarian-south.html (Accessed 03/02/2016)

McClanahan, Brion, "Please, 'Dump Dixie'", http://www.abbevilleinstitute.org/blog/please-dump-dixie/ (Accessed 12/12/2014)

McDonald, Forrest, "Why Yankees Won't (and Can't) Leave the South Alone," http://www.theimaginativeconservative.org/2015/07/why-yankees-wont-and-cant-leave-the-south-alone.html

McDonald, Forrest and Grady McWhiney, "The South from Self-Sufficiency to Peonage: An Interpretation," *The American Historical Review*, Vol. 85. No. 5, (Dec. 1980)

Oates, Stephen B., *American Heritage*, "Children of Darkness," October 1973, Vol. 24, Issue 6

"On Sectional Politics—Possibility of Division," *Letters and Addresses of Thomas Jefferson*, Parker & Viles, eds. Buffalo, NY: National Jefferson Society, 1903

Pew Research Center, "Trends in Political Values and Core Attitudes: 1987-2007," www.people-press.org (Accessed 03/28/2007)

REPORT ON ECONOMIC CONDITIONS OF THE SOUTH Prepared for The President by The National Emergency Council (1938), 1-2, pdf available at: https://ia600202.us.archive.org/21/items/reportoneconomic00nati/report.pdf

The Hill, "House votes to restrict Confederate Flag at national cemeteries," Christina Marcos, 5/19/16 http://thehill.com/blogs/floor-action/house/247171-house-votes-to-ban-confederate-flags-at-federal-cemeteries

Tomasky, Michael, "Dems, It's Time to Dump Dixie," http://www.thedailybeast.com/articles/2014/12/08/dems-it-s-time-to-dump-dixie.html (Accessed 12/14/2014)

USA Today, "Mortality Rates by States," George Petras, Mar. 7, 2016

Venkataramani, M.S., "Norman Thomas, Arkansas Sharecroppers, and the Roosevelt Agricultural Policies, 1933-1937," *The Mississippi Valley Historical Review*, Vol. 47, No. 2, (Sept. 1960)

Williams, Walter, "Education Disaster," https://www.creators.com/read/walter-williams/11/15/education-disaster (Accessed 11/18/2015)

Index

abolitionist, 20, 41, 44-48, 54-55, 63, 72, 74, 89, 93, 107, 140, 180, 190

Adams, John, 43, 126

Afghanistan, 3, 113

African-American, 29, 37, 42-44, 52-53, 63, 65-66, 90, 109, 127

Agee, James, 107, 109-110

Agricultural Adjustment Act, 102, 119

AIDs, 8, 133

Alabama, 22, 67, 81, 99, 107, 109-110, 156, 176, 182, 186

Alexander, E. Poter (Gen.), 22-23

Alien and Sedition Acts, 126

Allen, Henry W. (Gov.), 70

Allen, James S., 67

Allen, Joseph Henry (Rev.), 141

Andrews, Garnett (Judge), 139

Antebellum, 16, 19-20, 22-26, 28-29, 31, 41, 54, 63, 105, 135, 174, 183

Anti-Federalists, 38, 124-125

Appomattox, 4, 29, 61, 86, 101, 122-123, 128, 131, 133, 163, 166, 174-175, 177-181, 184, 186, 191, 198

Arizona, 4

atrocities, 70, 73, 75-76, 84

Austria, 28

Baltic States, 146, 157

Bancroft, Charles, 79, 167

Barron v. Baltimore, 38

Beauregard, P.T.G. (Gen.), 64-65, 133, 191

Benton, Thomas Hart, 39-40

Bible, 136, 194

Bible Belt, 166-167, 184

Biden, Joe, 10

Bill of Rights, 37-38, 126

Bismarck, Otto von (Chancellor), 73

bloodhound, 46-47

bondage (debt), 109, 179

Boston, 54, 63, 79, 196

Bradford, M. E., 85

Branagan, Thomas, 44

Brandon, Gerard (Gov.), 41-42

British Empire, 13, 17, 53, 121-122, 156

Brown, John, 46, 48-49, 57, 190

Buckingham, James S., 63

Buffalo Soldiers, 67, 84

Calhoun, John C., 123-124, 152

California, 4, 97, 156, 169

Camp Nelson, 79-80

capitalism (crony), 9, 12, 79, 87, 97-98, 100, 138, 143, 147, 157, 161, 163, 173, 180, 187, 189, 194, 198

Caribbean, 17, 26-27, 64

carpet baggers, 52, 178, 192, 197

Catholic, 13

cattle, 18, 22-23, 101, 106, 163, 176-177, 179

Celts, 13, 38

chattel slavery, 64, 74, 80-81, 105-106, 115, 117, 174, 181, 183, 193

cheap labor, 87, 157, 188

Chile, 28

Chisholm Trail, 22

Christian, 12-13, 34, 74, 85-86, 96, 115, 133, 136, 153, 165, 167-169, 171

church attendance, 151, 166

churches, 57, 163, 165-166

City on a Hill, 87, 107

Civil Rights, 133-134, 144, 190

Civil War, 7-8, 21, 67, 73, 79, 97, 99, 103, 105, 112, 116, 127, 139, 148, 167, 173, 188, 194, 198

civility, 11, 164, 166

Clans of Scotland, 13, 138

colonial, 15-19, 22, 31, 40, 45, 98, 122, 130, 150, 157, 179, 181, 183-184, 188-189, 195, 198

colonization (removing blacks), 42-43

Columbia, South Carolina, 60, 84

Confederate flag, 69, 143, 153

Confederate States of America (C.S.A.), 2-3, 5, 20, 24, 53, 55, 60, 66, 70, 75-77, 79, 84, 87, 96, 101-103, 106, 127, 132, 134-136, 142, 151, 154, 156-157, 160, 162, 173, 175, 179, 181-182, 184, 186, 188, 190

Conkin, Paul, 20

Connecticut, 25, 33, 44, 50, 89, 152, 156, 167

consent, 4, 8, 24, 37, 67, 75, 96, 121, 130, 139, 150, 198

Constitution (CS), 5, 19

Constitution (US), 4, 19, 31, 33-38, 40, 48, 53, 61-62, 74, 94, 121, 125-126, 135, 148, 191

Constitutional Liberty, 5, 121, 171-172, 198

Constitutional Republic, 5, 61

"coop him up", 75, 140, 147

cotton, 22-23, 26, 49, 82, 91, 95, 118, 162, 173, 176-178, 180, 182, 187

crime, 8, 56, 62, 75, 84, 138, 170, 173, 186

cultural distortion, 111, 122, 127-132, 134, 142, 161, 181, 186, 194, 198

D.C. Compensated Emancipation Act, 92

Davidson, Donald, 11, 148

Davis, Jefferson, 20, 97, 168, 172

Day of Jubilee, 140

Declaration of Independence, 4, 6, 39-40, 75, 96, 139, 171

de-humanize, 58, 73, 85

Democrat, 9, 51-53, 65, 132, 138, 144, 161

democratic, 9, 51-53, 65, 132, 138, 144, 161

Democratic Party, 93, 128, 131, 136, 138, 132-145

de-populate, 77, 190

DeRosa, Marshall, 121

destruction, 3, 10, 70, 76-80, 90, 97, 100-101, 106, 134, 163, 166, 170, 175, 177-178, 181, 183-184, 186, 188

dispossess, 160

divide and rule, 13, 51, 66, 84, 103, 123, 135, 189, 194

Dixie, 7, 16, 93, 99-100, 106, 111, 124, 128, 135-138, 154, 157-158, 161, 166-172, 174-175, 178-186, 189, 193, 195

dollar-worshipers, 21, 23, 50, 53

drugs, 3, 8, 12, 170

Earl, Arkansas, 108-109

EEOC, 5

emancipation, 9, 42, 45-46, 81, 90-92, 116, 144, 177

Emerson, Ralph Waldo, 56-58, 61

England, 13, 26, 28, 47, 92, 183

English, 4, 16-17, 148, 183

EPA, 5

erosion, 185-186

Estonia, 157

evicted, 116-117, 181

eviction, 80, 102, 118

evil empire, 67, 94, 134

exploitation, 8, 11, 54, 85, 89-90, 93, 96-97, 100, 102, 110, 125, 127, 137, 142-143, 146, 150, 162, 171, 179, 181, 183-184, 194

extermination, 58-59, 61, 69-74, 76, 77-78, 94, 96, 107, 118, 142, 177, 184, 190

Faulkner, William, 26

Federal Writers' Project, 64

Federalists, 33, 124, 126

Fifteenth Amendment, 93, 135

First Amendment, 37, 62

Fischer, David H., 148-149

flogging, 47, 195

Florida, 23, 137, 159, 168

Fogel, Robert, 28, 115

Forrest, N. B. (Gen.), 65-66, 133, 191-192, 194

Fourteenth Amendment, 93, 135

Ft. Sumter, 73

Gadsden Purchase, 97

Garrison, William Lloyd, 56, 190

Georgia, 16-17, 22, 39, 77, 83-84, 159, 90

Germany, 101, 167, 178

Giddings, Joshua, 55-56, 61

Goldberger, Joseph, 111

Grant, U.S., 52, 78, 140, 163

Grayson, William, 34-35

Great Britain, 5, 30, 148, 150

Great Depression, 95, 107, 117, 119

Great Recession, 107, 158

Haitian (slave revolt), 45-46, 64, 94, 190

Haley, Nikki (Gov.), 53, 143

Halleck, Henry W. (Gen.), 75-78, 82

Hannity, 51

Hardin, John Wesley, 67

Harlan, Justice, 132

Harper's Ferry, 48

Harvard, 167

hates polluted rag, 61

Hayes, Rutherford B., 140

Haynes, Leonard (Dr.), 141-142

Henry, Patrick, 2, 5-6, 31, 33-34, 38, 53, 125-126, 151-153

Hindu, 13, 138, 150

Hitler, Adolph, 57, 96

hogs, 22-23, 106, 163, 176, 179

Hollywood, 29, 31, 74, 92, 145, 167, 169

homeless, 116, 118, 162, 181-182

hookworm, 112

Hopkins, John Henry (Rev.), 44

housing, 16, 28, 115

Hungary (1956), 66

illiterate, 22, 30-31, 109, 135

imperial (imperialistic, imperialism), 20-21, 77, 85, 87, 93, 96-99, 110, 119

income inequality, 8, 164

Indian Wars, 129

Indians (American), 96

infant mortality, 113

Ingersoll, Robert G., 4

Ingraham, Joseph H., 29

Ireland, 13, 146, 150, 152, 154, 156, 183

Irish, 150, 152, 156, 183, 196

iron industry, 97, 99-100

IRS, 5

ISIS, 67

Italy, 28

Jackson, Andrew, 46

Jackson, Louisiana, 59

Japan, 101, 167, 178

Jay-Gardoqui Treaty, 89

Jefferson, Thomas, 2, 5, 49-50, 124-126, 141

Jim Crow, 9, 123, 128, 131-132, 145

Johnson, Chalmers, 13, 87, 96, 138

Johnson, Lyndon B., 95, 134

Judas payment, 136

Kansas, 48, 75, 82

kapo (Jewish guards), 129

Kennedy Twins, 1, 171, 212

Kentucky, 23, 79, 89, 126, 156

Kentucky & Virginia Resolves of 1798, 126

Kings Mountain, 102

kith and kin, 119, 127, 129, 139, 168, 173, 177, 181

KKK, 51

K-Street, 12, 131

Laden, Osama Bin, 57

Lancaster, William, 35

Lane, James H. (Gen.) 69, 75

Lane, Joseph (Sen.), 76, 149-150

lash, 29, 46-47

Latvia, 157

Levin, 51

"liberty and justice for all", 1, 103-104, 137, 155, 182, 189, 194-195

life expectancy, 28, 112, 115

Limbaugh, 51

Lincoln, Abraham, 3, 7, 12, 40, 42-44, 50, 59, 69-70, 73-79, 86, 92-93, 97-98, 100-101,

127, 131-132, 134, 140-142, 162, 188, 192, 197, 198

Lincoln-Douglass debates, 42-43, 96

Lind, Michael, 166, 184

Lindert, Peter H., 16, 19

literate, 30

Lithuania, 157

Livingston, Donald, 154

lobbyists, 12

Long, Huey, 132-134

Louisiana, 1, 22, 30, 59, 70, 78, 82-83, 91, 103, 114, 132-133, 141, 144, 165-166, 178

Lowndes, Rawlins, 36, 38, 153

Lytle, Andrew Nelson, 123

Maine, 165

majority, 11-12, 33-40, 45, 50, 55, 64, 89, 93, 106, 125-126, 132, 145, 147-149, 151-153, 171, 176, 182, 194-195

majority rule, 34, 89, 149, 152

malaria, 111, 114

malnutrition, 111-112, 180, 182-183

Manchester, England, 28

Marshall Plan, 101

Maryland, 16-17, 46, 77, 156-160, 160, 168

Madison, James, 22

Mason, George, 18, 21, 23, 148, 165, 168

Massachusetts, 17, 21, 26, 33, 43, 47, 50, 54, 71, 79, 89, 132, 152, 156, 165, 196

Mayflower, 16

McClellan, George B. (Gen.), 75

McPherson, James, 22

McWhiney, Grady, 18, 21, 23, 148, 165, 168

median household income, 156-159

Melish, Joanne Pope, 44

Melville, Herman, 47

Mexican War, 2

Michigan, 132, 195

milch cow, 31, 34, 50, 150

militia, 2, 37, 62, 138

Miller, Joseph (Pvt.), 80

minority, 10, 31, 33-34, 36, 50, 89, 125-126, 148, 152-153, 176

Mississippi, 18, 21-22, 26, 41-42, 49, 52, 55, 62-63, 66, 70-71, 106-107, 110, 119, 133, 137, 144, 156, 165, 175, 182, 186, 192, 195, 212

Mississippi River, 89, 97

Mississippi Territory, 2

Missouri, 39, 75, 81, 113

Moby Dick, 47

monopoly, 188

Moore, Rep. (African-American, Mississippi), 63

Morgan, J. P., 99-100

Murphy, Audi, 2

Muslim, 13, 57, 150

My Lai, 75

Myers, Mary Conner, 118

Myrdal, Gunnar, 116

NAACP, 143

Nashville Agrarian, 3, 123

Native American Scouts, 129

Nazi (National Socialist), 60-61, 67, 128-129, 134, 167, 189

New Deal, 95

New England, 13, 15-16, 19, 30, 35, 38, 43-44, 49, 55-58, 61, 65, 73-74, 85-86, 97, 107, 110-111, 127, 141, 146, 156, 165, 167-168, 179, 183, 187-188, 191-192, 195-197

New Hampshire, 33, 152, 165

New Jersey, 44

New Orleans, 65, 79, 83, 89, 97, 103, 191, 212

New South, 11, 37

New York (state), 47, 57, 63, 91, 111, 115

New York City, 28, 166

Ninth Amendment, 37

Nixon, Richard M. (Pres,), 75, 143

North America, 7, 17, 74, 92, 140

North American Review, 54

North Carolina, 10, 16-17, 19, 35, 52, 112, 126

Northern Ireland, 13

Northern Narrative, 54, 71, 107, 115, 157

Northup, Solomon, 91

Norton, Charles Eliot, 167

Nott, Josiah, 167

NSA, 5

nullification, 5, 158, 170-171, 189

numerical majority, 89, 149

numerical minority, 89

Obama Care, 152

Ohio, 53-55, 77, 84, 138, 189

Oklahoma, 114-115

Old Glory, 3, 61

Olmsted, Fredrick Law, 23, 25, 44

"one nation indivisible", 86, 94, 103-104, 130, 137, 142, 155, 182,

open range, 18, 22-23, 106, 117, 176, 178-179

opportunity cost, 163

outhouse, 84, 119

Owsley, Frank L., 16, 18, 21, 23, 30, 148, 194

Parker, Star, 9

Parliament (British), 91, 152

Pellagra, 111-112, 182

Pennsylvania, 46, 89, 102, 113, 134, 141

peonage, 70, 108-109, 116, 123, 174, 179-181

per capita, 7, 19, 21, 30, 109, 151, 178

per capita income, 103, 159, 175

Philadelphia, 46, 63, 212

Philippines, 96

Phillips, U.B., 27

Pickney, Charles Cotesworth (Gen.), 35, 126

Pierce, Franklin, 97

Pike, Shepherd, 140

plain folk, 16-18, 22-23, 105-106, 117, 176-179, 181

Plessy v. Ferguson, 132

political irregular warfare, 170

Politico Magazine, 166, 184

poor white, 16, 20, 22, 24, 89, 179

poor white trash (pwt), 118-119, 177

privy, 119

Profit minded Yankee, 89, 91, 97

progressive, 11, 69, 107, 110, 119, 123, 133-134, 145, 166-167, 180

propaganda, 3, 5, 26, 41, 51, 53, 55, 61, 71, 123, 146, 166, 189

propagandists, 8, 12-13, 73-75, 90, 92, 96, 105, 107, 127, 139, 145, 180, 189

Protestant, 13

punish (punishment), 7-8, 13, 52, 73, 76, 86-87, 99, 103, 106-107, 110, 113, 119, 139, 155-156, 159, 173, 178, 198

Puritans, 17, 86

Quisling, Vidkun, 128-129

Quislings, 129, 131, 134

race/racial hatred, 66, 192

Radical Republican, 4, 52, 55, 69, 132, 134, 136

rags (children in), 1-3, 8, 13, 107, 109-110, 112, 153

railroads, 17

Raleigh, Sir Walter, 17

Randolph, John, 47

rape, 26, 60, 76, 81, 83-84, 138, 171, 197

Rawle, William, 46

real States' Rights, 3-5, 62, 102, 124, 126, 128, 131, 136, 144, 156, 158, 160, 170-172, 198

Reconstruction, 2, 8, 65, 67, 71, 74, 86, 93, 96, 101, 111, 128, 131-139, 155, 162-163, 174, 178, 180, 184-185, 188, 190-192, 198

reparation, 164, 169, 170-171

repopulate (repopulated, repopulation), 69, 77, 157-159, 168

Republic of Republics, 6, 62, 94, 121, 134, 146, 158, 160, 170-172, 188, 195

Republican, 4, 8-9, 27, 51-54, 65-66, 70-71, 73, 76-77, 86, 93, 122, 128, 131-144, 153, 161, 175, 184, 191-193

Republican Party, 65-66, 84, 92-93, 128, 131-132, 134-135, 138-139, 142-144, 180, 191-192, 194

Resolves of '98, 126

Revels, Hiram (Sen.), 51-52, 66, 192

revenue, 39-40, 50, 79, 150

rice, 17-18, 23

Robber Baron, 99, 163

Roosevelt, Franklin D., 95, 101-102, 105, 107, 113, 118

Roosevelt, Theodore, 99

"root hog or die", 141

Roots, 26

Rothbard, Murray, 119

Royal authority, 4

ruling elite, 3, 11-13, 52, 74, 79, 84, 93-94, 101-102, 114, 118, 122, 124-126, 128, 130-131, 136, 138, 142, 146, 149, 155, 157, 161, 167-168, 170, 172-173, 189, 194

Ryan, Paul, 153

Satan, 87

scalawags (scallywags), 128-130, 143, 154-155, 178, 192

Schurz, Carl, 27, 63, 93, 100, 137, 140

secession, 5, 19-20, 35, 54-55, 57, 67, 70, 79, 86, 139, 150, 157-158, 170-171, 176, 198

secessionists, 7, 139

secular humanist, 34, 165, 166-169, 171, 184, 195

segregation, 9, 131, 132, 145, 190, 195

Semmes, Raphael, 38-40, 61

shackles, 86, 135, 173, 185, 194

sharecropper, 1, 95, 102, 106-119, 173

sharecropping, 29, 81, 95, 102, 105-106, 109-110, 112, 114-116, 119, 123, 163, 174-176, 180-183, 186, 193-194, 198

Sheridan, Phillip (Gen.), 73, 78, 177

Sherman, William T. (Gen.), 58-61, 72, 77, 82, 84, 87

Shiloh, 102

Simkins, Francis B., 16, 18, 20-21, 23, 25, 50

Slave Narratives, 64

soil erosion, 185

Sons of Confederate Veterans (SCV), 141, 198, 212

South Carolina, 15-17, 19, 35-36, 56, 60, 72-73, 78, 81, 83-84, 86, 126, 143, 162

Southern University, 142

Sovereign state, 4-5, 12, 121-122, 124-127, 149, 170, 175

Soviet Union, 150, 154, 157, 160

Sowell, Thomas, 9-10, 145

Spanish American War, 84, 96

Stalin, 57

Stampp, Kenneth, 110

Stars and Stripes, 61

States' Privileges, 130-131

States's Rights, 3-5, 62, 102, 124, 126, 128, 130-131, 136, 144, 156, 160, 171-172, 198

Stephens, Alexander H., 5, 171

Stevens, Thaddaeus, 69, 86, 134-135, 141

stools of everlasting repentance, 87, 110, 154, 171, 194

Strong, Josiah (Rev.), 85

sub-human population, 61

Supreme Court (U.S.), 38, 67, 121, 126, 132, 195

tariffs, 38, 40, 49, 55, 69, 79, 86, 97, 147, 187, 196

taxation, 34, 125, 137, 169

taxes, 5, 12, 33, 35, 124-125, 127, 130, 137, 162, 164, 169, 172, 188

Taylor, John of Caroline, 147-148, 150

Taylor, Joseph, 35

Ten Commandments, 67, 153

Tennessee, 2, 20, 23, 75, 81-82, 89, 99, 118, 136

Tenth Amendment, 37, 172

Texas, 2, 22-23, 55, 67, 97, 111, 114, 159, 190

The Daily Beast, 166

The South Was Right!, 171

Third Amendment, 37

Thirteenth Amendment, 65

Thomas, Norman, 102, 113

tobacco, 17-18, 23, 49

Tocquville, Alex de, 21, 24-26, 44, 184

toilet, 119

Tomasky, Michael, 166

Tories, 5

Transylvania, Louisiana, 108-109

treason, 5-6, 62, 130, 176, 195

Trumbull, Lyman (Sen.), 140

Trust Busting, 99

Tucker, St. George, 168

Turner, Nat, 47-48

tyranny, 29, 33, 35-36, 121, 137, 147-148, 150, 153, 170

Uncle Sam's Plantation, 9-10

Union, 3, 6, 31, 34, 36-37, 50, 53, 56-57, 70-80, 82-83, 86, 93, 100, 110, 125, 135, 137, 140, 143, 149-150, 152, 154, 162, 188

United States of America (U.S.A.), 2-3, 5, 7-8, 12, 19-20, 22, 24-26, 30, 36, 43-44, 46, 53, 59-70, 72-77, 80, 84, 89, 92, 94, 96, 103, 107, 112-113, 116, 121-122, 128, 132, 134-135, 140, 146, 149, 151, 156-157, 159, 161-164, 166, 168-169, 172, 175, 178, 184, 189, 192, 194

Utah, 11, 165

Vallandigham, C. L. (Rep.), 53-55

Vardaman, James K., 133-134

Vermont, 44, 47, 165

veterans' pensions, 162

Vichymen, 129, 131, 134

vigorous war policy, 59, 70, 73-74, 76-77, 100

virgin forest, 106, 163, 186-187

Virginia, 16-19, 23, 33-35, 39, 42, 47-48, 57, 76-78, 82-83, 121, 125-126, 137, 147, 156-160, 168, 189

Wall Street, 12, 99-100, 131, 158, 193-194

Wallace, Henry A., 95, 105, 118

War for Southern Independence, 2-3, 9, 18, 27, 61, 105, 107, 127, 148, 153, 156-157, 161, 168, 173, 175

War of 1812, 2, 55, 97

War on Poverty, 2, 55, 97

Washington (state), 165

Washington, D. C., 5, 9-12, 27, 50, 52, 59, 77-78, 82, 92, 94, 114, 119, 122, 128, 138, 142, 146, 154-156, 158-159, 171-173, 177, 189, 194

Washington, George, 2, 5

Weaver, Richard, 24, 148

Western Hemisphere, 26, 28-29

whipping-boy, 110

whipping-post, 47

White House, 42

white supremacy, 42, 123, 128, 131-133, 139, 142

Williams, Walter, 10

Williamson, Hugh, 35-36, 126

Williamson, Jeffery G., 16, 19

Wilson, Clyde, 172

World War I (WW I), 2, 73

World War II (WW II), 2, 73, 101, 129

York, Alvin, 2

ABOUT THE AUTHORS

The Kennedy Twins were born in Mississippi; both now reside in Louisiana. Ron and his twin brother Donnie are the authors of the bestselling book *The South Was Right!* with more than 135,000 copies sold. The Kennedy Twins have written four books together; their latest book together (prior to *Punished with Poverty*) was *Nullifying Tyranny*. Ron authored *Reclaiming Liberty, Nullification: Why and How, Uncle Seth Fought the Yankees* and *Dixie Rising—Rules for Rebels*. Ron is past Division Commander, Louisiana Sons of Confederate Veterans (SCV), a life member of the Louisiana Division and the National SCV. He is a frequent speaker at SCV, Southern Heritage and other pro-Liberty groups.

Ron received a Master in Health Administration (MHA) from Tulane University in New Orleans, a Master of Jurisprudence in Health Law (MJ) from Loyola University Chicago, a Bachelor's degree from University of Louisiana Monroe. He retired in April 2015 after serving over 20 years as Vice President of Risk Management for a Louisiana based insurance company.

Donnie is the author of *Myths of American Slavery* and *Rekilling Lincoln*; co-author with his twin brother of *The South Was Right!*, *Was Jefferson Davis Right?*, *Why Not Freedom*, *Nullifying Tyranny* and with Al Benson, co-authored *Lincoln's Marxists*. The Kennedy Twins have also edited, annotated and republished (1993) an 1825 textbook on the Constitution by William Rawle of Philadelphia, PA. Donnie is past Division Commander Louisiana SCV, a life members of the Louisiana Division and the National SCV and is a frequent speaker at SCV, Southern Heritage and other pro-Liberty groups.

Donnie received his bachelor's degree from the University of Louisiana Monroe and is a graduate of Charlotte Memorial Medical Center school of Anesthesia. He is a registered respiratory therapist (RRT), registered nurse (RN), and certified registered nurse anesthetist (CRNA).

Author's website: www.kennedytwins.com

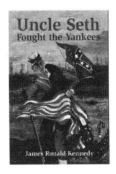

Available from Shotwell Publishing

Non-Fiction:

Annals of the Stupid Party: Republicans Before Trump by Clyde N. Wilson (The Wilson Files 3)

Nullification: Reclaiming Consent of the Governed by Clyde N. Wilson (The Wilson Files 2)

The Yankee Problem: An American Dilemma by Clyde N. Wilson (The Wilson Files 1)

Maryland, My Maryland: The Cultural Cleansing of a Small Southern State by Joyce Bennett.

Washington's KKK: The Union League During Southern Reconstruction by John Chodes.

When the Yankees Come: Former South Carolina Slaves Remember Sherman's Invasion. Edited with Introduction by Paul C. Graham

Southerner, Take Your Stand! by John Vinson

Lies My Teacher Told Me: The True History of the War for Southern Independence by Clyde N. Wilson

Emancipation Hell: The Tragedy Wrought By Lincoln's Emancipation Proclamation by Kirkpatrick Sale

Southern Independence. Why War? - The War to Prevent Southern Independence by Dr. Charles T. Pace

Dixie Rising--Rules for Rebels by James Ronald Kennedy

Green Altar Books (A Shotwell Literary Series):

A New England Romance & Other Southern Stories by Randall Ivey

Tiller by James E. Kibler (Clay Bank County, IV)

For more information, Please visit us at

www.ShotwellPublishing.com